What Time Is It?

What Time Is It?

A Deep Reading of Our Lives throughout
the Liturgical Year

WRITTEN BY

Gloria O'Toole Ulterino

EDITED BY

Elizabeth Maurer Webster

CASCADE *Books* · Eugene, Oregon

Cascade Books
An Imprint of Wipf and Stock Publishers
199 W. 8th Ave., Suite 3
Eugene, OR 97401

www.wipfandstock.com

PAPERBACK ISBN: 978-1-6667-0180-7
HARDCOVER ISBN: 978-1-6667-0181-4
EBOOK ISBN: 978-1-6667-0182-1

Cataloguing-in-Publication data:

Names: Ulterino, Gloria O'Toole, author. | Webster, Elizabeth Maurer, editor.

Title: What time is it? : a deep reading of our lives throughout the liturgical year / by Gloria O'Toole Ulterino ; edited by Elizabeth Maurer Webster.

Description: Eugene, OR: Cascade Books, 2022 | Includes bibliographical references.

Identifiers: ISBN 978-1-6667-0180-7 (paperback) | ISBN 978-1-6667-0181-4 (hardcover) | ISBN 978-1-6667-0182-1 (ebook)

Subjects: LCSH: Church year. | Liturgics. | Women in Christianity.

Classification: BV30 U50 2022 (print) | BV30 (ebook)

03/11/22

I dedicate this book to the full participation of women in
my beloved Church.

I trust that God will bring us there, through the ongoing
dedication of so many courageous souls.

Contents

Through narrative, poetry, imagined conversations with evangelists Matthew and Luke, some preaching words on John the Baptist, and a letter to his mother, Elizabeth, everyone is invited into the beginning of a new church year. It is hoped that each reader might experience the magnetism, perhaps even the magic, of this new beginning. The season concludes with an Epiphany story—the life-changing journey of St. Elizabeth Ann Seton—not unlike that of the magi of old.

This chapter introduces the Wisdom Woman, also known as the Wisdom of God. Although nearly hidden, she peeks out from behind some readings of the season, tantalizing us to know her better. Why is she important? How can we reclaim her after years, even centuries, of resistance to her ways? The chapter concludes with an addendum on Wisdom's voice in Scripture and a story of Joanne Cala, contemporary woman of wisdom.

Addendum

From the Ash Wednesday smudge on our foreheads until Lent's conclusion on Holy Thursday evening, this remains a season of introspection. The fullness of our Lenten tradition offers three different cycles: (1) preparation for the Easter sacraments in Cycle A, (2) exploration of our covenant with God in Cycle B, and (3) a celebration of reconciliation in Cycle C. In Cycle A, the Samaritan woman and Martha plunge us into the meaning of Baptism; Etty Hillesum inspires us with the depths of her sacrificial love in Cycle B; and in Cycle C, we celebrate a service of reconciliation, led by the woman with the lost coin (Luke 15:8–10).

Palm Sunday's passion sets the tone of these holiest of days. How can we tell the passion so as to move people's hearts? We enter into the Triduum on Holy Thursday evening with Jesus' tenderhearted command to wash disciples' feet. The solemnity of John's account of the passion carries us through Good Friday. Finally, emerging out of silence, we pull out all the liturgical stops for the Easter Vigil on Saturday evening. We proclaim God's Story with imagination. We baptize . . . celebrate . . . and believe. This chapter must include an imagined conversation with Mary of Magdala, Easter Sunday's apostle to the apostles. Finally, twentieth-century preacher extraordinaire Sr. Thea Bowman concludes this chapter with an account of her passionate life.

Easter is an entire season! As so often happens with events that are beyond our comprehension, we hear God's command, "Do not be afraid!" In response, Mary, the mother of Jesus, proclaims her experience of Pentecost. Not long thereafter, women leaders of early church communities—like Prisca, Phoebe, and Lydia— heeded that call. In our day, Scripture scholar Sr. Sandra Schneiders courageously responded to stifling Vatican orders. Finally, I introduce Ann Kurz, an extraordinarily brave friend, who lives abundantly with cerebral palsy.

Ordinary Time lasts nearly six months, from sometime in June until after Thanksgiving. Each of the three Synoptic authors (Mark, Matthew, and Luke) takes his unique turn in proclaiming the works of Jesus. Each is followed by a woman or women who reflects his style, in some particular way. Mark is first, because he was first to create the Gospel format. His style—brusque, no-nonsense, and powerful in its simplicity—is matched by the incomparable Dorothy Day.

Matthew is a teacher, par excellence. His twenty-eight chapters include many details and stories well beyond the sixteen chapters of Mark. Thorough is a word that comes to mind. What teacher, then, what professor, is so in love with Jesus that she must thoroughly probe our Tradition, always with the utmost regard for the students in her charge? To my mind, that person has to be Sr. Elizabeth Johnson. Her responses to my questions are found in this chapter.

Luke is the lyrical teller of stories. Above all, his storytelling Jesus is the One sent by God to seek out and save the lost. Remember Luke's "lost and found" chapter (15)? Jesus tells some stories to a bunch of whiny complainers. There's the shepherd who leaves ninety-nine sheep in order to save just one that was lost. A woman turns her house upside down to find just one lost coin. Finally, a father (of "prodigal" or "wasteful" love) waits endlessly for the return of his "prodigal" son. In today's Roman Catholic world, some women are in danger of being lost, for their call to the diaconate is not yet affirmed by the official church. A bit of their story appears in this chapter.

November has the "feel" of a "thin time," according to the Celts: a time when God draws near. It seems perfect, then, to conclude the liturgical year with this month of November, a time from "here" to "there." In doing so, I speak about a woman near and dear to my heart, Kathie Quinlan. As one of the founders of the local hospice movement, she has inspired and blessed many people. I trust that she will do the same for you.

Serving as a statement of purpose and profession of faith, this concludes the book with a blessing upon all readers. Sending everyone forth . . .

An Introduction to My Book

What Time Is It? A Deep Reading of Our Lives
throughout the Liturgical Year

Time. Fleeting time. Too little time. Time standing still. Time that changes everything. What time *is* it? At this very moment, the coronavirus has abruptly altered our experience of time. Perhaps our rushing-from-one-thing-to-another existence has stopped us dead in our tracks. Is there a sense of relief at imposed quiet? Or, on the contrary, is there a nagging anxiety? How will I earn the money I need to live on? How can I remain connected to those I dearly love? These and so many other questions keep on erupting. Most certainly, we have been thrust ever more deeply into our most intense human longings: to survive, to let go of past mistakes, to begin again, to follow longed-for hopes and dreams, to physically connect with loved ones. This much we've learned. Below the surface of day-in, day-out living, time can wake us up. Shock us, urge us, or even gently nudge us into a deep reading of our lives, so that we might continually become the authentic person rooted at our core, little by little, inch by inch.

Yet, how does this happen? The subtitle of my book suggests the church's liturgical year as the context for this ongoing discovery and unfolding. Why? Having fallen in love with the liturgical year, I know that it can be *precisely* the place where our deepest human longings can be found. Each season is a deeper telling of time, a more engaging telling of time, a time that plumbs our depths, all the while challenging the surface of everyday living. Each season has its own soul: the hope of beginning again (as in Advent); the recognition of falling short and dusting oneself off before proceeding further (as in Lent); the celebration of stunning, life-altering, life-giving events (as in Easter); the day-in, day-out living of commitments made (as in

Ordinary Time), as just one example. In other words, each season can reveal a deeper truth, perhaps a new-to-us truth, about following Jesus, the Christ. None of this can be done alone! Not without God, and certainly not without significant human companions on the journey.

We all need these faithful companions. In this book, I have carefully selected a few women, each of whom reflects something of the season for which she is chosen. Each one, in fact, simply exudes the power of her season. But we almost never hear about them on Sunday morning! Yes, they are right there in Scripture . . . or, sometimes located within our Tradition. Truth be told, they might even show up in our everyday lives. In any case, they are as capable as men—about whom we most often hear—of revealing the essence of each liturgical season. However, the Church I love has often neglected, ignored, or muted the voices of so many faith-filled women: age after age, year after year, season after season. We, God's People, are bereft without them. Therefore it is that I lovingly highlight the women in this book as models of discipleship for us *all*, men as well as women.

This book has been a long time in coming. The fruit of daily living and ongoing study, it reflects blessing upon blessing, often born out of struggle. For that struggle somehow, in some way, has been given meaning through my faith . . . through my experience of Church. From the time I was a youngster, I knew there was something special about "going to church." I still remember sitting in the pews with my parents, wondering "what on earth is that gibberish I keep on hearing?" (It was Latin, of course.) Then, without fail, at some point the priest would say "Gloria tua"—my maiden name was O'Toole—and I would sit up straight, thinking, "They know I'm here!" I belonged! Later, as a teenager, my parents and I would enter a darkened, hushed church before Midnight Mass. Until suddenly, at the stroke of midnight, lights flooded the entire place! Trumpets blared! And Jesus, the Christ, was born! The thrill of that moment has never left me! In middle age, after I'd returned to school to study theology and enter parish ministry, my husband and I were in London to visit our son and his family. We walked into Westminster Cathedral, and an Anglican Mass was underway in a side chapel. A woman was presiding! A woman not unlike myself, in love with the liturgy. Leading others in prayer, as I ached to do. And I wept, uncontrollably. Liturgy can do that. Liturgy can speak powerful truth by touching the depth of our souls, when done well.

Some might suggest that setting this book in the context of the liturgical year is nothing more or less than going around in circles, since we make the rounds every year. Nevertheless, I am convinced otherwise; for hopefully we begin each year, each Advent, in a place different from the year before. With more life experience and reflection. With ever-deepening convictions about the gospel and its meaning in our lives. Furthermore, we are given three *different* cycles of readings, varying from one year to the next, based upon the words and stories of the evangelist for the year: Matthew for Cycle A, Mark for Cycle B, and Luke for Cycle C.

To be specific, these three Gospel writers are named "Synoptic," for they reveal similar content in similar form. At the same time, their emphases often vary, since they wrote for different communities, with varying specific needs. We benefit from these differences, since our *own* hearts crave a response to our *own* specific needs. But, you might ask, "Where is John's Gospel in all this?" Good question! John's stories of Jesus are found sprinkled throughout the year, but most especially in Cycle A of Lent (the season of baptismal preparation) and every Easter season of life-beyond-all-imagining. We also hear John's account of the passion every Good Friday, since the Johannine Jesus majestically assures us: death can *never* be the end, either for Jesus or for us.

Finally, each Gospel selection sets the tone for the day, *always* connecting with the First Reading. During special seasons, outside Ordinary Time, it *also* connects with the Second Reading. Otherwise, in Ordinary Time, we hear from a variety of letters, one after another.

Drawing ever more deeply upon these roots, all the while peering ever more intently into the future, we live—I truly believe—at a most auspicious time. Undoubtedly, COVID-19 cannot possibly leave us unchanged. Neither can ongoing peaceful protests against racism in all its forms. Or challenges to our democracy, beyond imagining, until now. We are also living at a time when we're recognizing how very much science and faith, in concert with each other, can support us all. When evolution, for example, no longer evokes fear in us, but allows us to witness to our becoming. In this regard, I *love* Jesuit theologian Karl Rahner's image of God as the One-on-the-Horizon, beckoning us to become more of who we truly are! What a dynamic believing in this One who cherishes us all! In this One who nudges, invites, cajoles, urges us to become our very best selves. Surely, we are not unlike our ancestor Abram, called by God eons ago to set out on the adventure of a lifetime, to go "to the land that I will show you."[1] Not just once, but again and again and yet again. This endeavor, God assures us, will be one of blessing: "In you all the families of the earth shall be blessed."[2] Truthfully, then, in our daily travels, can we not *also* become a blessing?

It is in that Spirit (of God), then, that I offer this potentially life-changing journey of every liturgical year, companioned by women of passionate faith, substance, courage, strength, and love. I do so with the hope of inspiring, encouraging, and challenging all of us to enter unafraid into such a journey.

1. Gen 12:1.
2. Gen 12:3.

Preface

E ach of us is a word of God. Each of us "hears" God's voice and—on our better days—responds to what we hear, to the best of our ability. Our response becomes, then, that word, spoken out of our God-given gifts. We create poetry. We tell stories. We research and write clear narrative. We analyze and advocate, to the best of our ability. And so much more.

Why do I begin here? As you hold this book in your hands, it might help you to know how I have learned to respond to God's voice. I was trained, early on, to research and write good papers for my courses. Later on, as I engaged in parish ministry, I learned to speak in other ways: primarily through preaching and storytelling. This became a real fit. In fact, some twenty years ago, I formed the group "Women of the Well," in order to create venues—with music—to tell the stories of women in Scripture, Tradition, and contemporary life. Why? Because women's stories have so often been ignored or disregarded. Yet I knew that women's stories are every bit as important as men's, for men as well as for women. Their voices must be heard!

I also fell in love with the liturgical year of my beloved Roman Catholic Church. Why not, then, tell the stories of women within the various seasons of the liturgical year? Why not preach? Tell their stories in the first person? Create other ways of drawing the reader into these stories: like the use of imagined letters and conversations.

You will discover all these ways of speaking in this book. It is my profound hope that you will be drawn into the stories of these significant women and discover bits and pieces of yourself in the process. May you also find inspiration and courage to better become your own unique word of God, offering ever more life and hope to our world.

Gratitudes and Acknowledgments

In thanksgiving to the God of my life, who has continually offered so many "God nudges" of inspiration, along with the desire and encouragement to keep working at this life-giving endeavor.

In thanksgiving for my loving family: my ever-supportive husband, Gene, our three cherished children and their spouses, and our six treasured grandchildren.

In thanksgiving for my colleagues of the "Women of the Well," with whom I have created and presented programs on women for over twenty years now.

In thanksgiving for so many others who have supported and encouraged me over the years, including good friends Irene Goodwin and Mary Kallen, who have read some chapters of this book.

In profound thanksgiving for my dear friend Elizabeth Maurer Webster, who meticulously edited my manuscript in its final stages. With a degree in theology and some background in printing, Liz willingly gave *invaluable* assistance in the final preparations for publication. I am also grateful to Liz's husband, Donald Webster, a gifted computer programmer. He assisted in the final formatting of this book's chapters.

In particular thanksgiving to Father Kevin Murphy, who called me forth at a momentous time in my own life. He recognized possibilities in me of which I was totally unaware, including my budding love of liturgy; furthermore, he inspired my dedication to Church ministry and supported that ministry in a whole host of ways.

1

Advent/Christmas/Epiphany

An Introduction to the Season of Incarnation

In the beginning was the Word, and the Word was with God, and the Word was God . . . And the Word became flesh and lived among us. (John 1:1, 14a)

W e are flesh. Creatures/clay of the earth. Milking cows. Operating machines. Polishing furniture and words. Scrubbing floors. Cuddling babies. Nursing and washing them. Teaching, cajoling, nurturing them into adulthood. Baking bread. Anointing the suffering with compassion. Simply being present to one another.

Yes, we are flesh, clay of the earth. And yet, so much more besides! For we are "the work of" God's hand![1] Kneaded by our Potter. Imbued with God's Holy Spirit. For Jesus, the Christ, the Long-Awaited One, has actually taken on our human flesh! Will, then, the yearnings of the prophet Isaiah of old, *finally* root themselves in us, as well? "Arise, shine; for your light has come, and the glory of the Lord has risen upon you. For darkness shall cover the earth, and thick darkness the peoples; but the Lord will arise upon you, and his glory will appear over you."[2]

Oh, how well we know the darkness! Physical darkness this time of the year for those of us in the northern climes. Or, nagging anxiety-producing darkness. Straining to see beyond illness, financial insecurity, or even ruin.

1. Isa 64:8; in Mark's Gospel of Year B we encounter these words on the First Sunday of Advent.

2. Isa 60:1–2. These were words proclaimed by "Third Isaiah," prophet of the returned exiles, late in the sixth century before Jesus. Their longing to return home had been fulfilled, but they were still in need of further hope. Not unlike them, we are also consoled in this segment of the First Reading for Epiphany.

Pondering. Questioning. Aching from isolation, whether from loved ones or our deepest desires. Can we even *name* those desires?

Yet, the Light *has* come! . . . and with it, a shred of hope. For a new year begins! Will *our* longings and dreams sidle up to, or even embrace, current struggles? Will *our* wrestling produce newfound courage, strength, and even peace? Can *we* finally claim some measure of the deepest truth of all: that God—the Light and Love of Our Lives, the Heartbeat of the Universe—is simply *longing* to be birthed in *us*? To take root in us, breathe in us, hope and dream in us, take on *our* human flesh, again and again and again.

Will this be easy? No. So much life is crammed into this season. We're always in danger, each year, of settling for surface frivolities rather than engaging with God's deepest longings . . . *and* ours. But, is it possible? Yes, oh yes, indeed! Come and see, walk with me as we encounter so many, like Mary, who have said "Yes" to God, over and over and over again. We begin, then, with this season of incarnation: with Advent yearning and preparing, with Christmas birthing, and ultimately with Epiphany revelation/unveiling to the ends of the earth.

Advent: A Season of Longing, Yearning, Preparing

It takes guts, but we *dare* to begin another year, even as cold and darkness (in the northern half of the globe, at least) come knocking on our door. For we are *never* alone. Others, so many other people of faith, have withstood the shadows and emerged stronger, wiser, and fairly *bursting* with God's merciful compassion. Listen to the priest Zechariah, father of John the Baptist, now *filled* with the Holy Spirit at the celebration of John's circumcision. And do not forget that he and his wife, Elizabeth, had endured *years* of childlessness before the joy of this day.

> By the tender mercy of our God,
> the dawn from on high will break
> upon us,
> to give light to those who sit in darkness
> and in the shadow of death,
> to guide our feet into the way of
> peace.[3]

---

3. Luke 1:78–79.

In August 2005, on one morning in Vermont, I experienced something of what Zechariah might have felt, as a stunning sunrise birthed this poem in me.

> *This morning the angels*
> *left wispy puffs in their wake,*
> *like white cotton candy,*
> *clinging to the mountaintop.*
> *I watch . . . coffee brewing . . .*
> *as dawn shyly curtsies.*
>> *Her soft glance tenderly*
>> *brightening the Vermont skyline,*
>> *until . . . Ah!!!*
>> *A shimmering finger emerges,*
>> *urgently extending heavenward*
>> *from the crest of the hill.*
>> *And the sun bursts open the door*
>> *upon another day!*
>> *Gift! Hope! Promise!*
>> *Ours for the taking!*
>> *Ours for the making!*

*Conversing with Our Elders in Faith: Ancient Dreamers
and Evangelists of Good News*

Advent can startle, just like that! Or, more likely, remain hidden, lost, and alone, for *years.* That's how it had been for me. Here I was, forty years old, the newly appointed chair of the parish liturgy committee. Charged with helping folks prepare for the upcoming Advent/Christmas/Epiphany season. My first thought? "Where had Advent *been* all my life?"

Little by little, however, Advent began to speak to me. In treasured childhood memories. Of the annual Christmas carol "sing" around an enormous neighborhood tree. I never knew exactly how it happened, but every year we showed up, always on the proper night. And we would *joyously sing* our beloved Christmas carols! About the same time, there was the annual Christmas pageant in elementary school. At the sound of these words, I would perk up: "In those days a decree went out from emperor Augustus that all the world should be registered."[4] Ah, yes, *that* story, the one I *love*. But the rest of Advent remains a blur . . . of baking, shopping, writing out cards, buying gifts . . . just the right gifts, wrapping presents . . . of getting-ready-for-Christmas-time. I had missed Advent altogether!

Yet—as I was now slowly discovering—there's more, so very much more! This season is fairly bursting with beauty and hope, for it is nothing less than a time of pregnancy and birthing. Of longing for oneness with another/Another. Of exploding with joy at the moment of conception. Of hoping and dreaming: Who will this child resemble? Will this be a boy, or a girl? (In my day, we never knew ahead of time.) Which of God's many dreams for us will bear fruit in her? Or him? Will this pregnant time be an opportunity to begin again? To encounter Jesus—God's Word in human flesh—once again? Not merely the Jesus born over two thousand years ago, as uniquely momentous as that was, but the Jesus about to be born in us! Right here and right now! For we know that birthing takes time. Energy. Attentiveness. Hoping. Dreaming. Planning. Working, hard. Whether we've birthed a child . . . or a dream . . . or a project . . . or anyone/anything else that profoundly matters.

Thus began my ongoing conversation with our Advent elders in faith—from days of old through Gospel evangelists—as found in the readings. Will you join me in this conversation?

The Conversation Begins, Based upon Our Advent Readings:
Cycle A (Matthew's Year); Cycle B (Mark's Year);
and Cycle C (Luke's Year)

Gloria: Didn't our grandparents in faith, as far back as our elders from ancient days, experience those very same deep-seated yearnings? Didn't they also dream deeply of encountering the God of their lives in human flesh? What might *they* say?

Elders: Yes, of course we did. We're human, too. Just like you, with struggles and dreams. Hopes and failures. In *our* day (the eighth century before Christ, as you would say it), one of our great prophets, Isaiah, addressed us in words rooted in our Zionist tradition.[5] He believed—as did we—that God was the great

4. Luke 2:1.

5. The book of Isaiah has been divided into three sections. First Isaiah (chs. 1–39) pronounces judgment and hope from about 739 BCE until a few years into the next century. Second Isaiah (chs. 40–55) tenderly offers solace to a bedraggled people,

king of heaven and earth, that Jerusalem (Zion) was God's royal dwelling on earth, and that kings in the line of David were ruling in God's stead. So it was that he poured forth on us words of both judgment *and* assurance, in the face of the Syro-Ephraimite War, Assyrian attacks, and revolts against King Sennacherib. Listen.

> In days to come the mountain of the Lord's house shall be established as the highest of the mountains, and shall be raised above the hills; all the nations shall stream to it . . . . He [the Lord] shall judge between the nations, and shall arbitrate for many peoples; they shall beat their swords into plowshares, and their spears into pruning hooks; nation shall not lift up sword against nation, neither shall they learn war any more.[6]

Elders: And that's only the beginning! There's even more, so much more!

> A shoot shall come out from the stump of Jesse, and a branch shall grow out of his roots . . . . The wolf shall live with the lamb, the leopard shall lie down with the kid, the calf and the lion and the fatling together, and a little child shall lead them.[7]

Gloria: Ah, the peaceable kingdom! How well we know and cherish these words! For we hear them on the first two Sundays of Advent in Matthew's Year A. But here's my very favorite passage, from Second Isaiah, that sixth-century BCE prophet, seemingly alone in imagining a glorious homecoming for the people of Israel stuck in exile in Babylon. In fact, I chose it for my mother-in-law's funeral; for she had suffered greatly and was now surely at peace. (It is given to us all on the Second Sunday of Advent, Mark's Year B.)

> Comfort, O comfort my people, says your God. Speak tenderly to Jerusalem, and cry to her that she has served her term . . . . A voice cries out: "In the wilder-ness prepare the way of the Lord, make straight in the desert a highway for our God." . . . See, the Lord God

---

hoping against hope to return home to Jerusalem from exile in Babylon, beginning in the 540s BCE. Third Isaiah draws heavily from Second Isaiah but is writing after the exiles' return home in 539 BCE.

6. Isa 2:2, 4, from the First Sunday of Advent, Cycle A.

7. Isa 11:1, 6, from the Second Sunday of Advent, Cycle A.

comes with might, and his arm rules for him . . . . He
will feed his flock like a shepherd; he will gather the
lambs in his arms, and carry them in his bosom, and
gently lead the mother sheep.[8]

Elders: What healing balm for any of us in sorrow, suffering, and
throbbing pain! How could he so compassionately name what we
dared not even *begin* to conceive?

Gloria: And this is only the beginning! By our Third Sunday of
Advent, joy *multiplies*; it can even be tasted, touched, and em-
braced! Listen!

The wilderness and the dry land shall be glad, the
desert shall rejoice and blossom . . . . Then the eyes
of the blind shall be opened, and the ears of the deaf
unstopped; then the lame shall leap like a deer, and the
tongue of the speechless sing for joy.[9]
    The spirit of the Lord God is upon me, because the
Lord has anointed me; he has sent me to bring good
news to the oppressed, to bind up the brokenhearted,
to proclaim liberty to the captives, and release to the
prisoners; to proclaim a year of the Lord's favor. . . .[10]
    Sing aloud, O daughter Zion; shout, O Israel!
Rejoice and exult with all your heart, O daughter
Jerusalem! . . . The Lord, your God, is in your midst,
a warrior who gives victory; he will rejoice over you
with gladness, he will renew you in his love.[11]

Elders: *Explosions* of joy! Yes! We know them ourselves, however
fleeting.

How about us? How do these words impact us?
Do these words seem beyond imagining? And yet, don't we, like our
elders in faith, plead for peace in times of petty struggles and the horrors of
war? Don't we, too, long to come home, whatever that means to each of us,
just as deeply as did our ancestors, bound up in Babylon? Don't we know
the trashing of cruel name-calling and bullying, the scourge of political di-
visiveness, and the battling of endless wars across this tiny planet we call

8. Isa 40:1–2a, 3, 10a, 11.

9. Isa 35:1, 5–6a, from the Third Sunday of Advent, Cycle A.

10. Isa 61:1–2a, from Mark's Year B. This Third Sunday's First Reading also includes
Isa 61:10–11.

11. Zeph 3:14, 17, from Luke's Year C.

home? Of course we do! Our hearts break at the sight of children savagely thrust aside. Who can ever forget the five-year-old child of Aleppo, covered in dust, dazed into silence by his only reality of brutal war? I can't! Who can deny that his suffering goes on and on and on, in so many other innocents? Where is God in all this? Where is Advent hope in all this? Good questions. Great questions! *Our* questions, at one time or another.

Maybe, just maybe, *we* need to wake up! Feel the splash of cold water! The urgency of time running out! Our Advent evangelists—Matthew, Mark, and Luke—oblige us in this regard. Do you ever wonder why on earth we begin Advent with the adult Jesus, about to enter into his passion? Why this rude awakening by the Very One for whom we have been waiting? Where is the warm comfort of the Babe of Bethlehem?

Our Conversation Continues with Our Gospel Bearers of the Good News

Jesus fully intends to startle us . . . disturb us . . . provoke us . . . with foreboding images from his "end time" or "eschatological" discourses (in all three Catholic Lectionary cycles). Imagine an impending flood . . . a thief about to break into a house . . . heaven and earth about to pass away . . . signs of distress among nations and the roaring of the sea and the waves. Furthermore, St. Paul, in his Letter to the Romans, reinforces this wake-up call with a warning. "You know what time it is, how it is now the moment for you to wake from sleep. For salvation is nearer to us now than when we became believers; the night is far gone, the day is near."[12]

> **Gloria:** Those of us getting on in years understand that one! Then there are the moments we'll *never* forget. The pandemic, of course, and others unique to each of us. I was thirty-nine years old, driving early one Sunday morning to pick up my twelve-year-old daughter from Girl Scout camp. Distracted momentarily, I lost control of the car. It careened across the road (thankfully, no traffic was coming at me), and I landed upside down across the road. I only remember this: a heartfelt "God, *help* me!" before the sensation of being scooped up tenderly, only to land safely in the back seat. I emerged with only a tiny scar above my eye. *And* the beginning of a whole new life. God had certainly caught my attention! I would never again be the same.

> **A Gospel Evangelist:** Who can *continue* to provoke us, like it or not? Who can *alert* us to the ultimate truth: that the

12. Rom 13:11–12a, Cycle A.

Long-Awaited-One is *here, with* us, *alive* in our midst! There is only one: John the Baptist!

Gloria: Oh, how we need this rough-and-tumble truth-teller! To break through our busy, busy, busy lives! Our presumed need to meet everyone's expectations! Indeed, John does *not* take us on a saunter in the park on our Second and Third Sundays of Advent. Oh, no! Some thirty years ago now (as parish pastoral associate), I was about to preach on the Second Sunday of Advent, Cycle A.[13] Why not, I thought, enter and go down the main aisle . . . as John the Baptist? Complete with sheepskin clothing and a long wig? Shouting, "Repent! Repent! The kingdom of heaven has come near!" So I did! And I can assure you of this: it caught everyone's attention! What did I say after that? I have no idea, but *here* is what I can say now.

A Preaching Word for the Second Sunday of Advent, Cycle A

What on earth does that rough-and-tumble, harshly judgmental John the Baptist have to do with that powerfully poetic vision of First Isaiah? Total and utter peace: the lion lying down with the lamb. Or, in today's world, the refugee safely snuggled in the arms of the ICE enforcer. Enough food to go around for everyone. Where are *we* in this picture?

Hard to imagine, isn't it? Would it help to know that Isaiah's world, in the eighth century before Jesus, was *not* so very different from ours? With kings—rulers like dead stumps—striding around in self-importance. With divisions and hatred at every turn. With wars, even little firefights, everywhere. Surely, underneath it all was the profound yearning for the peaceable kingdom, so poetically proclaimed by Isaiah. Not unlike our own deepest hopes and dreams, in the face of constant name-calling and bullying. Sharply divisive points of view on a daily basis. Hate crimes and shootings. Impeachment proceedings and indictments for bribery. Add to that, stores shoving their wares in our faces: "Look at this!" "Buy that!" When even our best intentioned preparations—cookie baking, choosing just the right gift for a loved one, writing out cards—can simply feel like it's all too much! Don't we long for, yearn for, this peaceable kingdom? But, where and how is it to be found?

Can we listen to, can we really *hear*, the full-throated cry of John the Baptist: "Repent!" Turn around! But, we might say: How? What are we to

13. See Isa 11:1–10; Ps 72; Rom 15:4–9; Matt 3:1–12.

do? Here's a suggestion; it's become my treasured practice this time of the year. In fact, it's become balm for my soul. I get up early, in the darkness, and turn on the Christmas tree lights. I sit opposite the lights and intentionally invite God into my day. I take as much quiet time as possible. What will I discover? The patience that doesn't come easily? The joy of this one precious life I've been given? The hope and courage that peek out from behind struggles engaged? Maybe some answers to questions that endure? I never know what will emerge. But, oh, how I treasure these precious moments.

Of course, that's just the beginning. John the Baptist isn't done with us yet. He pushes and prods us: Produce good fruit! Show signs of turning around! This we know: John the Baptist has already prepared the way. He's already announced the good news. Now it's our turn. For we've already been baptized into his promised Holy Spirit, that fire of love and passion for justice. We've already been named priest, prophet, and royal person: fully responsible for our lives and our choices. Now what?

Remember now, we're pregnant with good fruit. Each and every one of us, pregnant with the good news. We'll know that this seed of life is growing within us whenever we can listen deeply to others, especially the ones with whom we disagree. Or find particularly cranky. Whenever we can hear their pain and struggle beneath the words they spew forth. We'll know that this new life is growing within us whenever we feel its kicks. Urging us to stand tall for what we know to be true. To speak our truth, even and especially when it is not comfortable. Perhaps most of all, we'll know we're on the right path whenever we give up trying to meet everyone's needs—like scattershot, all over the place—rather than responding only out of what is humanly possible. We'll certainly know this new life is taking form whenever we begin to feel ever more at peace with ourselves, so much so that we absolutely *must* share it.

Will, then, the "dawn from on high" break upon us this year? The full-blown recognition that Jesus needs you and me, right here and right now, to make his coming complete? Urging *us* to become our own unique version of John the Baptist, announcing loud and clear: "The kingdom of heaven is at hand!" And, we won't need to get dressed up in odd-looking clothes to do it!

Conclusion of Our Advent Conversation
with Our Gospel Writers

Gloria: Jesus, the One-and-Only Jesus! Matthew, how could you even begin to tell his story? We now know this: you and Luke each took two chapters to set the stage. Brilliant chapters. So different, one from the other. Written for different communities. With different needs. Yet the message remains the same: God is *always* there for the least likely, for those most in need. We have come to call them "infancy narratives."

I've been pondering: what is at the heart of your message for us all?

Matthew the Evangelist: In my case, it is the outsiders—from the outset—who are deepest in God's heart (gentiles, women, and more, as found in my genealogy of Jesus). Also, it is Joseph, not Mary, to whom the angel appears, in dream after dream. Yet Joseph lives in the shadows, does he not? The "strong, silent one," the protector of the Holy Family. What is he feeling in and through all this?

Gloria: I had not given this much thought, until Scripture scholar Kenneth E. Bailey suggested this possibility: Joseph is "fuming" at the news of Mary's pregnancy.[14] Even so, the compassionate Joseph decides to simply divorce her, quietly. Until he has another dream from another angel of God, as you describe it: "Do not be afraid to take Mary as your wife, for the child conceived in her is from the Holy Spirit."[15] Bailey goes on to suggest that Joseph determines to become Isaiah's "suffering servant" on behalf of Mary, even though he *still* does *not* understand.[16]

Luke, what inspired your telling of the story?

Luke the Evangelist: Some might say I write as though a symphony strikes up an overture, from the very first note, of the life/death/resurrection of Jesus. Even before the birth, I orchestrate the prophetic undercurrent of God's merciful love coursing throughout this entire Gospel. Upside-down love. Unexpected love . . . offered to and claimed by two women, Mary and Elizabeth.

Gloria: Yes. We call it the Visitation. The encounter between the two essential mothers of faith, not only of their sons, but also of us all . . . Elizabeth, mother of John the Baptist, and Mary, the mother of Jesus. You have no idea of the inspiration you

14. Bailey, *Jesus through Middle Eastern Eyes*, 44–45.
15. Matt 1:20.
16. See Isa 42:1–6 and Bailey, *Jesus through Middle Eastern Eyes*, 43–46.

have provided—age after age—to musicians, composers, artists, poets, and writers of every stripe. You have even inspired my reflection, as follows.

Reflection on Elizabeth

Won't you come with me to the home of Zechariah and Elizabeth, just outside Jerusalem? The very place deliberately sought out by Mary. What a long trek ... up, up, and up even more steps ... until finally, there you are! In May (when I was there), it's blossoming in Technicolor. Then, upon turning around, what a view! A deeply terraced hill, sandy in tone, but dotted with green scrub brush, here, there, and everywhere. Stubbornly daring to grow, but only after long hours of backbreaking labor. Perhaps this letter will help express what I was experiencing, in light of Luke's account of the Visitation, only to be found in his Gospel.

Dear Elizabeth,

You still stand in the shadows, though I have come to appreciate you more and more, year after year, as I age. Your courage in the midst of pain. Your faithfulness to the God of your life. Your hard-won wisdom. Your never-failing love in the midst of it all.

How can I imagine you in the flesh? Maybe by calling to mind my beloved Aunt Bess, Mary Elizabeth by name. My godmother. What a hardworking, faithful woman she was! In the Depression days, she was sent out to work after eighth grade, to help support her mom and dad and two younger brothers (the older of the two, my beloved dad). Maybe she complained, but I never heard any of it. When I would briefly come for a visit to the farm, she was always up early (so was I, never wanting to miss a beat), ready to head off to her factory job. Even then, I could feel her unconditional love for me, though the words were never spoken. Later on, when I was twenty years old, my dad died instantly, from a massive heart attack. She was the one who urgently insisted: "Finish college! Be sure you finish college!" I promised I would, and I did. Later, soon after our first child was born, I invited her over for dinner often, since we lived near her for a couple of years. What a gift to us!

Elizabeth, I see in you that very same faithfulness, that very same courage, that very same unconditional love, that very same wisdom. No wonder Mary sought you out! Here she was, a youngster by our standards, suddenly offered a mind-boggling

mission in life: become the mother—unwed, besides!—of the
Promised One, the Messiah! What on earth had she just done,
by saying "Yes"? Who could possibly understand and offer wisdom, support, strength, and guidance? It had to be you, Elizabeth, of course! Such a good, kind, faith-filled woman, you had
suffered for years from your shameful wound of infertility. From
endless whispers behind your back: "She seems so good, but she
must have done something wrong, somewhere."

Yet, God chose you, Elizabeth, to bear the son you named
John (the Baptist)! The one who would spade the ground for
the Messiah's coming. Oh, the balm, the quiet time of grateful contemplation you entered into, the prayers that must have
poured out of your depths, for a full three months. Without
realizing it, you were preparing for the visit of a lifetime, from
Mary, years younger, yet the one with whom you had always
felt a deep and abiding bond.

Were you jolted by the sound of Mary's voice at your
doorstep? For you apparently felt life for the very first time!
Moving in you, leaping, in fact, already announcing the words
that fell from your lips: "And why has this happened to me,
that the mother of my Lord comes to me?"[17] Spontaneously, in
response, Mary sang for all she was worth! The Magnificat, we
call it, though Mary knew it first as Hannah's Song. Hannah—a
once-barren woman—simply could not keep from rejoicing at
the birth and dedication to God of her precious son, Samuel.[18]
Was Mary honoring God's gift to you after all these years? Was
she even unwittingly nurturing in you the confident boldness
with which you would come to name your beloved son at his
circumcision? Yes, you, not his father Zechariah, contrary to
all the rules of the day.

Elizabeth, could you have possibly imagined at that moment
that your coming together with Mary was nothing less than the
first chord of a symphony of God's merciful love? And that your
two voices, Mary's and yours, would be tenderly recounted by a
man we call Luke, in a Gospel unknown to you? Indeed, in his
telling, we are given the very first prophetic words of this entire
Gospel! For you were first to proclaim Jesus as Lord. And Mary's
hymn of praise proclaimed the entire upside-down ministry of

17. Luke 1:43.

18. See 1 Sam 2:1–10; Hannah was named later on by the rabbis as the teacher of
intercessory prayer. She returned Samuel to the safekeeping and mentoring of Eli, the
priest, as promised; and Samuel became the last and greatest judge of Israel, before the
monarchy of Saul.

Jesus: to the lost, alone, rejected, hopelessly sinful, the hungry, the ones who have nothing. Surely, Mary would have needed the fortification of her time with you, to be able to hear the words of yet another prophet, Simeon: "This child is destined for the falling and the rising of many in Israel, and to be a sign that will be opposed so that the inner thoughts of many will be revealed— and a sword will pierce your own soul too."[19]

So it is, Elizabeth, that I rub my eyes, trying to see you in the flesh, trying to lock hearts with you, trying to take in your courage, strength, wisdom, and joy, even in the face of conflict and ongoing struggle. You, indeed, are prophet and model for us all.

Sincerely,

Gloria Ulterino

Reflection on Mary

No Advent season would be complete without Mary. Remember being thirteen years old? I do. We had just moved some three hundred miles from where I'd been born. Nearly every day that summer I would ride my bike all over town, just trying to get the lay of the land. This brought to mind another memory, a powerful memory. Of another perspective on this town: at night, looking down from on high at so many twinkling lights. Sparkling from home after home.

This memory stirred something totally new in me. For I connected as never before with the angel's annunciation to Mary. What if each of those lights represents a person? What if each of those lights represents a hope, a possibility of God's desire? As with Mary, each of them—each of us—gift- ed by God. In effect, each of them—each of us—a womb of God, seeded by the divine, to offer something precious to this dark, troubled, needy world. I could imagine a musician down there, comforting the world with a hushing lullaby, or awakening the world (perhaps by cacophony) to the taking on of an urgent dream. I could imagine someone else, gifted with wisdom and understanding, enough to bring integrity to politics. I could imagine the gift of science growing within the breast of yet another, who would eventually help create a life-saving vaccine, like the new coronavi- rus vaccines. I could imagine so many healing strains simply longing to be sung, for the good of us all.

19. Luke 2:34–35.

Is there doubt? Even fear? Maybe. And yet, from a young girl's deep well of passionate trust emerged these words: "Here am I, the servant of the Lord; let it be done with me according to your word."[20] God's ultimate dream took flesh then; God's dreams can still take flesh today.

Christmas: A Child Is Born!
The Child Is Born!

What are *your* stories of birthing? Perhaps your very own birth, as told by someone who loves you dearly. Or, the birth of a child. Your own, or someone else's. I remember so clearly the birth of my very first grandchild, Kayla Marie! It was a golden day in Chicago, late in October. Indeed, it seemed that all of nature's trees were welcoming this precious new life into the world with their golden hue. My daughter had invited me into the labor and delivery room, so I was there at the very moment of her arrival. I just couldn't resist heading over to the scale as the nurse took note of her weight. A bundle of energy, Kayla grabbed hold of my little finger for all she was worth. Life had won out, yet again!

But now: *The* Child is born! The Long-Awaited-One from of old! Remember Isaiah's bold promises to his people, at war with Syria in the eighth century BCE? God would act, lopping down mighty boughs, hacking down entangling thickets, until just the right time. And then: "A shoot shall come out from the stump of Jesse, and a branch shall grow out of his roots. The spirit of the Lord shall rest on him."[21] *This* Shoot would "decide with equity for the meek of the earth."[22] Bring peace. Between the wolf and the lamb, the leopard and the kid, between ICE and refugees today, between Democrats and Republicans, "and a little child shall lead them."[23] Yet, there's even more! When *we* are feeling lost and alone, disheartened and disconsolate, Second Isaiah's extravagant promises—two centuries later to a people in exile—can quench *our* deepest thirst, as well: "The wilderness and the dry land shall be glad, the desert shall rejoice and blossom; like the crocus it shall blossom abundantly, and rejoice with joy and singing."[24]

---

20. Luke 1:38.

21. Isa 11:1–2a, from the First Reading for the Second Sunday of Advent, Cycle A.

22. Isa 11:4b, from the same First Reading.

23. Isa 11:6c, the conclusion of that same First Reading.

24. Isa 35:1–2a, from the Third Sunday of Advent, Cycle A; this section likely belonged originally to the consoling book of Second Isaiah, chs. 40–55, written to weary people in exile in Babylon.

So it is that I kept wondering: what might Luke and Matthew each tell us about the *essentials* of their birth stories of Jesus?

Luke: First and foremost, this story is *not* magic. It does *not* alter the outward appearance of ordinary people. They were still poor. Still subject to political authority. If the emperor proclaimed a census, they would still need to obey. Although I am a gentile, I *knew* the promises of old to the Jewish people. I *knew* that Jesus *had* to be born in Bethlehem—the "city of David," just outside Jerusalem—even though Joseph and Mary lived up north, in Nazareth of Galilee. For Joseph was descended from the house and family of David. I *knew* that tiny Bethlehem would have been overrun with people in the midst of a census. So, why not have the birth take place in a barn? With only a manger—a feeding trough for animals—as the first place to lay Jesus' head? How fitting, of course, since Jesus would become Bread for all people! I *knew* that his birth was a fulfillment of all God's promises of old. A genuine God event! Yes, angels might well have been singing their hearts out. And shepherds—the lowest of the low, dirty and smelly because their work was out in the fields with no opportunity for ritual cleansing, never welcome in polite company—might well have been the very first to hear and respond to the great good news!

Gloria: By the way, as one approaches the center of the town of Bethlehem today, there's a field, with an enormous metal archway announcing its significance: *"Gloria in Excelsis Deo"* (Glory to God in the Highest)! Indeed, a small sign to the right identifies the place as "Terra Sancta" (Holy Land). We know it today as Shepherd's Field.

Luke continues: I *knew* that prayer was absolutely essential, just as it always was for Jesus. So, of course, right from the first, there would be people at prayer in the temple, a woman as well as a man. As for women, Mary's experience *must* take center stage. Oh, the questions she *must* have had! To whom could she go for advice and support? Ah, yes, how about Elizabeth, that wise, older relative, who had always been so kind, even in the midst of her own struggles to conceive. So it was that this story simply poured out of me.

Gloria: If only you knew how much we love your story! Given a boost, of course, by St. Francis of Assisi (1181/82 to 1226), who was enthralled by your portrait of events. Every year, in every parish, there's always a search for just the right baby to be Jesus. And, whose little girl will be Mary? How many angels and shepherds do we need? Could you have any idea of the music you have inspired over the centuries? From the tenderhearted "Silent Night"—now often introduced by the lovely "Night of Silence"— to the rousing "Angels We Have Heard on High,"[25] and so much more, classic as well as modern. Don't our deepest hopes today still well up at the sound? Will this One *finally* bring an end to terrorism? Walls that divide? Graffiti that denounces "the other," any other, oftentimes the very people who birthed Jesus in the first place? Millions spent on defense against "the enemy"? Name-calling, political strife that digs deeper than ever before, or so it seems? When, oh when, will there be an end to this nastiness, this certitude that only my view is the right one? When, oh when, can we hear the hopes and dreams of every human heart? When and where, if not in us and through us?

Matthew: As a faithful Jew, I would need to begin with a genealogy of Jesus, following the male line. But *my* genealogy included *women*! Holy women, like Ruth, though she was a Moabite, from a race denounced by the Jewish people. Others, like Rahab and Bathsheba—I never mentioned her by name, referring to her only as the "wife of Uriah"[26]—were left open to interpretation. And I completed the genealogy with Joseph, "the husband of Mary, of whom Jesus was born, who is called the Messiah."[27]

I would acknowledge that darkness still prevailed, from beginning to end. For the magi—from a different land and culture—simply *had* to travel at night, at the thrilling necessity of following that Promising Star. They might have been stalked by death at every turn, placing themselves at risk to robbers and ne'er-do-wells. Their danger even intensified, in fact, upon their arrival in Jerusalem. For their seeking after "the child who has

25. "Silent Night" was written by the nineteenth-century German pastor Joseph Mohr; Daniel Kantor wrote the words and music for "Night of Silence" (GIA Publications, 1984); "Angels We Have Heard on High" is an eighteenth-century French carol.

26. Matt 1:7. We know her as Bathsheba.

27. Matt 1:16.

been born king of the Jews"[28] stirred up tremors of fear in Herod and "all Jerusalem with him."[29]

Gloria: Indeed, our church still remembers Herod's maniacal massacre of the innocents on December 28, immediately following the joy of Jesus' birth.

Matthew continues: Even one of the magi's gifts smelled of death: while there was gold to honor a ruler, and frankincense (a fragrant resin used for worship), there was also myrrh (a resin used for embalming). Finally, the magi—warned in a dream of the danger lurking in Jerusalem—"left for their own country by another road."[30] And Joseph, *also* warned in a dream of Herod's intent to massacre all children under the age of two, fled to Egypt with his little family. Does he not remind you of Jacob's (Israel's) youngest son, Joseph (the "dreamer"), who ultimately saved his brothers in Egypt?[31] Is it not true, then, that Jesus became the new Moses, readying to deliver his people from death and destruction, even in the midst of darkness? Even in the midst of dominating oppression? This refugee family could only safely return from Egypt to the backwaters of Galilee upon the death of King Herod.

From beginning to end, I proclaimed: Jesus' birth, life, death, and resurrection would *disrupt* the status quo. Yes, earthquakes abounded! As Jesus entered Jerusalem just before his passion, I noted, "The whole city was in turmoil, asking, 'Who is this?'"[32] Upon his death, then, "The earth shook, and the rocks were split. The tombs also were opened, and many bodies of the saints who had fallen asleep were raised. After his resurrection they came out of the tombs and entered the holy city and appeared to many."[33] Finally, for the last time, "there was a great earthquake; for an angel of the Lord, descending from heaven, came and rolled back the stone and sat on it."[34] How fitting, then, that the angel proclaimed the *best* news of all to the women at the

28. Matt 2:2.
29. Matt 2:3.
30. Matt 2:12.
31. See Gen 37–49.
32. Matt 21:10.
33. Matt 27:51b–53.
34. Matt 28:2.

empty tomb: "He has been raised from the dead, and indeed he is going ahead of you to Galilee; there you will see him."[35]

Gloria: As you have said, these are *not* stories of magic. They are *our* stories, our *truest* stories: of the unfathomable love of our God for *us*, here and now. *Our* stories of the One who simply cannot ignore us in our miseries. *Our* stories of the One who refuses to erase them but works through them, with us, simple creatures of clay and flesh that we are, giving us hope despite everything. *Our* stories that proclaim: life is still tough but—in and through Jesus—God is *alive*! So . . . *nothing* is beyond the scope and power of God's unending love for us all!

The Gospel Given for the Vigil of Christmas: Matthew 1:1–17

Introduction: This is the Gospel passage we almost *never* hear! Even though it is the one given to us: the opening flourish of Matthew's Gospel, the genealogy of Jesus. But, it *was* the Gospel proclaimed in the first parish I served. It always fell to the deacon, who groaned—once again—that he was to be preaching on those "begats." (Because there were several preachers on staff, we were each assigned a different Mass for Christmas.) And I immediately responded to him, "Oh, I'd love to preach on that!" After he looked at me like I had two heads, I briefly explained why. For my beloved Scripture professor, Father Sebastian Falcone, had already given me the key; so, here is what I'd say.

A PREACHING WORD ON MATTHEW 1:1–17

I had so many memories of my grandmother, a great cook! It was how she made her living before her marriage. Aromas of dough rising on her old black wrought iron stove would draw me to the kitchen first thing in the morning when I would stay with them as a youngster. And my grandpa would regale me with stories. Though I couldn't have said so until years later, they were the ones who first taught me about Eucharist.

Which brings me to the genealogy of Jesus. Look at all those women! Why, it was unheard of to include women in a family's genealogy! There's Tamar, daughter-in-law of Judah, eldest of

---

35. Matt 28:7.

the twelve sons of Jacob.[36] She might well be accused of incest, since she tricked her father-in-law into having sex with her, which produced her twin sons. Why? Because, in those days, the widow Tamar could only be protected by marrying another son of Judah. But he had refused to honor this tradition. So, she plotted . . . and took action. In the end, Judah would proclaim, "She is more in the right than I, since I did not give her to my son Shelah."[37] Or, take the prostitute Rahab. An outsider, a sinner, a looked-down-upon woman, yet *she* is the one who assists the Israelite spies in their conquest of the Holy Land. Not only that, she enters the family herself, becoming another ancestor of King David! Then there's the sainted Ruth, a Moabite, from a people *detested* by the Israelites. Yet it is she who lives the spirit of the covenant more truly than any Israelite, becoming the great-grandmother of King David. There's the "wife of Uriah," known to us as Bathsheba, and finally, there's Mary herself, mother of Jesus.

What a slice of life! Honorable people and scoundrels, women and men. So it is that this genealogy is worth celebrating, isn't it? A God for us all, from way back then. A God for us all, to this very day! Our God, who is nothing less than Incomparable Love, the unfathomable Word-beyond-Understanding-Become-Flesh. One of us! Touching and being touched. Feeling our ups and downs. Struggling with anxieties and celebrating joys, from inside out. It's almost beyond human understanding, isn't it, that God chose to live the warts as well as the wonders of the human condition? God chose *us* as family! A mixed bag of weaknesses, sins, *and* greatheartedness. Us! What great cause for rejoicing!

Epiphany: Revealing/Unveiling This Word-Become-Flesh to the Ends of the Earth

Epiphany. In *Webster's Ninth New Collegiate Dictionary*, epiphany is an appearance or manifestation, especially of a divine being. For Christians, Epiphany is a celebration of the coming of the magi: outsiders, gentiles, beyond the pale of the Jewish faith. Who were they? Followers of a star, seekers of "the newborn king of the Jews." Bearers of gifts. Companions on a journey not unlike our very own: into the *beyond*, into *more*, into *life-changing truth*. How many were they? We can't say for sure. How did their

36. See Gen 38 and 1 Chr 2:3–4.

37. Gen 38:26.

lives change? We do not know that, either. But, they heeded a divine pull, then a divine warning before heading home *by another way*. Their lives mattered. So do ours, for we are the seekers, the magi of today.

A Preaching Word for Epiphany: Isaiah 60:1–6;
Ephesians 3:2–3a, 5–6; Matthew 2:1–12

Catherine was her name. You could easily spot her in church: tall, stately, usually wearing a stylish hat. A professional woman, of friendly demeanor, she always accompanied her husband and his daughter. Her husband, Tom, was one of the "pillars of the church," lovable and compassionate. On the day of Catherine's funeral, it was Tom—then in his mid-eighties—who gathered himself up tall to deliver her eulogy.

Although the pastor was a fine preacher, I cannot remember a word he said. But Tom? His words, I'll never forget! "When I was growing up," he began, "we lived at the very end of a cul-de-sac. At dusk I loved to go outside as the lamplighter arrived. I would watch . . . as he very carefully lit each lamp . . . one after another . . . until a soft glow covered the entire street. [Pause] Catherine was my lamplighter."

Tom was drawn to the light. As are we . . . in this clouded, darkened world, where bullying has become commonplace in politics. Where the earth cries out for our care. Where devastating storms rob so many of their homes. Where too many worry about lack of health care. Where physical and mental diseases sadly stake their claim on precious lives. And now, where COVID-19 literally turns life upside down.

Yes, we are drawn to the Light, for we are people of faith. Hardwired to seek out the Source of All Light. The One and Only, who created each and every one of us for good, caring, mercy, and setting things right in this clouded, darkened world of ours. We are seekers, not unlike the magi of old. Gentiles, from a far-away world. Not necessarily three, but an unknown number. Not kings, but people who had studied the heavens. Enough to be drawn by a star they could not explain, a star that promised more of life than they had previously known. A path to a Mystery they *had* to follow. Even at night, when their way would have been strewn with the danger of robbers and who-knows-what-else. They *had* to discover the Source. They *had* to offer the proper gifts: gold for royalty, frankincense for worship, and myrrh to proclaim that this king was one of us, yes, even in death itself. They had to go home by a different way, for their lives—after finding *this* king—would never, ever, be the same.

So it is for us. Hardwired, like the magi, to seek that Ruler of our very lives. That same Mystery who created each and every one of us. Who yearns for us beyond all telling—first, last, and always—never giving up on us. How privileged we are, then, to be baptized into this Mystery of Love. To be given a candle that is none other than the Very Light of this World. To be charged with keeping this Candle burning brightly all the days of our life, on into eternity. To set out on the journey of a lifetime: discovering, claiming, and living out our own unique God-given gifts in our own unique way.

Doesn't this journey flow out of companionship with others? Relationships of nurturing, caring, and mentoring? In and through nudges, challenges, and glimpses of "more"? Perhaps out of a desire to right wrongs and sufferings? Is it easy? No! Possible? Risky? Sometimes even dangerous? Courageous? And worth every step, even every misstep? Yes, yes, and yes, by the grace of God. I know. For at a certain point in my life, two people—a priest and a faith formation director—set me on a new pathway home. Never had I been more certain of anything! I *had* to discover this Source of All Life. I *had* to study theology. I *had* to enter parish ministry and wherever else this path would lead. The struggles have never ceased, but the joy has been beyond all telling.

Since the Second Vatican Council of the early 1960s, we—the Church, all of us—are called to be lamplighters, just like Catherine. People who glow with the Light of Christ, the Light of All Peoples (*Lumen Gentium*). Or, a "field hospital," as Pope Francis often likes to describe it. A place of continual reaching out to others rather than holding ourselves aloof. A place of building communities of health and healing rather than walls of schism. A place of listening, conversing, understanding, forgiving, helping make whole. This is our calling. This is our vocation, however we live it out. As people of clay: musicians, scientists, creators of families, pray-ers, politicians (yes, politicians), lawyers, teachers, priests, lay ministers, "techies," factory workers, laborers, and on and on. For the One we seek is the Lamplighter of our Hearts, the Source of all gifts, intended for our good and the good of our world, intended for healing, forgiveness and hope. This is the true meaning of Epiphany, the revelation of Christ to the entire world.

An Epiphany Story: The Life-Changing
Journey of St. Elizabeth Ann Seton

Now is the time for one final story. A story of this season: of pregnancy, giving birth, and of following the Star of Jesus wherever it led. It's the story of a young Anglican woman, wife and mother of five, whose life is totally transformed after a journey that will mark the death of her beloved husband. It's the story of encountering Roman Catholicism in Italy under the tutelage of dear friends, of becoming Roman Catholic, and of pursuing a dream to educate young girls and establish the first order of women religious in this country. I like to think of this woman as a "living letter of Christ," given her life's work and prolific letter writing to friends, even before the establishment of the United States Postal System. Not unlike Paul's image of the Corinthian community, she is certainly "a letter of Christ . . . written not with ink but with the Spirit of the living God, not on tablets of stone but on tablets of human hearts."[38] What follows is a story of her journey to Italy, which will change her life forever. What follows is a story of Elizabeth Ann Bayley Seton, the first native-born person in this country to be named a saint in 1975.

(Elizabeth comes in slowly and sinks into a rocking chair. She is wearing a long black shawl and black hat.) Do you mind if I sit here? I am old now—forty-six—and all worn out . . . (*now perking up . . .*) It is Epiphany, and I love that story. It always gives me energy. It is my story, too . . . following the star of Jesus . . . then, going home by another road. Let me tell you about it. (*Getting up, she places her black shawl and hat on the chair.*)

It all started some eighteen years ago, on October 3, 1803. I remember the date well. I remember *everything* about the voyage my husband, Willie, and I were about to undertake. Imagine with me, won't you? From on board our ship—the *Shepherdess*—we could look back on the tip of Manhattan, on our home. It was now a bustling little city of some thirty thousand people. I caught sight of Wall Street . . . the homes of some people I knew . . . some businesses, like Willie's merchant marine business. And most especially some of the most precious people in this world that I was leaving behind. Our oldest daughter—Anna Maria, now eight—was coming with us, but our four other little darlings . . . including our youngest, just weaned . . .

38. 2 Cor 3:3.

were left behind in the care of family members. Why were we *doing* this? Where were we headed that was *calling* to us so urgently? You need to know this: my precious Willie was dying from TB. I would come to call it the family disease. And the only hope for him, it seemed, was to accept the invitation of his good business friend and associate Antonio Filicci. "*Come* to us," he had insisted. Come, soak up the warm Italian sun, and you just might be healed. Many of our friends thought we were totally mad, though a couple of my dearest friends understood. How could we *not* take this chance? This one final opportunity for healing?

The voyage itself was healing. Precious time for reading . . . for playing with Anna Maria . . . for watching Willie become closer and closer to God. But, it was too long a journey, over two months. By the time we arrived, nothing about the Italian sun could save Willie's life. He died in my arms on December 27. And with him, it seemed that everything had died . . . our hopes and dreams . . . our plans . . . *everything.*

Yet the Filiccis took us in, and the healing rays of their warm welcome began to work their way into our hearts . . . Anna Maria's and mine. "Mama, how many friends God has provided for us in this strange land. For they are our friends before they even know us!"[39] Yes, week in and week out, they took us to church with them. The Catholic Church. For the Filiccis were faithful Catholics, good and loving Catholics. And their churches! Magnificent! Beautiful beyond believing. Back home, *my* church—into which I had been born, baptized and raised—was called the Protestant Episcopal Church. It was the church of nearly everyone I knew, certainly of professional people. There wasn't even a Catholic church in New York City back then. It wasn't long before I found myself writing to my dear sister-in-law, "How happy would we be if we believed what these dear Souls believe, that they possess God in the Sacrament and that he remains in their churches, and is carried to them when they are sick."[40] At that time, we Protestants only celebrated Communion four times a year. Where was the *vital*, Living Presence of Christ?

Over the spring of 1804—yes, we remained there for all kinds of healing—a new star began to rise in the heavens, peeking out from behind my clouds of grieving . . . nudging, emboldening, and questioning me. Could I imagine the unthinkable? Becoming Catholic? Would *everything* in my life change? Would my family and friends resist me at every turn? Would they even shun my children? Would they see us now as part of the lower class? For Catholics in New York were mainly immigrants. How

39. Bechtle, *Collected Writings*, 1:280; January 6, 1804.
40. Bechtle, *Collected Writings*, 1:292; February 24, 1804.

would I manage to support myself and my five children? Certainly I could teach: French and the love of God. But, would my friends *refuse* to send their children to my school?

As it turned out, my fears of being shunned were realized, even by some family members and my former friend and pastor, Dr. Henry Hobart. If it hadn't been for a few loyal friends and Antonio—who not only accompanied Anna Maria and me back home but stayed on this side of the Atlantic for three years—I hate to think. He introduced me to Bishop Carroll of Baltimore . . . to the Rev. Mr. Dubourg, president of St. Mary's College there . . . and to so many others. By now—March 25, 1805, to be exact—this new star of Jesus took lasting hold on my life. For on that date I announced my good news to Antonio's wife: "At last Amabilia—GOD IS MINE and I AM HIS—I HAVE RECEIVED HIM!"[41]

But, it would be another three years before I would literally head home by another road. The invitation came from the Rev. Mr. Dubourg: "Come to us, Mrs. Seton, and we will assist you in forming a plan of life, which . . . will forward your views of contributing to the support of your children. We also wish to form a small school for the promotion of religious instruction for . . . children whose parents are interested."[42] So it was that I left New York once and for all for the fertile ground of Maryland. (*putting on the black shawl and hat . . .*) So it was that I was part of building the first Catholic schools, where I made certain that Protestants were welcomed, as well. So it *was* that I fulfilled a dream to start the first order of women religious in this country, the Sisters of Charity of St. Joseph. Life has been full. God has been faithful . . . through good times and bad . . . through the excruciating loss of two of my three precious daughters to TB. Indeed, it has always been the star of Jesus that has led me home, by another road.

Postscript: Born on August 28, 1774, Elizabeth Ann Seton died on January 4, 1821, from the "family disease" of TB. Thus, her feast day is January 4, in the season of Epiphany. In September 2006, she inspired me to write the following letter to her.

Dear Elizabeth,

In your day, life was so hard, especially for a woman. No modern conveniences. No cures for diseases that don't even concern us today. No opportunities for higher education and professional life. No knowledge yet of family planning. And all the while,

41. Bechtle, *Collected Writings*, 1:376; March 25, 1804.
42. Bechtle, *Collected Writings*, 2:16, 18.

too many deaths in childbirth. But, *this* we share. Who among us has not known loss? Or been hemmed in by limits of gender, race, skin color, economic status, or something else . . . as dictated *still* by our culture or our church? Who among us does not need to "seek God in all things" . . . or to find comfort in our friends? Who among us does not need to know ourselves, and in that, find the Source of Life itself? Who among us does not need to discover our gifts and use them for the good of all? Who among us is not called to bear fruit and bear it abundantly? And so, we thank you for being a living letter to *us* and a model of encouragement. For giving us a window into your soul, that we might become—like you—a light to the nations, a friend of God and prophet. It is an honor to know you, dear friend Elizabeth. How true you are to your name. For God *is* your fullness.

With much appreciation,

Gloria

Some Final Thoughts on the
Advent/Christmas/Epiphany Season

Such is the stuff of which this season is made, the Mystery of God's Incarnation in human flesh: the pregnant human longing for "more," the fulfillment of what is hoped-for, along with the certainty that life will never again be the same.

These stories of Jesus' birth (the Big Story) are intertwined with our own personal and communal stories of birthing, we who inhabit this globe. They are stories of promise in the midst of darkness and doubt, of life in the face of death, of hope in times of despair, of God's upside-down, unexpected, life-changing ways of love. They are stories that create meaning for us, always connecting the Big Story of God in Human Flesh to our own.

As grown-ups, don't *we* have the same questions as our ancient ancestors in faith, the Israelites? Only *after* they knew themselves to be God's people—delivered out of slavery at the Red Sea, refined in their wilderness wandering of forty years, then given the promised land—could they ask questions. *Our* questions. If God is so good (a given), how is it that people suffer? Sin? Quarrel? Scrape by to make a living? And then die? How might it have been in the very beginning of it all? Only then could they create their own birthing stories, beginning with creation and the garden of Eden. Only then could they name their eagle-winged God who had hovered over them, guided them, and adopted them by divine choice as God's Very Own.

Today we are given new birthing stories by scientists, who can assure us of the big bang some 13.8 billion years ago and our development through evolution. As people of faith, we need not fear these truths. For they reflect the same One True God, Lover of Us All, from the beginning to the present day and beyond. In the words of Pope Saint John Paul II: "Science can purify religion from error and superstition; religion can purify science from idolatry and false absolutes. Each can draw the other into a wider world, a world in which both can flourish."[43] There has always been struggle. Pain. And darkness. Even more, there has always been our One True God to companion and champion us, nudge and summon us, from every horizon of possibility deep within and before us. Now it is *our* turn to ponder *our* questions, and create *our* truth-filled stories of beginnings and "becoming's."

Every generation is pregnant with new life. In our day, questions persist, demanding answers. How can we welcome refugees and strangers? Provide health care that services everyone? Respond to a scorched and muddied earth, crying out for care? For air that is gasping for breath? For dingy, polluted water eager to sparkle, once again? How can we heal a seemingly broken political system? And so much more. Always, we encounter profound yearning for "more" in the face of adversity, standing tall in the face of fear, and above all, the unbowed conviction that hope-filled compassion can and must prevail, no matter what. Such is the stuff of Advent/Christmas/Epiphany.

One final thought: as we proceed through the liturgical year, we are not playacting. We know, with everything in us, that Jesus has already come. Jesus, the eternal Word of God, has taken on human flesh. And that is only the beginning! For Jesus lived on this earth. Ministered on this earth. Revealed his God—*our* God—of mercy, compassion, justice-seeking and boundless love, for you and for me. Endlessly. His ministry lives on, with us and for us, over twenty centuries later. Christmas and Easter have become one, forever entwined in our lives. For *we* are the body of Jesus, the Christ! *We* continue to create the end of the story! Indeed, *we* dare to fully engage with this New Year, in Christ! And with one another! Walk on, with me, then, won't you, for the rest of the story.

Sending Forth Prayer and Hymn

Leader: Let us pray . . .

Holy One, you live and breathe in us, beckon to us and nudge us, sob with us in our sorrow and rejoice with us in

43. A brief segment of a letter by Pope John Paul II to Rev. George Coyne, director of the Vatican Observatory, in Delio, *Making All Things New*, xx.

our celebrations. You whisper to us, that we might know your tender love, passionately chasing after us in every turning away. So it is that we dare to bring our cares and concerns, our hopes and dreams to you, our Ultimate Companion-on-Our-Way.

Leader: Our response is *Come, Christ Jesus, Come.*

For *your* everlasting, ongoing desire to heal every human ill, we pray . . .

For the passionate *human* will—in people of every gender, race, religion, and nationality—to bring healing and wholeness into our broken, bruised, hungering, and thirsting world, we pray . . .

For the Church, the people of God, that we might know more nearly and follow more clearly, our responsibility for becoming a "field hospital," not only to heal our broken members but to remind our leaders of their need to welcome gospel change, we pray . . .

For all those seeking a better life for their children, especially all refugees, that they will find a welcome home rather than a hardened wall, we pray . . .

For the willingness to develop the gifts you have placed within us, that we might grow more and more into strength, courage and wisdom for this one earth we call home, we pray . . .

For a true celebration of this Christmas season: the ultimate recognition that we are all sisters and brothers, one with each other and one in you, we pray . . .

Leader: Your passion for our becoming never ends. Whether for picking us up and dusting us off, or delighting in us beyond measure, we praise and thank you, now and forevermore, in your name, we pray.

All: Amen!

Hymn: **"Awake, O Sleeper"**

Words by Marty Haugen, based upon Eph 5:7–14
Music by Marty Haugen, © 1987, GIA Publications, Inc.

2

Ordinary Time in the Wake of Epiphany

Introduction to the Season and
the Wisdom Woman

The Christmas decorations have been tucked away. Now it's back to Ordinary Time, at least in Catholic circles. Our Protestant sisters and brothers call it a continuation of Epiphany. In any case, it's an in-between time. A chunk of Sundays dressed in Ordinary Time green, for Catholics. A stretch of at least four, and up to nine, Sundays between the Feast of the Baptism of the Lord and the First Sunday of Lent.[1] Lest we think we're in for some "ho-hum" stuff, be forewarned.

The child is now grown up. He's been baptized in the Jordan and tested in the wilderness. As Mark tells the story, Jesus *springs* into action! *Now* is the time for mission! Calling his first disciples. Healing folks in dire straits. Teaching "with authority." Or, in John's words: the magnetic, compelling call of Jesus, "Come and see," resounds throughout the land. Not only back then . . . but throughout *all* the years . . . up to *now* . . . in this very moment . . . and beyond.

It's January. In northern climes, a dreary, dark, cold time. A time that *begs* for that spark of energy, *pleads* for abundant life! The kind that simply *oozes* out of Jesus. Where . . . and how . . . is such life to be found? Well, as it happens, an often-ignored woman makes her appearance, if only we have eyes to see. A woman of wisdom, grace, and unstoppable energy. Oh, she's clamored for our attention before. For *ages*! As far back as the Babylonian exile, some 550 years before the time of Jesus! "On the heights, beside the way, at the crossroads, she takes her stand."[2] Her cry *pierces* our souls.

---

1. This, of course, is determined by when Easter occurs each year.
2. Prov 8:2.

To you, O people, I call,

and my cry is to all that live.

O simple ones, learn prudence;

acquire intelligence, you who lack it.

Hear, for I will speak noble things,

and from my lips will come what is right;

for my mouth will utter truth;

wickedness is an abomination to my lips.[3]

Who *is* this bold woman? None other than the Wisdom Woman herself. Sometimes called Sophia, by sounding out the Greek letters of her name into English. Or *Chochma*, in Hebrew.[4] Did you know that the Israelites "discovered" her during and after the Babylonian exile, as they wrestled with new ways of speaking about God? That she first shows up in the book of Proverbs, written after the exile? That she evolved over the next few centuries, especially among Jews who lived in Alexandria? Did you know that by the first century before Jesus she had come to be known as "a spotless mirror of the working of God, and an image of his goodness"?[5] That *she* is the one leading the Israelites through the Red Sea, according to that same Book of Wisdom?[6] Did you know that one of the earliest names for Jesus was Wisdom?[7] Can this Woman offer us new, perhaps startling, ways to imagine and name the God who keeps beckoning us to "more"? Are we ready for this?

Consider this. We're grown up now, like Jesus. Eager to be in relationship with God, like Jesus. Doesn't that mean calling God by name, for how else can we be in relationship? By what names might we imagine speaking to God? Or, by what names might God be yearning to be known by us? Well, then, in the words of Jesus himself, "Come and see." Perhaps this prayer to Wisdom just might give us the nudge we need.

An Ode to Wisdom

O Holy Wisdom, Weaver of our souls,

From of old, at the beginning, you danced,

---

3. Prov 8:4–7.

4. The pronunciation of the "ch" is a guttural sound.

5. Wis 7:26.

6. See Wis 10:15–21.

7. See 1 Cor 1:24, 30, written by Paul about the year 51.

Rejoiced . . . playfully capered over the span of creation,

Delighting especially in the human race.

And ever since, age after age, you have shown mercy,

Weaving the thread of your heart through mortal flesh,

Entering into holy souls,

    And making of them "friends of God, and prophets."[8]

Entering into hurting souls,

And tenderly caressing human wounds,

Until they glow with compassion, beyond all knowing.

    But still, there's even more.

For your love is "strong as death,"

Your passion "fierce as the grave."[9]

So it is that you ignite, spark, enflame, enkindle

Our *own* mercy,

Our *own* passion for righting wrongs.

Your very breath tends, nurtures, cajoles, pokes, and prods

That spark for life within us,

Until its glow *bursts* into a raging flame.

    O Holy Wisdom,

It is you who cord us to yourself,

Making of our tentative next steps

A path of your desiring,

A wonder to behold,

A new creation, unfolding,

Today, tomorrow, world without end. Amen!

The Wisdom Woman Emerges on
the Second Sunday of Ordinary Time

Wisdom wastes no time in making her appearance, as early as the Second
Sunday in Ordinary Time, if only we have eyes to see and ears to hear.
For on this particular Sunday, regardless of the cycle, *all* the Gospel pas-
sages come from John's Gospel. Hmm . . . most unusual. Especially during

8. Wis 7:27d.

9. Song of Solomon (Song of Songs) 8:6b.

Ordinary Time, with Jesus now plunging headlong into his ministry. Does this signal to us something unique about the Jesus of John's Gospel? Let's take a peek. In Cycle A, we encounter John the Baptist pointing to Jesus as the Lamb of God and Son of God. Lamb of God: the Passover Lamb, whose blood on the doorposts of the Hebrew houses would save them from death, setting them free for a whole new life. Son of God: John the Baptist readily admits—*twice*—that he did not know these truths about his very own cousin. *Only the Spirit of God* gave him that insight and those words. In Cycle B, a confident Jesus eagerly invites his first disciples to "come and see" where he is "staying."[10] And *here* Jesus means much more than a physical location! (Aren't we—today's disciples—invited, too?) Finally, in Cycle C, we are treated to the very first sign of Jesus' joyful, healing power at the wedding feast of Cana. A love feast. A bountiful outpouring of wine, symbolic of great joy. But, where is Wisdom Woman expectantly lingering in these stories? And, what does she have to do with Jesus?

Jesus as Wisdom in the Gospel of John

Just this. None other than renowned Scripture scholar Raymond Brown assures us: John the Evangelist has drawn on Jesus' self-portrait—"In the world but not of it"—by identifying "Jesus with personified divine Wisdom as described in the Old Testament."[11] In fact, she threads her way through the entire Gospel. Jesus, like Wisdom, was with God, from the very dawn of Creation.[12] Jesus, like Wisdom, took delight in humanity.[13] Jesus, like Wisdom, longed to pitch a tent among us, to enter into all the messiness of our human condition.[14] Jesus, like Wisdom, revealed God's truth and enlightenment through lengthy pronouncements and dialogues, like those with the Samaritan woman, Martha, his disciples at the Last Supper, and Mary of Magdala on Easter morning.[15] Most of all, Jesus—just like Wisdom—offered

10. John 1:39. As is often the case, John's words have several layers of meaning. While the original question had to do with Jesus' earthly residence, we ultimately discover that Jesus "stays" now in his community of believers (that is, in us who believe).

11. Brown, *Gospel According to John, I–XII*, cxxii. Today we would say the Hebrew Scripture, rather than Old Testament. See the addendum to this chapter for details.

12. Prov 8:23–30; John 1:1.

13. Prov 8:31.

14. Sir 24:7–8; John 1:14.

15. See esp. John 4:4–42; 11:1–44; chs. 13–17; 20:11–18; compare to Prov 8:4–36; Sir 24.

life, the glory of God, to all with eyes to see.[16] (For more detail, please see the addendum at the end of this chapter.)

So it is that on this particular Sunday (Second Sunday in Ordinary Time) Jesus is roaming the streets, crying out, calling disciples, just like Wisdom herself: "To you, O people, I call, and my cry is to all that live."[17] Furthermore, just as Jesus performs the very first sign of his power at the wedding feast of Cana, the Wisdom Woman invites *everyone* to *her* feast of life: "Come, eat of my bread and drink of the wine I have mixed."[18] Yet she remains hidden, just as she was for the Baptizer. Only when our eyes are opened and our ears unstopped, can *we* claim her anew, in and through Jesus.

So it is that a passionate John the Evangelist urges us . . . compels us . . . to "come and see" . . . taste and know the goodness of God in Jesus, the ultimate gift of life in all its fullness. But that's only the beginning! Where, oh where, are we to find Jesus *now* . . . after his death and resurrection? Are you ready for this? Most astounding of all: we can now encounter Jesus—the goodness of God—in *us*! *We* are the body of the risen Jesus on earth!

Wisdom in Us, the Community of Jesus' Friends

How can this *be*? According to John, the cross of Jesus became his glory, his avenue of return to the Father. Furthermore, it's only upon his return to God that he can send his Spirit, the Advocate, to guide them—and us— "into all the truth."[19] Transform them—and us—inch by inch, into his true Community of Love. Therefore, as Scripture scholar Sandra M. Schneiders puts it: "The resurrection narrative [in John] is about what happened to *Jesus' disciples* after Jesus' glorification, namely that the Jesus who had gone to God had also *returned to them*."[20] Only then could this Spirit-filled community "become the *risen body of the glorified Jesus*, the temple in which God and humanity will meet."[21]

Wow! What a tall order! But, there it is! Yes, he has washed *our* feet. Yes, he has given *us* a new commandment: "that you love one another. Just

---

16. See John 1:14; 2:11; 11:4; 17:1–5, 22, 24. Chapters 13–21 are often called the Book of Glory; compare with Sir 24:1–6 and Wis 7:25.

17. See Prov 8:4, the conclusion of 8:1–4; see also Prov 1:20–23.

18. Prov 9:5.

19. John 16:13, words of Jesus at the Last Supper.

20. Schneiders, *Written That You May Believe*, 58; my emphasis in italics.

21. Schneiders, *Written That You May Believe*, 58; see also 58–62 and 162–79 on Jesus' community of friends.

as I have loved you, you also should love one another."[22] Yes, he has promised: "I will not leave you orphaned."[23] Yes, he has prayed for us: "As you, Father, are in me and I am in you, may they also be in us, so that the world may believe that you have sent me. The glory that you have given me I have given them, so that they may be one, as we are one."[24]

So, then, *we* are to become the very place . . . the *prime* location, in fact . . . of Jesus' bodily presence in our world. *We* are to nourish the starving. *We* are to assuage the thirst of the parched. *We* are to become light for any who sit on the dung heap of depression and loss. *We* are to become life for the addicted and other profoundly wounded souls in our day. *We* are to offer glimpses—however dim—of Jesus' light and Wisdom to so many desperate souls. The needs are enormous! But in loving community, we are so much greater!

Finally, although John the Evangelist makes these Wisdom connections in mystical ways, he's not alone in identifying Jesus with Wisdom. In fact, by the year 51, *Paul* had written to his Corinthian community that Jesus is the Wisdom of God![25] And yet, how easy it might be to miss this obvious point! To let our eyes skip right over this significant message . . . or our ears become deaf to this Word. And yet, some of the earliest followers of Jesus *must* have already made that connection. Paul *must* have picked up on that understanding, within the first generation after Jesus' death and resurrection.

I ask you, then, isn't this a Woman you would like to know? Where does she come from? How does she develop and morph, down through the ages? Why has it taken so long for us to discover her hiding in the folds of Jesus' garments? What can account for our human resistance to her? Even so, how might Wisdom stir our imaginations and fertilize our words about God today? In short, why does she matter to *us*, right here and now?

Part 1: Birthing of the Wisdom Woman, as Told by Wisdom and Two Voices

I pondered: how shall I tell Wisdom's story? This much is true: she emerges when the old stories of God no longer fit. Such has always been the case, for all people of faith. Haven't we, like our ancestors of old, probed new dimensions of God in the wake of evolution and the big bang theory? Don't we all

22. John 13:34, from Jesus' words at the Last Supper.
23. John 14:18, from Jesus' words at the Last Supper.
24. John 17:21–22, from Jesus' words at the Last Supper.
25. See 1 Cor 1:24; see also 1 Cor 2:6–13.

need to listen to our experiences, scrutinize our faith more deeply, intuit and
imagine new possibilities, and search out new answers, all the while remaining faithful to the inherited truth of an ever increasing, loving, and empowering God? In short, yes. So it is that Wisdom herself will join us to tell her
story, along with two voices, who raise questions and make comments, thus
moving her story along. Please welcome her with us today.

> **Wisdom Woman:** Thank you for inviting me here. I'm *delighted* to
> be with you today. Let me begin by asking: what comes to mind
> when you hear the word *wisdom*? Perhaps some unique strength
> or courage born out of a trying time. A treasure gleaned from
> life's difficult journey. A pithy statement—or proverb—to guide
> our pathways. An older woman of grace, who embodies those
> "roads less taken." A mysterious woman, someone you don't
> know but would *love* to meet. Or, even something else.
>
> Whatever your response, it can be said that I remain a Mys-
> tery. As I poke, prod, provoke, invite, and search out *everyone*,
> especially in the worst of times. In times of trauma. Utter aban-
> donment. And hopelessness. Because of my love for you.

> **Voice 1:** The time was about 550 years before Jesus. The place:
> Babylon. The last king of Judea—a descendant of David—had
> been killed, with no hope of another. But, God had promised!
> Through the prophet Nathan, God promised David: "Your house
> and your kingdom shall be made sure before me; your throne
> shall be established forever."[26]

> **Wisdom:** But now, your king was no more! And your beloved
> temple, the house of God, was no more! Your people—especially
> the leaders—were thrust into exile, with no hope of return. It was
> gone, all of it, gone. Your psalmist lamented, "How long, O Lord?
> Will you hide yourself forever?"[27] And your sobbing could be
> heard throughout the land!

> **Voice 2:** "By the rivers of Babylon—there we sat down and there
> we wept when we remembered Zion. On the willows there we
> hung up our harps. . . . How could we sing the Lord's song in a
> foreign land?"[28]

---

26. 2 Sam 7:16.

27. Ps 89:46a, from a very long psalm of lament.

28. Ps 137:1–2, 4.

Wisdom: But know this: *I wept with you*! Though you *still* kept asking, "Where is God?! Where are the promises of God? How can we ever connect again to the God who seems so very far away? Who can help us connect?"

Voice 1: It would need to be someone very different from before. Maybe a woman. Maybe a strong woman like one of our many mothers of Israel. Like Rebekah, wife of Isaac, or Rachel, beloved wife of Jacob. They had managed their households, taught their children, orchestrated banquets, even advised their kings, had they not?

Voice 2: Let's not forget Deborah, *another* mother of Israel, heroic leader, *and* one of the wisest of all the judges. Even named a prophetess . . . just like Miriam,[29] Huldah,[30] and Noadiah.[31]

Wisdom: The truth is this: I've been here all along, with you and your God. Yes, "the Lord created me at the beginning of his work, the first of his acts of long ago. Ages ago I was set up, at the first, before the beginning of the earth. . . . Then I was beside him, like a master worker; and I was daily his delight, rejoicing before him always, rejoicing in his inhabited world and delighting in the human race."[32]

How I cherished so many of your ancestors. Remember Mahlah, Noah, Hoglah, Milcah, and Tirzah?[33] They're commonly known as the daughters of Z. Remember how their father Zelophehad had died out in that long, forty-year trek in the wilderness? And how Moses was dividing up the new land among the *men* in the tribes? Of course, that meant no land for these women! So, the very next morning they "stood before Moses, Eleazar the priest, the leaders, and all the congregation, at the entrance of the tent of meeting"[34] and pleaded their case for land. Moses, incapable of deciding for himself, took the matter to God. And God said, "The daughters of Zelophehad are right in what they are saying; you shall indeed let them possess

29. Sister of Moses and Aaron; she is named a prophet at the banks of the Red Sea as she leads the women in praise; see Exod 15:20–21.

30. See 2 Kgs 22:14–20 and 2 Chr 34:22–28.

31. See Neh 6:14.

32. Prov 8:22–23, 30–31.

33. Their story is told in Num 27:1–11 and 36:1–12.

34. Num 27:2.

an inheritance among their father's brothers and pass the inheritance of their father on to them."[35] Not only that, but other
women shall also be given consideration.

Voice 1: But it took utter and total devastation for us to begin
searching for you more deeply than ever before. To raise questions. And consider new possibilities.

Wisdom: Yes, I know. I watched, and I *ached* when you brought so
much suffering on yourselves. Like turning your backs on prophets like Jeremiah. At the same time, I *longed* for . . . *craved* . . .
the possibility of your returning home again to kiss the ground.
To *joyfully* wend your way up to the gates of Jerusalem. To lift
up your eyes one more time upon the mountain of God's house.
Would you *ever* come home again?

Voice 2: Only Isaiah could imagine it. In poetry soaring enough
to comfort the most shattered heart.[36] *Finally*, after fifty *very* long
years, we were set free! Through King Cyrus of Persia, totally unaware that *he* was anointed by God for this very purpose.[37] Our
feet could *not* propel us home fast enough! Had God leveled the
rugged mountains before them? And filled in the rough valleys?
Indeed, so it seemed!

Voice 1: But, when we finally arrived home, our agony, wailing,
and groaning only grew louder! For our beloved temple, which
once had loomed large over Jerusalem, was now merely a pile of
rubble. Our land was in somebody else's hands! And the likeli-
hood of a kingdom? Gone, forever! Where was *God* in all this?
(*Pause*)

Wisdom: I was right here, waiting for your sages and rabbis to
recognize me. *Finally*, you heard me! *Somehow*, you began to
discover me . . . here, there, and everywhere.

Voice 1: "On the heights, beside the way, at the crossroads she
takes her stand; beside the gates in front of the town, at the entrance of the portals she cries out."[38] And a bold message it was!

---

35. Num 27:7.
36. See chs. 40–55 of the book of Isaiah, commonly known as Second Isaiah.
37. Isa 45:1–6.
38. Prov 8:2–3.

Wisdom: "I have good advice and sound wisdom; I have insight, I have strength. By me kings reign, and rulers decree what is just; by me rulers rule, and nobles, all who govern rightly."[39] As if *that* were not enough, I offered a feast of life to *all* people. "Come, eat of my bread and drink of the wine I have mixed. Lay aside immaturity, and live, and walk in the way of insight."[40] You even named me the ideal wife! I could do it all! Work with wool and flax, spinning and weaving . . . bring food from far away, like a merchant . . . rise before dawn to order my household, and work on into the night . . . "consider a field and buy it" . . . and open my "hand to the poor" and the needy. You claimed that I was strong and wise, an honor to a husband. Not only *that*, my works would praise me, publicly, in the city gates.[41]

Voice 2: You *had* been there all along! Only *now* could we see you and know you as the ultimate Mother of Israel. The face of proverbial Wisdom. The bridge to God that we so desperately needed.[42] Only *now* could we hear your insistent words to us.

Wisdom:

> To you, O people, I call, and my cry is to all that live.
> O simple ones, learn prudence; acquire intelligence,
> you who lack it. Hear, for I will speak noble things, and
> from my lips will come what is right; for my mouth will
> utter truth; wickedness is an abomination to my lips.[43]

Voice 1: Our ancestors finally discovered what is true for us all: once imagination is unleashed, there's no telling *where* it will lead.

Voice 2: For in time, some Jewish people chose to live outside Israel, in places like Alexandria. And they questioned: how could they keep their identity as God's people in a culture that was Greek? In a culture that spoke and wrote in a language other than Hebrew? In a culture that worshiped other gods . . . and goddesses?

39. Prov 8:14–16.

40. Prov 9:5–6.

41. See Prov 31:10–31, an Ode to a Capable Wife.

42. It is Scripture scholar Claudia V. Camp who offers this development of Wisdom Woman, out of the Hebrew experience of the exile, in her *Wisdom and the Feminine in the Book of Proverbs*.

43. Prov 8:4–7.

Wisdom: Yes, they began imagining me in new ways.[44] A way of *flourishing* life . . . like a stately "cedar in Lebanon and like a cypress on the heights of Hermon. I grew tall like a palm tree in *En-gedi*, and like rosebushes in Jericho."[45] And they praised me for producing the most fragrant perfume and the most luscious fruit. Enough to fill hearts, as well as bellies. In all this, I even became "the book of the covenant of the Most High God, the law that Moses commended us as an inheritance for the congregations of Jacob."[46]

Voice 1: By the first century before Jesus, in fact, faithful Jews in Alexandria began turning to *you* as their very own God of Israel, personified as a *woman*! They were surrounded by folks who worshiped the powerful goddess Isis—as Savior and *Kyria*—or giver of life. Certainly, Wisdom was more powerful than any goddess!

Wisdom: So it was that they named me "a breath of the power of God"[47] and "a spotless mirror of the working of God, and an image of his goodness."[48] I was so intimate with them, in fact, that I could renew all things, making them "friends of God and prophets," from one age to the next.[49] The truth is, I became "the personification of God's saving activity in the world."[50] I even became the God of the exodus. Listen!

A Reading from the Wisdom of Solomon (10:15—11:4)

A holy people and blameless race,
Wisdom delivered from a nation of oppressors.
She entered the soul of a servant of the Lord,
And withstood dread kings with wonders and signs.
She gave to holy people the reward of their labors;

44. See Sir 24:7–17.

45. Sir 24:13–14a, written as Ecclesiasticus in the second century before Jesus.

46. Sir 24:23.

47. Wis 7:25; this was written in the first century before Jesus.

48. Wis 7:26.

49. Wis 7:27.

50. "The Mother of Wisdom," in Robinson, *Future of Our Religious Past*; cited by Schussler Fiorenza, *Jesus*, 137.

She guided them along a marvelous way,
And became a shelter to them by day,
And a starry flame through the night.
She brought them over the Red Sea,
And led them through deep waters;
But she drowned their enemies,
And cast them up from the depth of the sea.
Therefore, the righteous plundered the ungodly;
They sang hymns, O Lord, to your holy name,
And praised with one accord your defending hand;
For Wisdom opened the mouths of those who were mute,
And made the tongues of infants speak clearly.
Wisdom prospered their works by the hand of a holy prophet.
They journeyed through an uninhabited wilderness,
And pitched their tents in untrodden places.
They withstood their enemies and fought off their foes.
When they were thirsty, they called upon you,
And water was given them out of the flinty rock,
From hard stone a remedy for their thirst.

Wisdom: As one rabbi—Rami Shapiro—would say, some twenty-one centuries later, this was the work of people with "spacious minds."[51]

Voice 2: Yes, *open* minds! Generous minds! Listen, also, with the ears of your heart, to a description of Wisdom's nature, as found in the Wisdom of Solomon (7:23–28).

Voice 1:

> There is in her a spirit that is intelligent, holy, unique, manifold, subtle, mobile, clear, unpolluted, distinct, invulnerable, loving the good, keen, irresistible, beneficent, humane, steadfast, sure, free from anxiety, all-powerful, overseeing all, and penetrating through all spirits that are intelligent, pure, and altogether subtle.
>
> For wisdom is more mobile than any motion; because of her pureness she pervades and penetrates all things. For she is a breath of the power of God, and a pure emanation of the glory of the Almighty; therefore nothing defiled gains entrance into her. For she is a

51. Shapiro, *Divine Feminine*, xiii.

reflection of eternal light, a spotless mirror of the working of God, and an image of his goodness.

Although she is but one, she can do all things,
and while remaining in herself, she renews all things;
in every generation she passes into holy souls and
makes them friends of God, and prophets; for God
loves nothing so much as the person who lives with
wisdom.[52]

Wisdom: Do these words ring a bell? Are they at all familiar?
Do you ever hear these words of Scripture?[53] Probably not, for
they are *nowhere* to be found in the lectionary, the book of readings used in worship. How, then, will you remember me? *Please*
remember me! Please, do *not* forget me!

Part 2: Remembering, Rejecting, Reclaiming Wisdom ...
A Reflection on the Wisdom Woman in Light of the Coronavirus

The coronavirus, COVID-19. Doesn't it feel like *everything* has been tossed
up in the air? Where will it land? Where will *we* land? Will everything
change? Will God change? If so, what will we do then? I recall a few years ago
that a good friend, a parish pastoral associate, told me of her experience in
preparing a family for a funeral. They had chosen a reading from the Book of
Wisdom for the First Reading, but the man who was to proclaim the reading
simply could *not* make himself say *She*. He was, however, able to struggle
through this new territory by saying "Wisdom" in her place.

Where are *we* in this picture? Are we in exile, too, like our ancestors of
old, from so many familiar routines in our daily lives? Working at home, in a
new way, if we're fortunate. Unable to connect physically with so many family and friends. Yet, all the while gifted with modern technology, so that we
might consider new ways of staying in touch, through the power of Zoom,
for example. Where is *God* in all this? Might we *now* begin to enter into
relationship with this Wisdom Woman, when the very ground seems to be
shifting under our feet? In short, yes. Whenever we heed Wisdom's call, we
need to: (1) remember all the names we've given to Jesus, one of which is
the Wisdom of God, (2) examine how we have rejected Wisdom Woman

52. In her book *Friends of God and Prophets*, Elizabeth Johnson explores sainthood
as "friends of God and prophets," based upon these words from the Book of Wisdom.

53. These words are in Catholic Scripture, but Protestants do not include the Book
of Wisdom and a few other deuterocanonical books, since they were not originally
written in Hebrew.

from our vocabulary and our hearts, and then, (3) engage in the possibility of reclaiming Jesus as Wisdom Woman.

The Essential, Hope-Filled Task of Remembering Jesus as the Wisdom of God

Remembering matters. Remembering rightly is essential to the well-being of our lives. As gifted Presbyterian minister, theologian, and author Frederic Buechner puts it: "For as long as you remember me, I am never entirely lost. When I'm feeling most ghost-like, it's your remembering me that helps remind me that I actually exist. When I'm feeling sad, it's my consolation. When I'm feeling happy, it's part of why I feel that way. If you forget me, one of the ways I remember who I am will be gone. If you forget me, part of who I am will be gone."[54]

Wow! *"If you forget me, part of who I am will be gone!"* Think about it! Can this apply to Jesus Christ? To us together, as his body of Christ? Even to God? And the Wisdom Woman herself? Put another way, if we forget the Wisdom Woman, might we be in danger of forgetting something significant about our very selves? Even about God and Jesus? This is worth exploring.

The Coming and Naming of Jesus

In the fullness of time, Jesus entered our world, and it seemed as though *nothing* would ever again be the same. Who can imagine how it might have been to actually see him in the flesh? Hear his voice of authority. Experience his compelling call to follow. How was it possible to do otherwise? Benefit time and time again from his compassionate healing, even of those beyond his cultural and religious boundaries. How, then, could anyone imagine the devastation of his cruel, shameful death? No! This cannot be! He was too good, too compassionate, too loving, too challenging to anyone and anything that would keep people down! No!

He *seemed* dead, even totally abandoned by God. But, the tomb was *empty*! To some of the men, it seemed an idle women's tale, at first. But, little by little, the eyes of their hearts were opened. He *seemed* dead . . . but he *wasn't*! He was *alive* . . . still *with* them . . . in a *new* kind of body . . . transforming stuttering fear into powerful witness! God had raised him from the dead! God was *there* for him, all along! Could it possibly be that

54. Buechner, *Whistling in the Dark*, 100.

everything keeping people dead . . . exploited . . . misused and abused . . . was now being rolled away, as well?

How shall we name this Jesus who has made all the difference in our lives? Back then, communities would gather. Remember and name him, in good and truthful ways:

- ✣ **Lord**: A title of respect and authority. Even divinity. For God *did* raise him from the dead.

- ✣ **Messiah**: The Long-Awaited-One who would set all things right.

- ✣ **The Anointed One, the Christ**: Like kings and prophets of old.

- ✣ **Son of God**: Like kings of old. (Of course, he kept telling us that *his* kingdom would be different. Like yeast that a woman kneaded in dough. And also, that anyone who wanted to lead such a kingdom *must* do it by serving others.)

- ✣ **Son of Man**: Genuinely human, except for sin. Alongside his unique ability to shatter narrow boxes, while tantalizing folks to see as God sees.

- ✣ **Suffering Servant**: How could this all-good man be *crucified*? Surely, he fulfilled the prophetic imagination of Second Isaiah: the gentle teacher who would never break a bruised reed, while faithfully bringing forth justice.[55] The "light to the nations."[56] The one who listened intently to God, and followed God's path, no matter the cost.[57] The righteous one, who had been "despised and rejected" through a "perversion of justice," but who willingly "bore the sin of many" for the sake of releasing people from their bound-up ways.[58] Indeed, some recognized him after his death and resurrection precisely by the nail wounds in his hands and the spear wound in his side.[59]

- ✣ **Emmanuel**: God with us *always*![60] In his suffering, and in ours; in his joy, and in ours, just as he had promised!

These names simply rolled off the tongues of the early disciples. But there was one more name, and she has been nearly forgotten.

---

55. See Isa 42:1–4, the first "suffering servant song."
56. Isa 49:6, from the second "suffering servant song."
57. See Isa 50:4–7, the third "suffering servant song."
58. Isa 53:3, 8, 12c, part of the fourth "suffering servant song," 52:13—53:12.
59. See John 20:19–29.
60. This is a name given by Matthew the Evangelist.

☙ **Wisdom/Wisdom Woman:** Paul knew her well and proclaimed her in the early 50s.[61] Yet she did not catch on as quickly. Did it somehow suggest the "femaleness" of God? Surely, God is not a big man in the sky, as some have often imagined. God is so much more, inclusive of women as well as men. We often name God by analogy to what we experience, like the comforting mother of Isa 66:13. Indeed, we *know* that women, as well as men, are made in the image of God (see Gen 1:27). That Jesus had regarded women, as well as men, with dignity and worth. That women, as well as men, had followed him. Women like Mary of Magdala, "and Joanna, the wife of Herod's steward Chuza, and Susanna, and many others, who provided for them out of their resources."[62] Jesus had even been stretched in his own ministry by women who *insisted* upon his healing, like the Syrophoenician woman of Mark's Gospel and the Canaanite woman of Matthew's Gospel.[63] And finally, we *know* that Jesus sent Mary of Magdala—apostle to the apostles—as the first proclaimer of the ultimate good news: "I have seen the Lord!"[64] And yet, on Easter Sunday morning—in Roman Catholic readings assigned for the United States—we have yet to hear this absolutely essential proclamation of God's good news!

Rejecting the *Femaleness* of God, Including Wisdom

Women were considered "less than men" in the centuries before Jesus. In fact, in the century *just* before Jesus, Jewish theologian and philosopher Philo put it crudely and succinctly: Femaleness is "weak, easily deceived, the cause of sin, lifeless, diseased, enslaved, unmanly, nerveless, mean, slavish, sluggish."[65]

Surely, one would hope and expect that the coming of Jesus would make a difference when it comes to women. But no! Prejudice against women stubbornly persisted. Despite Jesus' warm welcome of women as disciples. Despite his sending Mary of Magdala—apostle to the

61. See 1 Cor 1:30; it is found in the Second Reading in Ordinary Time, Cycle A.

62. Luke 8:3, referring to the women who followed Jesus.

63. See Mark 7:24–30 and Matt 15:21–28.

64. John 20:18, concluding the resurrection appearance to Mary of Magdala; she was first to see and hear the Risen Christ, and first to be sent by him to proclaim the good news.

65. Baer, *Philo's Use of the Categories of Male and Female*, 42; cited by Schussler Fiorenza, *Jesus*, 137. Like Aristotle, Philo believed that the male alone is perfect; females are imperfect.

apostles—with the good news of Easter. Despite the Gospels' witness that women can be . . . and are . . . preachers, entrusted with the good news.[66] Despite Paul's profuse praise of women—like Prisca, Junia, and Phoebe— with whom he worked as equal partners.[67] Despite New Testament stories of women who led communities in Corinth, Ephesus, Rome, and Philippi at the very dawn of Christianity.[68]

Why such prejudice? Why such rejection? This much is certain. There was something in the air favoring men over women, even after the coming of Jesus. Something claiming that men were the norm (androcentrism) and, therefore, rightly able to rule over everyone else, women included (patriarchy).

Listen to how these attitudes seeped into Scripture itself by the end of the first century. And be aware that the person who wrote the First Letter to Timothy was not Paul, but someone who claimed to be his disciple, some forty years after his death, despite Paul's respect for women. "Let a woman learn in silence with full submission. I permit no woman to teach or to have authority over a man; she is to keep silent. For Adam was formed first, then Eve; and Adam was not deceived, but the woman was deceived and became a transgressor. Yet she will be saved through childbearing, provided they continue in faith and love and holiness, with modesty."[69]

Sexist? Yes. But remember that in Jesus' day there was no such word as sexism. In our day, here's how Webster defines the word: "prejudice or discrimination based on sex" (the body) . . . or gender: "behavior, conditions, or attitudes that foster stereotypes of social roles based on sex." In fact, by a few decades after Jesus, such attitudes would coalesce around questions of orthodoxy, or right teaching of the Church.

Take one complicating factor, for example, that of the so-called gnostic communities, formed within the first couple of centuries after the death and resurrection of Jesus. Many of them produced their own Gospels, like the Gospel of Mary Magdalene or the Gospel of Thomas. Contrary to popular opinion, "Gnosticism" was *not* a system of thought. But it *was* a label attached to these diverse communities, each of which believed that a special knowledge or "gnosis" was available to those who opened themselves up to God. And the label stuck.

There's much that might be said—and has been said—about these communities. Their desire to follow Jesus. Their insights into Jesus through

66. See John 20:17–18; Mark 16:6–7; Matt 28:1–10.

67. Rom 16:1–7.

68. For example, see Acts 18 and Lydia's story in Acts 16:9–15, 40.

69. 1 Tim 2:11–15.

the Gospels of Mary Magdalene, Thomas, and others. But, suffice it to say here: many of them ultimately ran afoul of the broad parenthesis of recognized Christian belief. Ultimately, those drawn to "gnostic" communities sought an escape from the trials of this world. They shuddered at the world's evil, even regarding *all* matter as evil. It was only Spirit that mattered; it was only Spirit that could point the way to ultimate freedom. So it was that these communities fostered a mystical element, the search for one's inner divine self. Or, one might say, the search for wisdom deep within. But they *also negated the sacredness of our bodies.*

Here's the irony. "Orthodox" Christianity theoretically opposes the dualism of matter and spirit, as well as the belief that the material world is evil. And yet, both dualism and apprehension about the body have made their way into Christian thought. But the great saints had it right, proclaiming the uniqueness of Jesus *alongside* the divinity within each person. Teresa of Avila, for example, *insisted* that Jesus was *the* way to God. At the same time, she also believed that God was to be found at the core of every single person, at the core of each person's Interior Castle. For her, as for so many great saints, it was only possible to know God by knowing oneself.

In the end, the close association of these "gnostic" cults with Wisdom was disastrous for Wisdom's development in "Orthodox" Christianity. Wisdom was to be avoided at all costs. And women, along with Wisdom, were to be shunned. Just listen to what some men had to say about women down through the centuries!

Tertullian, for example, the Carthaginian theologian (ca. 155–240), pronounced one of the most egregious statements ever made: "You are the devil's gateway: you are the unsealer of that (forbidden) tree: you are the first deserter of the divine law. . . . On account of your desert—that is death— even the Son of God had to die."[70] Furthermore, St. Thomas Aquinas, a thirteenth-century "great" in matters of theology, was rooted in the Greco-Roman belief system of procreation. Devoted to Aristotle's work in this regard, Aquinas believed that only men, biologically speaking, have enough "heat" or "vital spirit" to produce seed. Therefore, women are, in fact, "misbegotten" males.[71] And this view prevailed through the eighteenth century! At the same time, it must be noted that Aquinas held Mary, who brought Christ into the world, in the highest regard.

70. Tertullian, "Time Changes Nature's Dresses."
71. Aquinas, "Question 92."

Reclaiming the Wisdom of God Today

Now, I am certain that folks are not out there suddenly remembering the Wisdom Woman at this cataclysmic, profoundly uncertain time of the coronavirus. At the same time, people have professed to be praying, singly and often together, on the internet. Might not the experience of our ancient ancestors in faith during *their* exile shed light on our own? Might we not begin to discover this one who has remained hidden to our eyes, hearts, and imaginations? This Wisdom Woman who seeks us out, as well?

I don't know. But I can say this. By whatever name, her evidence is becoming increasingly real. Consider the heroic strength, courage, and wisdom of our health care providers, doing whatever they can for sick patients even in the face of their own possible illness. Consider neighbors everywhere, sharing pictures of blooming flowers or offering to stop and pick up some needed items at the grocery store. Consider the story of a man in my hometown who loves to play "Amazing Grace" on his bagpipes at 9:00 every evening. People in his neighborhood open their windows and doors just to allow that grace to seep into their lives. Her spirit is certainly no longer hidden!

And yet, there's even more. Consider the boldness of the Wisdom Woman found in the book of Proverbs, chapters 8 and 9! A compelling preacher of God's truths! A presider of a magnificent feast! An advocate for those in need! A lover, delighting in people. Where—and in whom—does she show up today for you? What questions does she raise about remembering her, ourselves, and others?

Many responses come to mind for me. There's Mary, the mother of Jesus. I especially love the "Millennial Mary" I encountered in a side chapel of St. Joseph Church in Nazareth. An olive-toned statue, she's moving forward, in full stride! A woman of strength, courage, confidence, and boldness! Now *here's* a Mary I long to know!

Oftentimes, when I reread chapters 8 and 9 of Proverbs, I see a woman leading sacramental worship in my Catholic Church. How can God's call upon the lives of some women—so genuine, so compelling, so assured by people who know her well—be denied by mere human regulation? We believe, surely, that women are made in the image of God, just like men. We believe, surely, that girls, as well as boys are baptized into the body of Christ, *all* of them named priest, prophet, and royal person. We believe, surely, that each one is a bundle of her own/his own unique gifts, as God deigns. We believe, surely, that it is up to us, the Christian community, to help each person discern their own gifts for the good of the community. And yet, when it comes to ordaining women—who are gifted and called by God, who have engaged in the hard work of honing their gifts, who are called by their communities for such service—we hit a brick wall, a human law. Who is forgotten when this happens? She is, of course. How about the body of Christ, the entire community she would love to serve? Are they forgotten? Is God also forgotten?

Let me simply conclude this section with a tiny bit of good news that always tickles me. A few years ago, when I served a parish as pastoral associate, I would always head over to church to help set up before the Saturday afternoon 4:30 p.m. Mass. A gentleman arrived early each week, always in a wheelchair. When it was time for the community to add prayers to the General Intercessions, he would always pray for the "poor souls in purgatory." On one particular Saturday, before Mass started, he said to me, "I think I'll write a letter to the pope." So I then inquired, "What would you like to say to the pope?" His response? "I think I'll tell him it's time to start ordaining women."

A New Year's Resolution: Naming God in New Ways?

Naming matters. When we bring a child for baptism, we are asked: "What name do you give this child?" Naming reveals relationship. Profound care and concern. Desire for the very best for this beloved one. My mother often told me, as a youngster, that she named me after the American flag. (You know: "Old Glory." Yes, she was patriotic.) While I've been grateful for my name, upon preparing for Church ministry, I renamed *her* inspiration into my own: praising God in liturgy, hymns, and daily living, however limited that might be.

We're never far from the beginning of another new year. Right now, it's the beginning of a new year impacted by the coronavirus. Might we consider and try on new ways of naming the God of our lives? Knowing that we humans most often speak about God by analogy to our limited experience. Knowing that God is way beyond Anyone/Anything we can possibly ever imagine . . . within and among us all . . . threading backward through generation upon generation . . . connecting all human life, of whatever race, religion and stripe right here and right now . . . sending us forward into a future known only by Our Holy Mystery. To this end, Richard Rohr, Franciscan priest and contemporary spiritual guide, loves to pray "in all the holy names of God." So, in quiet and reflection, we might ask ourselves: How might I name God now? Are there any new names that come to heart? Any name that might call forth the "femaleness" within the Mystery of God? Perhaps the following prayer might help open the floodgates.

A Prayer in Honor of Wisdom

Leader: Let us pray . . .

O Holy One, Veiled One, Mysterious God beyond imagining, Age after age, you have offered tantalizing glimpses of your glory, vulnerable majesty, tenderness, and irrepressible life.

In response, your beloved ones have rejoiced in you, naming what they have seen, heard, touched and tasted of your compelling, intimate, passionate love.

We pray, then, for such longing . . . and be-longing, in You, O Holy One.

Leader: Our response is *That we might rejoice in You.*

With Isaiah the prophet, who knew you as panting, laboring mother,[72] or a mother who can never forget her nursing child,[73] help us experience you as the best of all possible mothers, we pray . . .

With Irish saints, like Patrick, Brigit, and Columcille—who recognized you in all the "thin places" of creation, whether on land, sea, or in the air—awaken the eyes of *our* hearts to you at every moment, in every circumstance, we pray . . .

With Hildegard of Bingen, Benedictine abbess and multiply-gifted woman of twelfth-century Rhineland, help us know the "juiciness" of your abundant life, we pray . . .

With Julian of Norwich, prayerful teacher in troubled fourteenth-century England, who named Jesus as mother, laboring on the cross for us, help us discover you in the depths of any piercing sorrow, we pray . . .

With Catherine of Siena, lay Dominican who admonished the pope out of her certain conviction that you alone were her "Sweet First Truth," strengthen the steel of our own backbones, we pray . . .

72. Isa 42:14.
73. Isa 49:15.

With Therese of Lisieux, who discovered you in *every* instance of love, even the tiniest and most difficult, gift us with this profound desire to love, we pray . . .

With each of us, who allow our senses to be penetrated by you, that we might give voice to our most unlikely experiences of you and share your love with anyone and everyone who crosses our paths, each and every day, we pray . . .

With our newfound upside-down world of coronavirus, revealing our profound need of you at all times, we pray . . .

Leader:

May we all find wisdom in a tender touch of delight,

and a whisper of love that heals ancient wounds,

in the urgent cry of a newborn life,

and the surrendering sigh of a dying one,

in the rustling of trees, the roaring of oceans, and the very core of our hearts,

propelling our compassion into flourishing for all,

both now and forevermore, in Wisdom's name we pray.

All: Amen!

Joanne Cala: A Contemporary Woman of Wisdom, Woman of Mission

What follows is the story of a woman who captivates my heart: Joanne Cala. And, wouldn't you know: her name is the feminine of John, the Gospel writer who uses multiple Wisdom images of God in describing Jesus. Indeed, I've known for awhile that she is full of wisdom, that she has risked enormous change to follow God's compelling call on her life. But where does she best belong, within the liturgical year? Could it be Advent? For she has unabashedly said yes to the God of her life, over and over. Just like Mary, "Our Lady," to whom Joanne has an enduring devotion. And, just like Mary, Joanne knows about lifting up the lowly. Or, does she properly reflect the spirit of Christmas, giving birth to a dream and a hope for so many people? How about Epiphany, for she has certainly followed the star emblazoned on her heart. But, then, at Mass, as I proclaimed the First Reading for the Second Sunday in Ordinary Time (also known as the

Second Sunday of Epiphany in the Revised Common Lectionary), I knew. This was it! For hers is the story of young Samuel, eagerly responding to an insistent call in the middle of the night. Was it Eli, the priest and his mentor, calling? Oh, no, Eli assured him. It was God . . . the Holy One of Israel! Why, that's Joanne! And this is her story.

> Her name means "Yahweh is gracious." What a fit! Here's what I love about Joanne: her sparkling eyes . . . her calm, yet lively demeanor . . . her love for God (yes, she knows God well!) . . . her desire to do God's will, above all else . . . her obvious love of people (with her beloved husband, Bill, topping the list), and her equally obvious need for quiet time with her God. Finally, there's her strong, driving sense of mission. I especially love her image of being in a valley with so many others before arriving here, on this good earth. And eagerly waving her hand at God's call, "Here I am, send me. Yes, send me!" *Yes* is writ large throughout her entire being.
>
> I first met Joanne several years ago, at a women's spirituality group. Even then, she kept speaking about a dream: to work in Africa, empowering people—especially children—to answer their own calls from God. A few years elapsed. But then, I became aware that her dream now had a name, "Joining Hearts and Hands." Shared with her husband, Bill, it now had a mission: "to promote dignity, opportunity and hope." Specifically, their nonprofit agency "promotes improved educational, health and economic conditions for African orphans and their communities by building schools, sponsoring health clinics, providing secondary scholarships, and nurturing sustainable development and initiatives, all to promote dignity, opportunity and hope." (See for yourselves on the web, www.joiningheartsandhands.org.) They often spend a month at a time in Kenya. Making connections. Listening to the needs of the people. Working with and training leaders on the ground. Building schools. Building infant businesses. Building lives. One dream fulfilled leads to another, and now their newest venture is adult literacy.
>
> I had so many questions. How did she, along with Bill, come to this great endeavor? What gifts have they brought to this dream? What has she been learning as they continually give birth, again and again? How has this journey into her dream changed her? Joanne graciously met with me, as I peppered her with all

these questions. As she spoke, I listened. And in the process, I discovered another soul sister.

Early on, Joanne said, she could date her dream back to 1978, upon graduating with her master's degree in elementary education. But now she realizes it goes back much further. To her family, she says. Like building blocks, one generation after another was lifted up on the shoulders of the ones who went before. Hers is a family of great faith, providing numerous vocations to the priesthood and religious life. And "Our Lady," for whom she has an intimate devotion, has become an important part of this family. Then there's Bill, with whom she has partnered a new generation. The love of her life, a complex personality like herself, an educator and social activist who uses his gifts and skills well, Bill agreed to be part of her adventurous dream, to see where it would take them for the rest of their lives, upon retirement. In her view, they could model lay couples of faith: not pointing to themselves, but to God working through them.

What else, who else, has formed and shaped Joanne? Writers on the spiritual life, like Bede Griffith, Bruno Barnhart, and Henri Nouwen. Scripture, of course, especially passages describing the great wonders of God (like Sir 42:15–25) and God's tender, insistent call upon us (like John 21:15–17), where Jesus urges Peter, "Feed my lambs . . . Tend my sheep . . . Feed my sheep." Loving relationships with children and grandchildren. Smiling in joy at the tender love shared by son Christopher with his wife, Caroline. Cherishing daughter Lisa as she strives for excellence while loving her children with all her heart. Watching her children parent is a source of joy, for surely they are not unlike Jesus' tenderhearted touch of the children he welcomed. Then, of course, there are women of wisdom currently in their mid-nineties: like her mom, Audrey Leising, and aunts Dorothy Mary, Blanche, and Florence Leising, each of whom is a school sister of Notre Dame.

There are also fearless, holy women religious in Kenya who have shown the way. Among them are Sr. Mara Frundt, SSND; Sr. Rose Nagacha, SSND; Sr. Bea Leising, SSF; Sr. Joanne Gangloff, SSF; Sr. Maurice Michael, FSJ; and Sr. Helen Pius, FSSA. It was Sr. Mara, from the United States, who became an early guide, serving as leader of the novitiate house for new SSND sisters in Kisumu, Kenya. For more than fifteen years, Sr. Mara listened to, encouraged, prayed, and worked with Joanne and

Bill. Together they mourned and buried a dear Kenyan colleague in his home village, after he had committed suicide. They also shared many times of joy, as when Sr. Mara hosted lively political discussions on what's happening in the world, complete with big bowls of popcorn and homemade cake. Currently serving in Rome, Sr. Mara mentors and guides all novitiate sisters, always motivated by God's good grace.

Joanne knows how privileged she is to work alongside so many who continually encourage and model ways to pray, sing, dance, laugh with, and love others. At the same time, she has learned this: even sandpaper relationships with adversaries can stretch us into growth. Then, of course, prayer is essential. Prayer of all kinds: like Mass, Adoration of the Blessed Sacrament, the Rosary, Chaplet of Divine Mercy, the Spiritual Exercises of St. Ignatius, and more. And there's her precious "Dear God" journal. But always, it is God's call upon her heart that is central.

What has she learned along the way? That we are all blessed and cherished by God, gifted with talents and a reason to be in this world. That we are also broken, because something is wrong and/or missing, thus providing yet one more way to connect with people. And that we are chosen to fulfill our own special path in this world. Because of her ongoing openness to these pieces of truth, she has grown in compassion and trust. Her journal has helped her here. Often, while writing, she suddenly discovers that the voice simply changes; no longer hers, it is God who is speaking, to her, unbidden. And the message is always one of love and encouragement. Though she does admit to often struggling to wait upon God. Why not *now*, God?!

But 2005 became her *now*, the beginning of her journey, with Bill, to Africa. Once there, she felt that they were in God's heartland. As she puts it, we brought our skills—Bill's in education and management, mine in counseling, compassion, and management—and our connections with us. We help people find their own voice, alongside clergy and natural leaders on the ground. When we see unhealthy conditions, we nudge gracefully and work together to find alternatives and solutions.

Wouldn't you love to meet Joanne? People here in Rochester continually invite her and Bill into their hearts, parishes, prayer group meetings, and interfaith gatherings: to speak, to inspire others, and then connect folks of all ages from here to there. In the process, her faith is continually enlivened, she says, by the certainty that God will direct us all and keep us in divine care. Who could ever ask for more?

As a matter of fact, I did ask for more. A few years had transpired since I had written this piece, intending to reveal Joanne's passion. Now, at this point, was there anything more she would want to add to what I hoped would become another book? She began by acknowledging her wonder at God's many blessings. As she spoke, I couldn't help but be reminded of Jesus' parable of the sower and seed. Surely, I thought, God's seeds in her and Bill are bearing fruit a hundredfold! Not only in their neighborhood, but halfway around the globe! Indeed, as Joanne had believed, they had arrived at God's heartland, the very place—according to scientists—from which human life had emerged.

Her face shone as she emphasized: relationships have always been at the core of their mission. Prayer of so many supporters. Ongoing donations to their mission. People in Africa who continue moving forward "on the ground" in their absence, though they faithfully continue to spend a month at a time there on this dream. Among the ongoing relationships she treasures is that with women religious and priests, some of whom have led them into neighboring Tanzania. She glowingly speaks of the Sisters of Our Lady of Usambara, in Tanzania's Diocese of Tanga. Their ministry incorporates medicine and education, alongside pastoral ministry in parishes and homes. Joanne's face lit up as she described the recent visit with their leader, Mama Gaspara. Who knows what collaboration lies ahead? Ultimately, it is all about relationship with God, for she often intuits God's presence in fleeting moments. She feels protected, knowing that God is leading them, that they are simply agents of God's work. For God is the link . . . the connection . . . working in and through their human relationships. Joanne experiences this connection more and more often in daily activities.

What has Joanne continued to value in this mission? It is very clear, she maintains, that these relationships help reveal the needs of the people. For example, Joining Hearts and Hands is now seeking scholarship money from donors so that teenagers might complete high school. Everything they do is a way of showing "you can do something."

What's next? Joanne again asserted her need of prayer to point the way. It is the fuel, absolutely central to their ongoing mission. Therefore, she has continued confidence that their projects will be sustainable, that their plans will grow into new physical realities. We parted with her exclamation, "I love it!" Her passionate energy is shared by Bill, and there can be no doubt that their seed will continue to flourish.

Jesus as Wisdom: An Addendum

Who is Jesus? What did he mean to his first disciples? How did they name him? Those who first followed Jesus gave him titles ... and images ... that expressed some of the truth they had come to know of him. Lord, a title of reverence. Messiah, or Christ, Anointed One. Suffering Servant. Son of God. Emmanuel, God-with-us. Wisdom of God. As Paul clearly said, circa 54 CE: "God is the source of your life in Christ Jesus, who became for us wisdom from God."[74] Later, in the 80s, the Jesus of Matthew's Gospel (11:29) compares himself to Wisdom (Sir 51:26–27): "Take my yoke upon you, and learn from me; for I am gentle and humble in heart, and you will find rest for your souls. For my yoke is easy, and my burden is light."

However, it is in John's Gospel that this comparison goes deep and wide. As Scripture scholar Raymond Brown puts it: "The evangelist has capitalized on an identification of Jesus with personified divine Wisdom as described in the Hebrew Scripture."[75] What follows is a comparison of Wisdom Woman, as found in the Hebrew Scripture, with the Jesus of John's Gospel.

	Hebrew Scripture	John's Gospel
She was with God in the beginning.	Prov 8:22–31; Wis 6:22; Sir 24:3–6	John 1:1–2
She descended from heaven to dwell with humanity.	Prov 8:23, 29b–31; Sir 24:8–12; Bar 3:29,3 7; Wis 9:10, 17	John 1:14; 3:13; 16:28a
She roams the streets, mixing with humanity, seeking disciples.	Prov 1:20–23; 8:1–4; Wis 6:16	John 1:36–46; 7:28–31; 9:35–38

74. See 1 Cor 1:30.

75. Brown, *Gospel According to John, I–XII*, cxxii.

	Hebrew Scripture	John's Gospel
She gives life, truth, enlightenment, and knowledge to humanity.	Job 11:5–7; Wis 7:26; Prov 4:13; 8:32–35; Sir 4:11–12; Bar 4:1–2	John 1:4–5; 8:12; 9:5; 12:44–50; 14:6
She speaks of herself in long Discourses: The Way, Truth, and Life True Vine Bread of Life Light of the World	Prov 8:4–6; Sir 24; Prov 8:32–35; Sir 24:17; Prov 9:5–6; Sir 24:19–21; Wis 7:26	John 13–17 (Last Supper); John 14:6; John 15:1–7; John 6:48–58; John 8:12; 9:5
She forms disciples as her children.	Prov 8:32–33; Sir 4:11; 6:18	John 13:33
She is rejected by some.	Prov 1:24–25, 28; Bar 3:12	John 3:19–21; 8:46; 10:25
She displays the glory of God.	Sir 24:1–6; Wis 7:25	John 1:14; 2:11; 11:4; 17:1–5, 22, 24

All Jesus' signs offer a choice: believe . . . or not.

Wisdom Books and Themes in Scripture

Where is Wisdom found in Scripture? There are several places: (1) in five canonical books of the Hebrew Scripture, (2) in three deuterocanonical books of the Hebrew Scripture, and (3) in sections of some New Testament books and letters, besides John's Gospel. The ones with an asterisk (*) give voice to the Wisdom Woman.

Canonical Books of the Hebrew Scripture

1. **The Psalms.** While there is no total consensus on which are "Wisdom" psalms, there is agreement that the following offer Wisdom instruction: Pss 1, 11, 34, 37, and 112.

2. *****The Book of Proverbs.** See especially 1:20–23; 8:1—9:6; and 31:10–31.

3. **Song of Songs/Song of Solomon.**

4. **Ecclesiastes (Greek translation of the original *Qoheleth* in Hebrew).** Although written in the persona of King Solomon, it was written several centuries later.

5. **Job.**

Deuterocanonical Books of the Hebrew Scripture

These books, written within the two centuries before Jesus (BCE), are not part of the Hebrew canon because they were originally written in Greek, not Hebrew.

1. *****Baruch.** Written in the second to first century BCE. See especially 3:9—4:4.

2. *****Ecclesiasticus, or Sirach (the Wisdom of Jesus, Son of Sirach).** Written in the second century BCE. See especially 1:1–20; 24:1–34.

3. *****Wisdom of Solomon.** Written in the first century BCE.

New Testament Books and Letters, Besides John's Gospel

1. **1 Corinthians 1:24, 30.** Written by Paul in the early 50s.

2. **Luke's Gospel.** Written in the 80s. See especially 13:20–21 (woman kneading dough); 15:8–10 (woman searching for the lost coin); 18:1–8 (the persistent widow); 19:10 (Jesus "came to seek out and save the lost"); 24:13–35 (Jesus, as Wisdom, encounters two disciples on the road to Emmaus).

3. **Matthew's Gospel.** Also written in the 80s. See especially 13:33 (woman kneading dough); 11:18–19 (Jesus compares himself to Wisdom); 11:25–30 (Jesus is a gentle, humble servant).

Who, then, is Wisdom? How shall we describe her? She is . . .

- Dancer at the dawn of creation, delighting in the human race, delighting in all that is (Prov 8:22–31)

- God's delight/beloved/abundance (Prov 8:25–30)

- Order *and* creativity (Wis 7:22b–23; 8:1)

- Seeker after the lost (Luke 15)

- Liberator at the exodus (Wis 10:15–21)

- Street preacher, calling disciples; bold advocate for justice (Prov 8:1–9)

- Teacher of insight into the ways of God: the Way, the Truth, and the Life (Prov 8:14–16; John 14:1–6)

- Food for the hungry, drink for the thirsty (Prov 9:1–5; John 6:48–58)

- Life in a parched land: a stately cedar, an olive tree, a palm tree in *Engedi* (Sir 24:14–15)

- Book of the covenant (Sir 24:23)

- Spotless mirror of the working of God (Wis 7:26b)

- A breath of the power of God (Wis 7:25a)

- An image of God's goodness (Wis 7:26c)

- She is for us. She is mobile: for she enters into "holy souls," making them "friends of God, and prophets" (Wis 7:27)

3

Lent

L ent is different. Stark. No more "Alleluias." No more "Glorias." No more flowers. No more bright colors. Purple is everywhere. Simplicity is everywhere, stripping us to the core. Confronting us . . . with messing up? Or even with our mortality, our reason for being?

Ash Wednesday Sets the Stage

Each Lent begins the same way . . . on Ash Wednesday. With the exact same readings.[1] I recall an Ash Wednesday some thirty years ago now. I was at work in the parish office, and the phone rang. "Hi, Mom! I just wanted you to know I went to church today!" Her chipper voice conveyed the good news as much as the words themselves. It was my daughter, calling from college. She was a freshman at the time, and she hadn't darkened the door of Sunday Mass more than a few times since she'd arrived. But, it was Lent. Ash Wednesday, to be precise. And something drew her there.

There's something about Ash Wednesday, isn't there? That day seems to attract more people than any of the designated "holy days." Is it something we do just because we've always done it? Or, does that smudge on our forehead connect us to some deeper truth? Something, perhaps, about our mortality? Vulnerability? Our needs/limits/failures . . . and our need for forgiveness, God, someone to count on, meaning in life? A longing for life, for even the tiniest green shoot, when everything—at least in our neck of the woods—appears to be deader than a doornail? (For the word "lent" *does* mean springtime.) What has seeped into the crevices of *your* consciousness, into your very bones about this day?

---

1. See Joel 2:12–18; Ps 51:1–4a, 10–12, 15; 2 Cor 5:20—6:2; Matt 6:1–6, 16–18.

I can't say for sure why my daughter was drawn to church that day. But this much is true. Every year, we come. With our stories. Our losses and grieving. Our celebrations, as in a job promotion. Our sicknesses, perhaps even a cancer diagnosis. Our commitment to health, strength, and weight loss. Yes, we come. I came that year, thirty years ago. And yet, did I *really* *hear* the words we *always* hear on Ash Wednesday? Did I really hear their urgency? Gather an assembly! "Sanctify a fast"![2] . . . "We are ambassadors for Christ, since God is making his appeal through us; we entreat you on behalf of Christ, be reconciled to God . . . . See, now is the acceptable time; see, now is the day of salvation!"[3] No. Back then, I did not.

But every now and again an event can leave an indelible mark on our very being. An imprint that cannot and must not be ignored. For me, that event was the pandemic called COVID-19: an ugly, invisible, pervasive, global virus attacking everyone and anyone, of every nation, class, and culture, like it or not. Social media—Facebook, tweets, all of it—brought everyone into our living room. The pain and suffering, hopes and dreams, chasms of division among us were laid bare. Now, *finally*, the urgency with which Paul had written his challenging words to the Corinthians, would hit home for us, as well. Soon there would be thousands—even millions—of people worldwide dying from this virus. The gulf between haves and have-nots stared back at us. Those people in power, who cared more about themselves than the people they served, became increasingly obvious. Of course, it continually takes time for all this to sink in.

And yet, I have hope. I hope and trust that these memories can serve us well on future Ash Wednesdays. That the urgency of Paul's words, written to his own divided community with the profound hope of their coming together, will help us "listen up." *Become* ambassadors for Christ. *Remember* the greatheartedness of God, in the face of our tenuous promises. *Remember* the fragility of our gifted lives. *Respond*, then, with everything in us. *Turn*, and turn again—*now*, today, and every today of our precious lives—to the Only One who can stand us tall, with conviction, to serve our needy neighbors, next door and around the world.

How shall we do this? In exactly the same way urged on us by the evangelist Matthew, writing to his *own* divided community back in the 80s CE (some fifty years in the wake of Jesus' death and resurrection). *Pray.* Daily. In secret. In quiet. Listening . . . listening for the God who created our hearts, our very being. Listening to the God who *longs* for those hearts. Listening as well to the human cries for justice that pierce the heavens. Listening again

2. Joel 2:15b.

3. 2 Cor 5:20; 6:2c.

to God's nudges to become agents for healing and righting wrongs. Then, *fast*. From name-calling. From blaming and shaming. From prejudgments, made hastily and harshly. From any sense of superiority. From separating ourselves out from our neighbors, whether they live next door or halfway around the world. And, of course, *give alms*. A healing touch. A kind and compassionate word. A challenging word, an advocating action for any-one—*anyone*—who needs it most. This year, like *every* year, we *must* develop the tough discipline of returning hatred with love—not soft, mushy love but divine love—the kind that *refuses* to see an enemy in *anyone* and *everyone*. The kind of love insisted upon by the Rev. Dr. Martin Luther King Jr. The kind of love that alone can create the Beloved Community of healing and reconciliation. The kind of love that can energize a people into working for health care for everyone. Into *nonviolently* attacking the roots of poverty in the wealthiest nation on earth. Into facing head-on the many challenges to mold an inclusive and pastoral Church. Only then can disconnected human hearts be transformed into true ambassadors for Christ: Jesus, our brother, whom we follow. Every Lent *must* be different! *Must* point beyond ourselves, by the grace of God, into a future dripping with hope! Not only for ourselves, but for *everyone's* sake. What do you say?

The Sundays of Lent

Ash Wednesday sets the tone for the entire Lenten season of repentance, healing, and reconciliation. Letting God be God in our lives, the God who took an unlikely, ragtag assembly of slaves and covenanted with them: "I am the Lord your God, who brought you out of the land of Egypt, out of the house of slavery; you shall have no other gods before me."[4] And a time of entering into the power of our baptism into Christ, for the first time or yet once again.

We enter the Sundays of Lent in the same way. In the wilderness. With Jesus. "Driven" there, as Mark dares to put it. Now, Matthew and Luke soften the word, but "driven" says it best for me. For who would ever *choose* to enter that disorienting space? That vast expanse of endless shades of white . . . in sand and mountain . . . where only the mountain goats, called *ebeks* in Israel . . . are at home. Who would ever seek to wan-der a space that seems to have no end? Where all signs of life are fleeting? Perhaps a Bedouin tent here . . . or a camel there . . . munching on only a sparse blade of grass or two? Where oases *seem* to pop up, only to deceive, yet one more time? Like clutching to an addiction, desperately hoping

4. Exod 20:2–3, from the First Reading for the Third Sunday of Lent, Cycle B.

that *this* time that ancient wound will be healed? Only to discover, yet one more time, that looking into the bottom of an empty bottle . . . or at an unnecessary purchase . . . or some food that will *never* nourish the body, let alone the soul . . . that *none* of this will *ever* give life.

Jesus went willingly. So do we, in our most courageous moments. Knowing, as did Jesus, that *only* encountering . . . and facing . . . these demons head-on will truly set us free to walk the path of life itself. Some commentators suggest that this journey might well have been literal for Jesus. And *also* metaphoric, a continual temptation throughout his ministry to *human* greatness, rather than greatness as God sees things: a continual temptation to false sources of praise and so-called nourishment rather than the genuine article of God's wisdom and strength. A continual temptation to reign supreme by *human* religious standards rather than to serve as *God* would have us serve.

So it is that we begin in the wilderness before gaining a glimpse, on the Second Sunday of Lent, of Jesus' true identity, in the transfiguration. After this, each cycle of readings diverges, retaining one particular focus for the season. In Cycle A, we encounter familiar guides on all it means to be immersed into Christ: the Samaritan woman, the man born blind, and three siblings profoundly loved by Jesus: Martha, Mary, and Lazarus. In Cycle B, we explore God's covenants made with God's people, for the sake of being ever more deeply plunged ourselves into the life of our "I am with you, I am for you" God. Finally, Cycle C brings us face-to-face with powerful stories of healing and reconciliation, for *our* sake, for *everyone's* sake. So, then, into what new territory are *we* being summoned, nudged, and cajoled *this* Lent? *Every* Lent?

Cycle A: The Baptismal Cycle, in Prose, Poetry, and Story

Our Christian life begins here. At the font. We are welcomed here, most typically as babies. Brought here by our parents and godparents, our nearest and dearest community, the ones who now take responsibility for raising us "in the practice of the faith." We are signed by the Church, with Christ's cross. Soon we will be baptized. But only after the entire participating community has listened to the word of God, renewed baptismal vows yet one more time, and rejected Satan's power, yet once again. For this is a very big step. *Now* we are immersed . . . literally or metaphorically . . . into the waters of baptism. Anointed with fragrant oil, the chrism of salvation, as members of Christ's body. Clothed with the white garment that is the "outward sign" of our

"Christian dignity," which is to be brought "unstained into the everlasting life of heaven." Given the Light of Christ, which is "to be kept burning brightly."[5] Is it any wonder, then, that we encounter Jesus as Living Water, Light of the World, and Resurrection and Life in *this* Lenten cycle?

Like most of us, I was baptized as an infant. As it happens, my first parish ministry assignment included preparing parents for their children's baptism. It wasn't long before I became increasingly jealous of those few adults I kept encountering who had made their baptismal commitment as *adults*. I will never forget inviting a woman to our parish liturgy committee, to share her story of being baptized in an *immersion* font at her parish Easter Vigil. In the telling of *her* baptismal story, she became radiant, transformed before our very eyes.

Then, in May of 2008, I finally had my *own* adult experience of baptism. It happened in the River Jordan, near the place where the Jordan begins. There were thirty-one of us on a pilgrimage in the Holy Land, guided by three veteran leaders. On the night before we left Galilee to head south into the wilderness, we were asked to prepare two brief statements for the following morning. What had we come to believe, deeply? And to what would we commit ourselves, as a result? It must be said that most of us brought considerable life experience to these requests. For most of us were in our sixties and seventies. Imagine, then, as we waded into the Jordan River, one at a time, each answering those questions in our own words. My words? I believe that God embraces *all* people, women included. Furthermore, I recommit myself to work—alongside so many others—toward the full equality of women in the Roman Catholic Church. Imagine, as we experienced the waters of the Jordan poured over our heads and fragrant oil rubbed onto our brows. On that day, our salty tears flowed readily into the Jordan waters, erupting from convictions that had been rubbed into the depths of our souls.

Since Vatican II, we have been urged to make our sacramental signs large enough, generous enough, to more truly reflect our sublimely merciful God. So it is that a number of parishes have constructed large immersion fonts by now, big enough for adults, pregnant with the power of baptism. If you're anywhere near Chicago, there's a baptismal font at St. Benedict the African Church in Chicago's South Side that's worth a visit.[6] In fact, its abundant life is announced even before you arrive at the church. (At least, this was true when I visited the church some twenty-five years ago.) Built in a rough neighborhood, this church beckons *everyone* to *life*,

---

5. The quotes are from the Roman Catholic Rite for Baptism.

6. There are pictures and descriptions of this font in Kuehn, *Place for Baptism*, 45–50.

through colorful banners a block from the church in every direction. And, upon arriving, at least in good weather, it's impossible to miss the carefully tended gardens that surround the house of this church. Then you enter . . . through a hallway, marked on each side by artistic creations. You make a full 180-degree turn . . . and your breath is taken away! A magnificent stone font welcomes all seekers just within the threshold of the sanctuary. This round font—a huge step-down pool—is twenty-four feet in diameter, and three and a half feet at its deepest end! There's no mistaking that in baptism we die and rise in Christ Jesus! And, just to make certain that everyone can witness this most important event, the chairs in the sanctuary can be turned to face the font, the place of beginning, again and again.

Living Water

Living Water!
Lavish! Lush! Cascading
like pebbles artfully tossed,
lightly tapping a playful two-step
across the shimmering sea,
or like birds swooping elegantly in flight,
lithesome, slowly sweeping a romantic Tango.

Cleansing water,
washing away blindness;
Oh, and in the process,
a mixture of earth's clay and saliva
by God's Sent One,
a down-to-earth Jesus.
(For Jesus *did* command the man born blind
to wash in the Pool of Siloam, which means Sent.)

Re-birthing water,
erupting like God's tears
from an empty, deep well of grief,
gushing from the bowels of the soul,
from the compassionate womb of Jesus,
at the loss of a dear friend, Lazarus,

and at all human anguish.

What about *our* tears of Living Water?
Are they God at work, rivering through us?
Bursting the dammed up walls of denial,
softening the stiffened ridges of unforgiveness,
cleansing out the dross of all bitterness,
that we might turn, yet once again,
to . . . Living Water!
The Gushing, Gurgling Fountain
erupting! From the very depths of our being!

A Story, as Told by the Woman of Samaria

This day began just like any other . . . just like every other. *Nothing* would ever change. I was sick and tired of the constant whispers behind my back. Sick and tired of my neighbors' stinging judgments. Sick and tired of trudging to the well in the scorching, searing sun of noonday. Sick and tired of being lonely. Sick and tired of being sick and tired.

Off I trudged, yet one more time, to the well. Only, this time, I *wasn't* alone! A *stranger* was sitting there. A *man*. Would he *leer* at me? Did I need to *defend* myself? No! He gave me a look I wasn't accustomed to: a look of kindness. And then he did something he wasn't supposed to do. Or so I'd always been taught. He *spoke* to me! Kindly. *He* needed something from *me*! A drink of water! I could tell immediately by his accent that he was a Jew. One of my enemies . . . or so I'd always been taught. Jews and Samaritans *hated* each other, from way back. With a *visceral* hatred. Like a family, split apart. We *were* family—he and I—descended from the patriarchs and Moses. But, along the way, we ended up in different camps. With different beliefs. And different places of worship. Besides all that, Jewish men were taught that we Samaritan women were totally unclean. To be banished from thought, word, and deed. But, *look* at him. He's calm . . . assured . . . polite . . . gentle . . . indifferent to everything I've ever been taught. Why, there's even an air of *freedom* about him. Who *is* this man?

Okay, I admit it. He's piqued my curiosity. Especially with his offer of Living Water. A gift, from him, to me. But, I don't understand. He doesn't even have a *bucket*, and this well is deep! What on *earth* is he talking about? I *had* to engage. I *had* to find out. I *had* to allow my assertiveness to take over. He actually rather seemed to like that (*said with a little chuckle*). Now I must tell you: many people consider his next statement a change of subject, a distraction. But it wasn't. He was actually very much on point. "Go, call your husband,"[7] he said. He might just as well have said, "So, tell me about yourself." By now I was totally disarmed. By now I knew this man would never condemn me . . . or find me wanting. So, I poured out my heart and my soul. And he listened intently. Compassionately. Like he already knew my entire story anyway. Like what was done was done. Like what *really* mattered was what lay in the future. And then the strangest thing happened. I could feel the stirring of *something* deep inside. Like Living Water? Dredging out all my fear, pain, and suffering? Splashing insight in its wake? For the very first time, I felt connected to my very own people. I wasn't so very different from any *one* of them! From way back, when the Assyrians—and so many others—had defeated us, we had *all* gone chasing after false gods: five of them, just like my five husbands. But our past did *not* define our future! Living Water was erupting in me! What a strange, new, powerful feeling! With something like *hope*!

Suddenly, there was even *more*. There were memories. Compelling memories. Ancient memories. Of the time—way back when—we were about to enter the promised land. I could almost see . . . and hear . . . Moses saying his goodbyes to us. Assuring us that God would *never* leave us orphaned. God would someday raise up a prophet like Moses from among the people. And that prophet would tell us *everything*! Why, it was happening! To me! Right now! With Jesus! I ventured the guess that was welling up inside me. "I know that Messiah is coming" (who is called Christ). "When he comes, he will proclaim all things to us."[8] How can I ever forget the smile of total delight that came over the face of Jesus? As though he *wanted* to say, "Look at you! You've engaged with me. You're just the person I was waiting for!" What he *did* say was even *more* astounding. Simply, "I am he."[9] Not unlike God's disclosure to Moses at the burning bush. Jesus identified himself to *me*—a woman from Samaria—an outcast to my own people, and a double outcast to the Jewish people. Unbelievable!

By now, the Living Water of Jesus was simply *gushing* out of me. No more water jug for me! *I* became the vessel myself! Would you believe that I headed straight for the folks with pointed fingers and stinging tongues? Only *God* could set this up! Come and see! "Come and see a man who told

7. John 4:6.
8. John 4:25.
9. John 4:26.

me everything I have ever done!"[10] So they came. And they saw. In the way of all believers, they invited Jesus in . . . to remain . . . and grow in them . . . that they might claim believing for themselves.

Afterward, I just knew. It was like a love story. For I was loved—*treasured*—just as I was. Given space to grow, expand, and become all I could be. You know what I mean, don't you? Truth be told, it's *only* the power of love that can propel us into this kind of confidence. Courage. And speech never before imagined. Yes, here I was, a Samaritan woman . . . unwanted and rejected . . . become *apostle* to my very own *people*! "Come, meet the One we've all been waiting for! Come and see! Come and see for yourselves!"

A Conversation among the Samaritan Woman, the Man Born Blind,
and Martha (Sister of Mary and Lazarus)

Now, what if we could listen in on a conversation among this Samaritan woman, the man born blind, and Martha? What insight, hindsight, and courage might these grandparents in faith reveal to us? How did *they* discover the abundant life promised by Jesus?[11] Listen.

> **Martha:** Welcome, everyone! My name is Martha. And I can tell from your knowing looks and smiles that you know me well. So, I may as well take charge, as I often do. All right, some people call me bossy; and I'll admit, I *am* assertive. It probably goes with being the firstborn. In my case, the older sister to Mary and my brother, Lazarus. But not everyone appreciates my finer qualities, it seems. I can honestly say that I'm warm and welcoming, and I *certainly* know how to set a fine table. Jesus always appreciated my giving him a place to lay his weary head, right here in Bethany, whenever he was in the neighborhood of Jerusalem. What good friends we became with him! What memories we cherish of conversations on into the night about the people he'd met! Like the Samaritan woman and the man born blind. Look, here they are!

> **The Samaritan Woman:** Yes, I can see that we Samaritan women are still all lumped together. Because we're "different," at least in someone's eyes. My story raises lots of questions about separating people out like that. You know what I mean? Let me introduce myself by name. I'm Rachel, named after my ancient ancestor, who met her beloved Jacob at a well.

10. John 4:29.
11. John 10:10.

The Man Born Blind: (*with a smile*) My name got lost, too. It's Benjamin! Named after Jacob's youngest son and his wife Rachel![12] (*Gives a smile to Rachel, as he says,*) "Well, look at this! Strangers a moment ago but now connected, from way back! Who would ever have imagined?" But, now, back to my story.[13] Until Jesus came along, I was *lost*! Dependent. Stuck. A *victim*. Living on the margins of life. By the side of the road. Begging . . . daily . . . for my next denarius. It's how things were. It's how things would *always* be! That is, until the day that Jesus came along. There I was, listening, as usual, to the people who went by. This time it was a small group, with someone asking about me: "Who sinned . . . that he was born blind?"[14] "Nobody!" The response was strong, swift, and sure. Who *was* this person, so unwilling to blame? So confident. So willing to shatter my world with compassion.

The Samaritan Woman: Yes, I know *exactly* what you mean. *Nothing* was ever going to change for me, either. Not the pointed fingers that shoved me to the well in the scorching heat of midday, rather than the cool comfort of early morning. Not the shaming. Not my endless search for love that always turned up wanting. Nothing! But I was never *dependent*. Oh, no. I was *tough*. Nobody was *ever* going to get close enough to hurt me, not ever again! I had no idea how parched I was! For genuine love! For *life, gulps* of life! That is, until Jesus came along.

Martha: I guess I'm the fortunate one. I *knew* I was loved. By Jesus. With the same love he poured out on Mary, Lazarus, and *all* his disciples. I *knew* his compassion. His healing on the Sabbath, despite the stubborn resistance of some religious authorities. You'll understand, then, why he shattered my world at his *delay*. Lazarus was so sick! Of course, Mary and I sent word to Jesus. Immediately! "Come! Quickly!" But he *didn't* come. Day in, day out, we *waited*. Day in, day out, we *looked* for him. But he didn't come. Not for four . . . whole . . . long days. And Lazarus, my beloved, gentle brother, died. Where was *Jesus*? Why hadn't he come?

---

12. I imagined the names Rachel and Benjamin; they seemed to fit with the stories of their ancestors.

13. See John 9:1–39.

14. John 9:2.

The Man Born Blind: How sad for you! Especially because of your friendship with him! I can say this: I felt abandoned by him, too, at least at first. Now remember, Jesus came into my life so suddenly. I was *still* blind when I felt the strong yet gentle pressure of his hands, smearing my eyes with mud. I was *still* blind when I heard the kind but firm command, "Go, wash in the pool of Siloam."[15] Which means *sent*, by the way. Hmm. Was Jesus *sent*? To *me*? So I *did* wash. And I *saw*! But, where was *he*? Gone! *Who* was he? There I was, all alone, embroiled in conflict. My neighbors weren't even sure I was the same person! As for the Pharisees, they interrogated me *twice*, the second time after they questioned my parents . . . who, by the way, kept their distance from me. Talk about being abandoned! Some of the religious leaders were really irate at my testimony! "How dare this man Jesus heal on the Sabbath!" Others weren't so sure. Maybe he *was* the Promised One. But I became more and more convinced as I considered, and spoke . . . and spoke again. "Never since the world began has it been heard that anyone opened the eyes of a person born blind. If this man were not from God, he could do nothing."[16] Wow! I was developing a backbone! Courage! I could even stand tall and speak my truth!

The Samaritan Woman: Yes, he had that same effect on me, too. Though I never felt abandoned by him. Not at all. In fact, it was just the opposite. We talked. He listened. *I* listened to the truth emerging in *me*. Why, I couldn't *wait* to drench my neighbors with the Living Water of good news! Yes, my *neighbors*: the very ones who had turned their backs on me! Wow! Where did my courage come from? And who can account for their about-face? For bringing us together as family, once again? Why, only Jesus, of course, "truly the Savior of the world."[17]

Martha: Oh, yes, Rachel, I agree! For his love had shattered *all* our puny expectations. He could do anything! Even the impossible, for Lazarus. But Jesus pushed me even further: "I am the resurrection and the life."[18] His words stunned me. Could I *believe* that? Yet, I trusted him with everything in me. "Yes, Lord, I

15. John 9:7.
16. John 9:32–33.
17. John 4:42.
18. John 11:25.

believe that you are the Messiah, the Son of God, the one coming into the world."[19] And I meant it!

The Man Born Blind: I, too, came to believe in Jesus. I could see, of course, but my little-by-little, inching-along insight would be sorely tested! By neighbors . . . even parents . . . unwilling to claim me. By religious leaders who tossed me out of the synagogue. Only later would I learn that Jesus returned *precisely* because of this. Remember now, I didn't know him by sight. Only by that same strong, familiar voice, now pressing me, "Do you believe in the Son of Man?"[20] Yes, Lord, yes. I am totally changed! Brand new! Yes, "Lord, I believe!"[21]

Martha: Indeed, Jesus had a way of continually pushing and prodding those he loved to become "more": more loving, more courageous, more genuine. How can I ever forget that moment he called Lazarus forth from the tomb? He'd done the impossible! Obviously, he didn't need *us* for the rest of the story. Or . . . did he? "Unbind him, and let him go."[22] Those words . . . that responsibility . . . were on us! He would always do the heavy lifting, but he would never take away from us what *we* could do for ourselves.

Some Questions: Where has Jesus been a magnetic force for good, healing, and love in *our* lives? What people and events have revealed his continual, compelling call upon us? Where has his powerful pull drawn us into a new land, a place of belonging, a place of becoming our best selves? Despite a personal cost to our very lives, can we risk being drawn further into Christ? What does it mean that Jesus came so that we might have life, and have it abundantly?

19. John 11:27; Martha's profession of faith parallels that of Peter in the other three Gospels.

20. John 9:35.

21. John 9:38.

22. John 11:44.

Cycle B: Covenanted by and with God,
Promises Made, Promises Kept

Cycle B almost gets lost. Whenever there are catechumens in the parish, Cycle A may always be used. And, the emphasis on reconciliation in Cycle C is something for which we yearn. Can the tender story of the prodigal son, so near and dear to many a heart, be ours as well? But, Cycle B? What do we make of the raging Jesus in the temple? Eyes flashing, heart pounding for the sake of God's reign! It's no polite Jesus that we encounter on *this* day!

At the same time, what a gift is wrapped up in this cycle! For it is on *this* day—the Third Sunday of Lent—that this zealous Jesus is paired with the Exodus account of God's passionate love for our Jewish ancestors in faith.[23] God so loved the Israelites that God delivered them "out of the land of Egypt, out of the house of slavery."[24] Could *anyone* imagine more? And yet . . . there *is* more! For, on the following Sunday, we hear this: "God so loved the world that he gave his only Son, so that everyone who believes in him may not perish but may have eternal life."[25] Doesn't this unbounded, passionate, divine love fulfill Jeremiah's tender prophecy, as proclaimed on the Fifth Sunday of Lent? "I will put my law within them, and I will write it on their hearts; and I will be their God, and they shall be my people."[26]

God is with us; God is for us. God is out to liberate anyone held captive: whether in Egypt, or in addictions, or in so many forms of cruel hardheartedness delivered by both society *and* church. Make no mistake. God *intends* to set us free. Free *from* servitude. Free *for* service, to *all* our sisters and brothers. And God keeps those promises. By nudging, urging, cajoling, and tenderly touching our hearts, that *we* might partner in that great work of midwifing creation, yet one more time. Such is the great hope . . . *and* the great challenge of Lenten Cycle B.

The Exodus Today, for Jews and Christians

Passover: the high point of the Jewish year. Telling, re-creating the story of the people of Israel. Not just in the past, but today. This year. Every year. It is *the* foundational story of being set free from slavery, from the rigid, narrow, enslaving place of Egypt. *The* story of being set free by divine love, for the

---

23. Exod 20:1–17 and John 2:13–25.
24. Exod 20:2.
25. John 3:16.
26. Jer 31:33.

sake of serving God and God's people. Not just back then . . . but today, and every day.

The Christ Event (the life, death, and resurrection of Jesus): the high point of the Christian year, the *ultimate* exodus event. It is Jesus, the Christ, who sets free. And yet Jesus, the Jew, was formed, shaped, molded, and challenged by the original exodus event . . . the event which shaped the Israelites into God's "treasured possession . . . priestly kingdom and a holy nation."[27] That is why, as descendants of the Israelites, we *must* hear the exodus story of liberation at every Easter Vigil, the high point of our church year. That is why it behooves us to explore the meaning of that original exodus event for ourselves. That is why we begin here.

Each spring, Jewish people gather in homes around the globe, to celebrate who they are. At these Seder suppers, the past becomes present, heavy-laden with meaning. Leonard Fein, American social activist, puts it this way:

> Each cup we raise this night is an act of memory and of reverence. The story we tell, this year as every year, is not yet done. It begins with them, then; it continues with us, now. We remember not out of curiosity or nostalgia, but because it is our turn to add to the story.
>
> Our challenge this year, as every year, is to feel the Exodus, to open the gates of time and become one with those who crossed the Red Sea from slavery to freedom.
>
> Our challenge this year, as every year, is to know the Exodus, to behold all those in every land who have yet to make the crossing.
>
> Our challenge this day, as every day, is to reach out our hands to them and help them cross to freedom land.
>
> We know some things that others do not always know—how arduous is the struggle, how very deep the waters to be crossed and how treacherous their tides, how filled with irony and contradiction and suffering are the crossing and then the wandering.
>
> We know such things because we ourselves wandered in the desert for forty years. Have not those forty years been followed by thirty-two centuries of struggle and of quest? Heirs to those who struggled and quested, we are old-timers at disappointment, veterans at sorrow, but always, always, prisoners of hope.

27. Exod 19:5b, 6a.

The hope is the anthem of our people (*Hatikvah*), and the way of our people.

For all the reversals and all the stumbling-blocks, for all the blood and all the hurt, hope still dances within us. That is who we are, and that is what this Seder is about. For the slaves do become free, and the tyrants are destroyed.[28]

On this night, then, the Jewish people renew their covenant with God. And all present, from oldest to youngest, have a role. It is worth noting that the Hebrew word for Egypt means "narrow place." A stifling place. A place of constriction. If the exodus is about birthing new life, then Egypt had become the womb, the place of beginning. For Egypt had once—in the time of Joseph (of the coat of many colors)—been a welcoming, nurturing place, where starving Israelites had been fed. But, it had become a place of cruel oppression, under a fearful pharaoh, "who did not know Joseph."[29] So, the Israelites cried out to their God. And the slow, painful process of giving birth to God's people was set into motion. For faithful Jews, this night:

- Is the night for reckless dreams, for impossibilities to become God's surprises. It is hope, believing in what is not yet seen. "Next year in Jerusalem!"

- Is the realization that the turning point from slavery to freedom begins with the human shift from passive resignation to resistance of oppression.

- Is trust in the God who hears and responds to human cries, who bleeds in and through human suffering, who longs for human freedom.

- Is the recognition that even the suffering of our enemies reduces our joy, which is why we shed a drop of wine at the naming of each plague.

- Is the recognition that in this incomplete and imperfect world, God abundantly showers us with gifts. And for that, we give thanks and praise. *Da-yeinu*, the song of thanksgiving that traditionally ends the telling of the story, is a lengthy list of God's miracles on our behalf, any one of which "would have been enough" for us to experience God's love.

- Is the time for *everyone* to see themselves coming out of Egypt *now*, just like the first generation, just like every generation ever since; good

---

28. Zion and Dishon, *Different Night*, 117. The four cups mentioned at the beginning of the celebration are the ones blessed and drunk on this night, each with its own meaning. In addition, a cup is poured in hope for the coming of Elijah.

29. Exod 1:8.

leaders are essential to an ever deepening understanding of this night for each generation of Jewish people.[30]

Can we not hear the questions raised by the Hebrews as our very own? What does it mean to be enslaved? Or persecuted? What does it mean to be set free? Internally, by becoming an authentic person, externally by serving the Living God and God's people? What does liberation feel like? Is it instantaneous? Or a process? What is the impact of suffering on life? Has it become a source of vengeance, bitterness, and harsh judgments? Or, has suffering become a source of compassion and advocacy for those still enslaved? Or, perhaps both, at different times, even at the same time? What does it mean to become a liberator of others?

Etty Hillesum: Jewish Woman Set Free for Unconditional Love

So it is that I now turn to a young Jewish woman of the early and mid-twentieth century, Etty Hillesum. A Dutch Jew, Etty is twenty-seven years old when we encounter her in Amsterdam in 1941. Given the name Esther, she grew up in the town of Deventer in the eastern Netherlands. Her family might well be described as "chaotic," one of Etty's favorite words. Her father, Dr. Louis Hillesum—a professor and scholar of classical language— was small, brilliant, quiet, and yet witty. Her mother, Rebecca, a Russian Jew, was lively but unstable. All three children were brilliant and gifted: (1) Etty, the oldest and only daughter, in writing and language; (2) Jaap, a scientist who became a doctor; and (3) Mischa, an exceptionally gifted concert pianist. At the same time, all carried within them the seeds of mental illness, which blossomed into schizophrenia in Mischa. Etty's diary and letters—written over two and a half years—witness to her intentional, profound transformation during the horrific Nazi occupation. It remains, for me, nothing less than an immersion into the depths of love and forgiveness. An immersion into covenant with God.

I was so moved by her story, as found in *An Interrupted Life and Letters from Westerbork*, that I simply *had* to respond to her by letter, her primary form of communication. What follows is that letter, written in February 2010, in her words and mine.[31]

---

30. Zion and Dishon, *Different Night*. My bulleted list summarizes their thoughts.

31. Etty Hillesum's diary and letters form the substance of *An Interrupted Life* (1996), and all footnotes that follow are from this book. I thank my storytelling colleague Marilyn Catherine, who urged and assisted me in transforming this letter from my voice alone to mine and Etty's, for performance and writing.

Dear Etty,

I had heard of you and read little snippets of your writing, enough to know I simply had to know more. So, I picked up your *Diary and Letters from Westerbork*. Built by the Dutch as a refugee camp in the eastern Netherlands for Jews fleeing Germany, under the Nazis, Westerbork became a barbaric holding camp for Jews, before being shipped east to Auschwitz.

I was not prepared for what happened. We seemed so different, you and I. Here you were, a Dutch Jew, cigarette in hand, tasting the modern enjoyments of your day. And I, an American Catholic Christian, was raised in a more "straight-laced" household. But your eyes . . . direct . . . honest . . . intense . . . searching . . . drew me in. And, surprise! You made a home in my heart! We actually shared two and a half years together on this globe, in the early 1940s. And so much more. Our love of books. Studying. And writing. Your phrase . . .

Etty: "I should like, as it were, to caress the paper with just the right word."[32]

Gloria: . . . *tickled* me. Then there's our joy in little things . . . a few flowers . . . wearing a pretty blouse. And our struggle to be comfortable in our own skin and claim our full dignity as women. But it's *you*—your intense, probing, inspiring journey—that I simply *had* to share with so many others who had never heard of you! We begin, then, with your first entry, dated March 9, 1941.

Etty: "I seem to be a match for most of life's problems, and yet deep down something like a tightly wound ball of twine binds me relentlessly, and at times I am nothing more or less than a miserable, frightened creature, despite the clarity with which I can express myself."[33]

Gloria: Oh, but how you would grow over the next year, in fits and starts, chronicling it all—the tussling and doubts, discouragement and joy. Surely it was no accident that the beginning of a profound, complex relationship with Julius Spier at this time would sow the seeds of your intentional growth into wisdom

32. Hillesum, *Interrupted Life*, 120.
33. Hillesum, *Interrupted Life*, 3.

and courage itself. Take, for example, your determination to stay grounded in reality.

Etty: "One must keep in touch with the real world and know one's place in it . . . . To live fully, outwardly and inwardly, not to ignore external reality for the sake of the inner life, or the reverse—that's quite a task."[34] The truth is: "I am sometimes so distracted by all the appalling happenings round me that it's far from easy to find the way back to myself. And yet that's what I must do."[35]

Gloria: But it was your daily immersion in prayer . . . your desire to grow God within you . . . that became your mainstay and source of counsel. A discipline, not easy at first.

Etty: "There is really a deep well inside me. And in it dwells God. Sometimes I am there too. But more often stones and grit block the well, and God is buried beneath. Then He must be dug out again."[36]

Gloria: And dig you did . . . until your prayer became an act of intimate love. How I smiled when you called yourself . . .

Etty: "a kneeler in training."[37] It seemed that I was "forced to the ground by something stronger than myself. . . . I was still embarrassed by this act, as intimate as gestures of love that cannot be put into words either, except by a poet."[38]

Gloria: So that, by November you could pray, on your knees,

Etty: "Oh, Lord, let me feel at one with myself. Let me perform a thousand daily tasks with love, but let every one spring from a greater central core of devotion and love."[39]

Gloria: As if in answer, you were given moments of profound peace.

Etty: "Oh, God, I thank You for having created me as I am. I thank You for the sense of fulfillment I sometimes have; that fulfillment is after all nothing but being filled with You. I promise You to strive my whole life long for beauty and harmony and

34. Hillesum, *Interrupted Life*, 25.
35. Hillesum, *Interrupted Life*, 41.
36. Hillesum, *Interrupted Life*, 44.
37. Hillesum, *Interrupted Life*, 74.
38. Hillesum, *Interrupted Life*, 74.
39. Hillesum, *Interrupted Life*, 70.

also humility and true love, whispers of which I hear inside me during my best moments."[40]

Gloria: Even so, the ups and downs continued.

Etty: "Oh, Lord, this day, this day—it seems so heavy to me, let me bear it well . . . But Lord, help me not to waste a drop of my energy on fear and anxiety, but grant me all the resilience I need to bear this day."[41]

Gloria: It's not too strong to say that you were blossoming into a mystic, in love with God's presence. But here's what absolutely stirred the depths of my soul, from the very beginning. Your *compassion*! Even for the enemy! Or, as you put it, early on,

Etty: "hatred of Germans poisons everyone's mind." . . . But, "if there were only one decent German, then he should be cherished despite that whole barbaric gang, and because of that one decent German it is wrong to pour hatred over an entire people."[42]

Gloria: And this compassion settled in your very core, making ready to overflow that deep well of your very being, even after a most significant turn of events. The date: April 29, 1942. From that day forward, you and every other Jew had to wear the yellow Star of David. And then, little bit by little bit, the noose kept tightening. No longer could you be served by green grocers. No longer could you take the trams. No longer could you even ride your bicycles. They must be turned in, so that all your bruised, blistered feet swelled . . . as you walked . . . and walked . . . and walked . . . to fill your needs. Finally, the darkness descended with an 8:00 p.m. curfew. And yet, you could still proclaim:

Etty: "Something in me is growing, and every time I look inside, something fresh has appeared and all I have to do is to accept it, to take it upon myself, to bear it forward, and to let it flourish."[43]

Gloria: It wasn't long, however, until you grasped the full reality of events.

Etty: "What is at stake is our impending destruction and annihilation, we can have no more illusions about that. They are out

40. Hillesum, *Interrupted Life*, 73–74.
41. Hillesum, *Interrupted Life*, 109.
42. Hillesum, *Interrupted Life*, 11.
43. Hillesum, *Interrupted Life*, 131.

to destroy us completely, we must accept that and go on from there."[44] "I accept it. I know it now, and I shall not burden others with my fears. I shall not be bitter if others fail to grasp what is happening to us Jews. I work and continue to live with the same conviction, and I find life meaningful—yes, meaningful— although I hardly dare say so in company these days."[45]

Gloria: Whirlpools of hatred swirled around you. Genuine moral indignation. Alongside petty personal hatred. No, you would *not* be partner to *that*. Life was *far* too precious. Yes, you could "see visions of poisonous green smoke"[46] in Poland. And yes, you could be with the hungry and the dying, but you could also be . . .

Etty: "with the jasmine and with that piece of sky beyond my window; there is room for everything in a single life."[47]

Gloria: Oh, how you had grown! Enough, in fact, to accept your "destiny," in your words.[48] And how did you name this destiny of yours? You claimed so many pieces of it over the next year and a half . . . oneness with all who suffer, no matter what . . . a burning love for everyone, no matter what . . . becoming peace in a world gone mad, no matter what. But, it was on September 30, 1942, that you pleaded with God for your deepest desire:

Etty: "Let me," O God, "be the thinking heart of these barracks"[49] in Westerbork.

Gloria: Yes, despite the protests of your friends, you remained a member of the Jewish Council, to stay with your Jewish family at large. Despite illness in the fall of 1942, which took you away for a short while, you became their thinking heart. How? By first of all coming to terms with suffering.

Etty: "It is possible to suffer with dignity. . . . I mean: most of us in the West don't understand the art of suffering and experience a thousand fears instead. We cease to be alive, being full of fear, bitterness, hatred, and despair. God knows, it's only too easy to

44. Hillesum, *Interrupted Life*, 153.
45. Hillesum, *Interrupted Life*, 154.
46. Hillesum, *Interrupted Life*, 152.
47. Hillesum, *Interrupted Life*, 152.
48. Hillesum, *Interrupted Life*, 130.
49. Hillesum, *Interrupted Life*, 225.

understand why."[50] But "I can sit for hours and know everything and bear everything and grow stronger in the bearing of it, and at the same time feel sure that life is beautiful and worth living."[51]

Gloria: *Here* is what I *really* love. This was not some kind of pious "stuff," the prayer of a person disengaged from reality. On the contrary—and you were very clear about this—it must be *real* suffering, not *imagined* suffering.

Etty: "Man suffers most through his fears of suffering." On the contrary: "Reality is something one shoulders together with all the suffering that goes with it, and with all the difficulties. And as one shoulders them, so one's resilience grows stronger." Only then will you "also have the strength to bear real suffering, your own and the world's."[52]

Gloria: It was redemptive suffering you were talking about. And you made sure we could see it for ourselves, on one hellish night in Westerbork. One of those early Tuesday mornings, while it was still dark, week in and week out, when hundreds of prisoners were being loaded on cattle cars headed for Poland. There were the sneering, bestial faces of the guards.

Etty: "I looked at them, each in turn, . . . and I have never been so frightened of anything in my life. I sank to my knees with the words that preside over human life: And God made man after His likeness. That passage spent a difficult morning with me."[53]

Gloria: As if *that* wasn't enough, you saw . . . you *felt* . . . the anguish on every side. The "tiny piercing screams of the babies, dragged from their cots in the middle of the night."[54] And the young boy who ran off when he realized he was going; he was caught, of course; but the commandant saw to it that another fifty people had to go, just because . . .

Etty: "There was a little woman in the washhouse, a basket of dripping clothes on her arm. 'I've got to go, and I won't even be able to get my washing dry by tomorrow. And my child is sick,

50. Hillesum, *Interrupted Life*, 152.

51. Hillesum, *Interrupted Life*, 153.

52. Hillesum, *Interrupted Life*, 220.

53. Hillesum, *Interrupted Life*, 340, from a letter dated August 24, 1943, just two weeks before Etty's deportation.

54. Hillesum, *Interrupted Life*, 341, from the same letter.

he's feverish, can't you fix things so that I don't have to go'?"[55] And then, sobbing, 'They take the sick children away and you never get them back.'"[56]

Gloria: One after another, so many in agony: the woman who mistakenly said she couldn't stand, so they made her stand for hours . . . the woman stuffing down molding sandwiches for fear there would be no food . . . the woman nearly a full nine months pregnant. Yes, Etty, you brought us there, in the midst of it all. And yet, and yet, you—the thinking heart of the barracks—could still proclaim, in a letter from Westerbork,

Etty: "New thoughts will have to radiate outward from the camps themselves; new insights, spreading lucidity, will have to cross the barbed wire enclosing us and join with the insights that people outside will have to earn just as bloodily, in circumstances that are slowly becoming almost as difficult."[57]

Gloria: It is almost as though you had heard "the Jew Paul," as you named him, whisper into your heart: "suffering produces endurance, and endurance produces character, and character produces hope, and hope does not disappoint us, because God's love has been poured into our hearts through the Holy Spirit that has been given to us."[58] Indeed, God's love was not only poured into your heart, but out of that heart, for so many others. Upon the death of your special friend, Julius Spier, in September of 1942, you could say,

Etty: "I now realize, God, how much You have given me. . . . With the passing of people, I feel a growing need to speak to You alone. I love people so terribly, because in every human being I love something of You. And I seek You everywhere in them and often do find something of You."[59]

Gloria: How tenderly you persisted in this great love.

Etty: "I thank You, God, for the great gift of being able to read people. Sometimes they seem to me like houses with open doors . . . . and every one must be turned into a dwelling dedicated to You,

55. Hillesum, *Interrupted Life*, 343, from the same letter.
56. Hillesum, *Interrupted Life*, 344.
57. Hillesum, *Interrupted Life*, 250–51.
58. Rom 5:3–5.
59. Hillesum, *Interrupted Life*, 198.

oh God. And I promise You, yes, I promise that I shall try to find a dwelling and a refuge for You in as many houses as possible."[60]

Gloria: Knowing that the end of this war would unleash two torrents—loving kindness and hatred—you vowed to "take the field against hatred."[61]

Etty: "Ultimately, we have just one moral duty: to reclaim large areas of peace in ourselves, more and more peace, and to reflect it toward others. And the more peace there is in us, the more peace there will also be in our troubled world."[62]

Gloria: You even prayed that God would turn your life into "one great peace."[63] In your words . . .

Etty: "They [the Nazis] can harass us, they can rob us of our material goods, of our freedom of movement, but we ourselves forfeit our greatest assets by our misguided compliance."[64] "True peace will come only when every individual finds peace within himself; when we have all vanquished and transformed our hatred for our fellow human beings of whatever race—even into love one day, although perhaps that is asking too much. It is however, the only solution. I am a happy person and I hold life dear indeed, in this year of Our Lord 1942, the umpteenth year of the war."[65]

Gloria: Your last diary entry, Etty, left me in awe.

Etty: "We should be willing to act as a balm for all wounds."[66]

Gloria: There's one more final word of yours I simply cannot resist, this time from your very last letter to your dear friend Maria. As it turned out, this was written only five days before you, yourself, were transported from Westerbork to Auschwitz:

Etty: "If we just care enough, God is in safe hands with us despite everything."[67]

60. Hillesum, *Interrupted Life*, 205.

61. Hillesum, *Interrupted Life*, 208.

62. Hillesum, *Interrupted Life*, 218.

63. Hillesum, *Interrupted Life*, 224.

64. Hillesum, *Interrupted Life*, 144.

65. Hillesum, *Interrupted Life*, 145.

66. Hillesum, *Interrupted Life*, 231.

67. Hillesum, *Interrupted Life*, 359, in a letter dated September 2, 1943.

Gloria: *reflectively,* "If we just care enough, God is in safe hands with us despite everything."

With eternal gratitude,

Gloria

A POSTSCRIPT

On one of those horrific Tuesday nights—September 7, 1943—to be exact, Etty and her family were forced to take their turn, boarding the infamous cattle cars, bound for Auschwitz. They all handled it with grace, Etty flinging one last postcard out the window. It was found and sent to the intended recipient. On November 30, 1943, Etty Hillesum died at Auschwitz. And yet, Etty had entrusted her letters and diary to a dear friend. But it would take another forty years for a relative of that friend to find a publisher. Her words live on, for us, thanks be to God!

In the summer of 2012, my husband and I traveled to the Netherlands. One of the two places I simply *had* to see was Etty's house in Amsterdam. Much to my surprise, very few people knew about Etty. But the hotel concierge found the information I needed on the internet. As might have been expected, she lived in a cultural section of the city. With my back to her house, having the same view as she did—from the window of her room on the top floor—I could see the concert hall off to the left. Directly across the street was a park, bordered on the other side by the Rembrandt Museum. Yes, this fit; it was her place, all right. But then came the ultimate surprise. Suddenly, without warning, as I turned around and faced her house, an unbidden surge of energy charged through me! Might it not be true that her spirit is still alive . . . still challenging . . . still empowering . . . still overflowing her beloved Amsterdam and us all with the unquenchable power of God's love? Might it not be true that she has revealed to us a way to heed God's summons to the ultimate new land of love beyond all telling, even in and through profound pain and struggle? I wonder.

Cycle C: Repentance, Healing, and Reconciliation
Finding and Claiming the Lost

From the days of the early Church, Lent was set aside as a time for repentance and reconciliation, along with baptismal preparation at the Great Event of Easter. Luke's Gospel (the Gospel of Cycle C) is replete with stories of God's extravagant forgiveness and healing. Chapter 15, in particular, overflows with God's mercy, through the stories of the lost sheep, the lost coin, and the lost son(s), the latter commonly known as the "prodigal son." For this cycle, I offer a prayer service of reconciliation. While this service concludes with general absolution, it might also be celebrated without general absolution as prayerful community preparation for one-on-one sacramental reconciliation.

Both communal *and* one-on-one sacramental reconciliation are rooted in our Catholic tradition. Both are pastorally valuable, in my view. Communal services drive home the point that our personal sins affect others; one-on-one offers an opportunity to examine the weaknesses that result in sin, along with the profound, forgiving love of God in Jesus. It is my abiding hope that Communal Penance Services will once again be offered on a regular basis, to satisfy the thirst of those desiring this kind of prayer.

"Lost and Found": A Celebration of Reconciliation[68]

(Greeters welcome everyone with a program and a candle.)

Opening Hymn: "All Are Welcome"

> Text by Marty Haugen; tune is TWO OAKS
> © 1994, GIA Publications, Inc.

Greeting by the Presider

(A priest, if general absolution is offered or a qualified lay person if not.)

Opening Prayer

Presider: Forgiving, pursuing, pardoning God,

All: **Your compassion for us is beyond all imagining.**

Presider: When we are lost, You hunt us down,

---

68. There might be a concurrent program for young children, focusing on the story of the woman with the lost coin. After the story is told, the children might act it out, taking turns being the woman and the lost coin. Children might then talk about what it feels like to be lost. And found. And, what does it feel like to be the one doing the searching? They might be also invited to give a variety of names for God. In this process, they could be introduced to a fine resource for children, *Heart Talks with Mother God*, by Bridget Mary Meehan and Regina Madonna Oliver. This has some lively pictures and meditations for children on several Scripture stories, including a meditation on the woman with the lost coin.

All:	**even and especially in the darkest corners of our hearts, our fears, our shame, our wanderings.**
Presider:	You embrace us, salve our wounds, and restore us to You, delightedly leading the joyful celebration of our being found.
All:	**Can we—the Beloved you claim for your very own—**
	Soak up Your forgiveness, as it flows into every cell of our being?
	Enough to forgive those who have wounded us?
	Yes, but only with You. Amen!

The Word of God

First Reading:	Hosea 11:1–4
Psalm 103:	**"Loving and Forgiving"**
	Text and tune by Scott Soper, © 1992 OCP Publications. All rights reserved.
Gospel:	Luke 15:1–10
	(This is best proclaimed "by heart," so that people will connect more closely with the story.)

Reflection

She's almost lost herself, tucked in between some very familiar men. It happens all the time! There she is . . . so ordinary, so common, an often-overlooked woman with a broom. The "housewife." Only this time, she's sandwiched in between two other people we know well. On one side, the shepherd, who searches up hill and down dale for one lost sheep. One out of ninety-nine, who are safe and sound. On the other side, the abundantly merciful . . . we might even say prodigal . . . father, unlike any patriarch of his day and age. He's keeping daily watch at his gate: waiting, longing, hoping against hope that his younger son will come to his senses and return home. And . . . hope against hope . . . the son returns! Later, when the elder son pouts and turns his self-righteous back on the party, this same father goes chasing after him, as well. These men are well-known images of God. But, this woman with the broom? What do we make of her?

Jesus makes quite a bit of her. An image of God, as well, though he's careful how he puts it. Jesus does *not* say to his dinner companions, most pointedly to the Pharisees and scribes, "Which one of you, having ten silver coins . . . ," as he did when he said, "Which one of you, having a hundred sheep . . ."[69] No, Jesus only means to get their attention. And that he does, when he compares them to a smelly, dirty, disparaged shepherd! (Shepherds, you see, are *not* included in polite company in his day.) But, compare them to a woman? Heaven forbid! That would be insulting beyond their endurance! Carefully, then, he continues, "Or what woman having ten silver coins . . ."[70] And yet, Jesus tells the exact same story . . . with the exact same message. The point? It's *both* the shepherd . . . *and* the woman . . . who are like God. The Divine Seeker. Or, should I say, the Divine Pushy One. And his dinner companions get the point. God can be found working through the most un-likely, the most ordinary, yes, possibly even through their dispar-aged "tax collectors and sinners." Though we never know if they, like the elder brother, return to Jesus' party.

What, then, is the point of all this? God, just like the woman, turns up the light on all the ones the world calls worthless. Yes, God takes the time. Makes the time to do precisely that. We see it all the time, if only we have eyes and heart to see. Not only that, our prodigal God expends the energy—oil for the lamp, what-ever it takes—to poke around all the darkest corners of our lives. That *we* might be found. And treasured. But there's even more. God, in the form of a woman, gleefully leads the celebration. And restores the lost one to a rejoicing community. When does this happen? Whenever passionate seekers diligently push and prod . . . to restore people to full human dignity. This is precisely what happens when mentors walk with children, introducing them to Dr. Seuss and to love. This is precisely what happens whenever people go into prison to help inmates rebuild their lives . . . when-ever people in recovery walk with the ones still stuck in addic-tion . . . whenever people advocate for those stuck at the border of hatred and exclusion . . . whenever people of differing views can listen to one another, really listen, before responding. This is precisely what happens whenever passionate seekers shed light on, and refuse to let go of, God's dreams for God's daughters.

69. Luke 15:4a.
70. Luke 15:8.

Whenever daughters are as fully welcomed as sons to the feast of life. Whenever God-gifted women, as well as men, whose calls are affirmed by their communities, are ordained to *lead* the celebrations at the Feast of Life. In short, this is precisely what happens when the Church lives out the gospel of Christ.

Today, then, we celebrate our God, Good Shepherd and Pushy Woman with a Broom, who never, ever gives up on any of us. We celebrate that we are all made in God's image, and that God keeps after us, so that we might fully become God's treasured daughters and sons.

Examination of Conscience

(*It is essential to read these questions slowly, so that people have time to reflect on their answers. It might also be very helpful to have some quiet flute music played in the background, to assist in the reflective nature of this examination.*)

Leader: We now pray that God's light will shine on our hearts . . . that our imaginations might be stirred . . . and that we might make faithful and honest responses to the following questions.

To what extent am I like the lost coin? Passive, lying in dark corners of resentment or desire to blame another whenever I get stuck. Lost, because I hide from making tough choices. *(Pause)*

To what extent do I give into the untruth that I am not worth much? To what extent do I indulge in self-pity, rather than taking action I know is necessary? *(Pause)*

To what extent do I take the time to give God thanks for continuing to search me out, as often as I need it? *(Pause)*

To what extent do I find myself grumbling and complaining? *(Pause)*

To what extent do I make harsh judgments on others, without knowing the truth? *(Pause)*

Where and how might I become more like the woman with the broom? Where and how might I grow in compassion and persistence? Where can I search out vulnerable people in need? How might I advocate for them? How might I join with others to confront the systems that keep people vulnerable and passive? *(Pause)*

What gifts do I bring to such a struggle? To what extent have I used my gifts well for this purpose? To what extent am I ready to lead a celebration of God's abundant goodness in some nook or cranny of creation? *(Pause)*

Where and how might I become more like Jesus? To what extent am I willing to confront self-righteousness in others? To what extent can I see God in the most ordinary— even unexpected—people and places? To what extent can I see the seeds of God in myself? To what extent am I ready to plant those seeds in my everyday world?

Rite of Reconciliation

Sign of Desire for Reconciliation

(The presider invites everyone to come forward and light their candle from larger candles held by the proclaimers of the word. You will be asked: "Do you desire to live in God's light?" You're encouraged to respond, "Yes, I do." During this time, the following hymn (or another healing one) may be sung in a reflective way by one or two people:)

Hymn: **"Hosea"**

> Text and tune by Gregory Norbet, ©1972, 1980
> The Benedictine Foundation of the State of Vermont, Inc.

Assignment of Satisfaction/Penance

(The presider makes some suggestions, which would include our initiative in restoring or healing a relationship and/or some kind of outreach or advocacy for an individual or group.)

Hymn: "Christ, Be Our Light"
(Led by song leaders, as people return to their seats.)

> Text and tune by Bernadette Farrell, © 1994
> Published by OCP Publications. All rights reserved.

General Confession: *(All are invited to kneel.)*

> I confess to almighty God,
>
> and to you, my brothers and sisters,
>
> that I have sinned through my own fault,

in my thoughts and in my words,

in what I have done,

and in what I have failed to do;

and I ask blessed Mary, ever virgin,

all the angels and saints,

and you, my brothers and sisters,

to pray for me to the Lord our God.

Leader: Our response [R] is *Hear us, Gracious God.*

Our God is persistent in seeking after us, that we might have life.

Grant us life in its fullness. [R]

Shine your light on our darkness. [R]

Restore us to your image, O God. [R]

Lead us to your celebration, with family, friends, and strangers. [R]

That we might shed your light on our world. [R]

The Lord's Prayer *(All stand, if able.)*

Exchanging the Sign of Christ's Peace

General Absolution:

Offered by a Priest:
(He extends hands in blessing over the people with these words:)

Our persistent, pushy, passionate, and compassionate God seeks us out,

that we might joyfully celebrate life.

May God always find us in all our lost places

and restore us to ourselves and one another.

All: Amen.

Priest: Our Brother Jesus came to heal and challenge.

Through the ministry of the church,

may God grant you pardon and peace.

All: Amen.

Priest: The Holy Spirit is in our midst,

calling us all out of darkness

into God's marvelous light,

that we might live as children of the light.

All: Amen.

Priest: And I absolve you from your sins,
          In the name of the Father, and of the Son, +
          And of the Holy Spirit.

All: Amen.

*(If this is a prayer service led by a lay person, the following prayer can
replace General Absolution and precede the sending forth hymn.)*

Lay Presider: Our persistent, pushy, passionate, and compassionate God
          seeks us out, to set us free from every sin.
          Go, therefore, in peace, committing to make amends
          and ever more become agents of healing.
          In Jesus' name, we pray.

All: Amen!

Sending Forth

Leader: Our Gracious God has freed us from our sins,
          and restored us in love to shed God's light in our world.
          Go in peace.

All: Thanks be to God.

Hymn: "We Are Marching in the Light of God"
          South African text and tune, ©1984, Utryck
          Walton Music Corporation, agent.

4

Holy Week and the Triduum
(Three High Holy Days)

Introduction to Holy Week and the Triduum

W e are about to enter into our high Holy Days, the Triduum: three days of Love-beyond-All-Telling-for-Us. Three days that reveal—through profound agony to the fullest ecstasy—the true, essential nature of God. The Paschal Mystery (dying and rising) of Jesus, the Christ, and of the body of Christ. But first, we need a doorway, a hinge, a way through that will give us pause, a way to profoundly reflect on this most sacred week of the year. We are given that doorway on Palm/Passion Sunday, the final Sunday of Lent. Come with me, won't you, as together we enter into these days of the dying and rising of Jesus, and into our own ultimate journey.

The Hinge from Lent into the Triduum:
The Passion of Palm Sunday

It's called the passion for a reason.
It's the encounter of red hot, blazing, searing, transforming love
of the Holy One's unfathomable yearning and longing for every
human heart . . . from the very beginning . . .
to this very moment . . . to the very end of time,
personally encountering
stone-frozen fear . . . jealous rage . . .
depths of human degradation . . .
the absolute horror that one human can inflict upon another.
Jesus, the Holy One of God, stood firm in its midst.

What's your experience of Palm/Passion Sunday? Until a few years ago, here's how it was for me. We walked in and were given palm branches. Everyone was invited to be part of a procession, complete with song. To enter Jerusalem, with Jesus, victorious. To feel and see the adoring crowds . . . jubilant crowds, waving palm branches. But . . . it often fell flat. Even before the adulation morphed into disaster. Even before we sat through that very long reading of the passion. Oh, the readers did their best. But most often the rest of us were *only* invited to chime in on "Crucify him! Crucify him!" Is there not a better way to prepare for the holiest week of the year?

Imagine *this* instead. People—all of us—are sitting in the pews, utterly rapt by the story we're encountering. Storytellers come forward, one at a time, telling their part, about fifteen verses each, seamlessly moving from one to the next. Totally immersed in this telling, we're *all* right there, glued to the spot! We *see* everything that is happening. *Hear* everything that is going on. The pain. The doubt. The wrestling. The denials. The horror. All of it! We are even given a chance to catch our breath, to catch up with our emotions by singing a simple refrain at three different points in the story.

How can this be? It was August 2004, and I was attending the annual Festival Gathering of the Network of Biblical Storytellers for the first time.[1] *There* I encountered Dennis Dewey, a leader of the network. I'll *never* forget his words! The process of storytelling is *not* about memorizing words. It's *not* a head trip. Rather, it's a head, heart, entire-being trip . . . absorbing the entire passage so that it literally *begs* to be told, as accurately as possible. Then, in another workshop, Jerre Roberts led us through a process of discovering *ourselves* within a Scripture passage. What's the setting of the story? Who are the characters? What are they feeling? What am I feeling? What images and actions move the story along? And, where does this story stick "like Velcro" to my own? (Anyone familiar with the Jesuit Nineteenth Annotation—the prayerful, imagining style of St. Ignatius of Loyola—will recognize the similarities.) They both ignited in me a spark . . . a raging flame . . . a passion for storytelling! I took it home with me! Thus began a much anticipated annual event in my parish, the telling of the passion by heart on Palm Sunday.

What does it take for this to happen? Making a commitment: fueled by love of Scripture, liturgy, people in the pews, the power of the Gospel, and the power of good storytelling. Gaining approval by the pastor and the liturgy committee. Dividing the passion into sections of about fifteen verses each, depending upon the movement in the story. Recruiting a "Passion Team" of

---

1. This ecumenical network office is located in Indianapolis, Indiana, 46208. The email address is nbs@nbsint.org. Ellen Handlin is the office manager; telephone is (800) 355–6627. The web site is https://www.nbsint.org.

nine to a dozen folks, willing to devote time and energy to this Big Event. Preparing for three or four months. (That first year we began in November, when Palm Sunday was the following March 20.) Immersing the team, from the beginning, into the Synoptic Gospel writer for the upcoming passion, since his particular "take" on Jesus will show up in the passion. Inviting everyone to choose their own selection. Engaging in faith sharing for the next couple of sessions, to begin building genuine community. "Stumbling through" the early attempts of each telling by heart. (Please note: this is *not* about simply memorizing words. Rather, it *is* about *accurately* internalizing the Scripture, in order to release its power in proclamation.) Allowing time for the story to "gel," with a seamless flow from one person to the next, from one microphone to the next. (We used just two microphones.) After this, rehearsing in church, enough times for each teller to feel prepared. *Finally*, being gifted with comments like these: "I felt like I was right there!" "It was one of my best experiences in all the years I've been at St. John's!"

One participant offered this: "It was a wonderful experience living and praying with a section of the Passion. By the end of the experience, I believe we all did in fact become 'Passionate People'! My personal experience was daunting because in the past I have totally blanked out information that I knew inside and out before, when nervous. My mind would truly go blank. As we practiced, this phenomenon happened a few times, though not as seriously as it had in the past. Yet, with the encouragement of the team, I persevered. My big question as Palm Sunday neared was: what will actually happen when I am up in front of the faith community? The result? I proclaimed and told the story the way I believed this section of the Passion should be told. Why? Because I needed to share the story with the people attentively sitting before me—waiting to discover again what happened as Jesus was laid to rest. The story came to life because of the people. I needed the people!"[2] Indeed, "the Word became flesh and lived among us" (John 1:14).

A Preaching Word for Palm Sunday,
upon Entering into Holy Week: Jesus Stayed

(Note: This word must be short, to the point,
given the length of the passion.)

Jesus stayed . . . and *that* has made all the difference. But I *must* be very clear. Jesus' staying had *everything* to do with his purpose,

---

2. These are the words of Liz Maurer Webster, one of the proclaimers of the passion.

his mission in life. It had absolutely *nothing* to do with staying in a situation of abuse and misery, which some have experienced in marriage or other relationships. In those situations, resistance is essential. Leaving is essential. But Jesus stayed out of a healthy and healing love for us all. And *that* has made all the difference.

After supper, as he led the disciples to the top of the Mount of Olives, he could gaze down upon the valley of Gethsemane . . . and then up to the magnificent temple, where he had taught so often. He might have turned in the opposite direction. Onto a familiar path, sloping ever so gently to Bethany and the home of dear friends: Mary, Martha, and Lazarus. He might have entertained the thought—ever so briefly—of betraying his truth and hiding there. But he didn't. He stayed.

He *had* to stay. He *couldn't* back off now from everything he believed in . . . everything he had taught . . . everything he had done. He *couldn't* back off now from all the ways he had proclaimed and lived the poured-out, unending love of God for *everyone*: *each* of us, *all* of us, no matter what.

He stayed . . . even as the disciples slept through his agony down in the garden of Gethsemane. He stayed . . . even as he *might* have agonizingly questioned, in the full fragility of his humanity: Had he done it right? Had he done all that he could? Had he expected too much? Where might he have done more? Done better? Even so, he stayed . . . through the kiss of betrayal. Through the denial of his dear friend Peter. He stayed . . . through the torture and taunting. He stayed . . . abandoned by the men, though never by the women. Because, out of integrity, out of intimate companionship with his Wholly Other, he could do no less.

Yes, Jesus stayed, that *we* might stay our course. Through the worst that life can hurl at us. Jesus stayed, so that *we* might know how very profoundly we are loved, no matter what. And *that* has made—and continues to make—all the difference.

The Triduum
(Holy Thursday Night through Easter Sunday):
An Introduction

What does it mean to be "holy"? Frederick Buechner (a Presbyterian minister who has a "way with words") offers us this: "Only God is holy, just as only people are human. God's holiness is his Godness. To speak of anything else as holy is to say that it has something of God's mark upon it. Times, places, things, and people can all be holy, and when they are, they are usually not hard to recognize."[3] He then goes on to describe a very ordinary workshop in these words: "I have no idea why this place is holy, but you can tell it is the moment you set foot in it if you have an eye for that kind of thing. For reasons known only to God, it is one of the places he uses for sending his love to the world through."[4] Doesn't he imply that we can *all* reveal God's holiness? God's "whatever-it-is that we just know is holy"? Perhaps vulnerability, joy, profound love—unconditional, unwavering love. *You* name it; you know you can.

Three days . . . three all-important days . . . days blending seamlessly into one another, days making present for us, yet one more time, the life, death, and resurrection of Jesus, the Christ. Days of tender parting, anguish, agony, and celebration of love-beyond-all-telling. Days that reach deep down into the font of our truest identity—participants in the Risen Body of Christ—only to erupt with lavish hope-beyond-all-telling. Dare we allow our puny, withered dreams to *explode* into so much more? Dare we allow our fears, weaknesses, and sorrows to literally burst open at the seams of our lives? Dare we reach out and grab hold of resurrected life, again . . . and again . . . and yet again? In effect, dare we risk being transformed by the power of resurrection into people of vision, courage, wisdom, and perseverance? Dare we claim the power of our baptism, the power of our fragrant anointing into Christ? Dare we, as disciples of Jesus, proclaim that we, *too*, are being sent "to bring good news to the poor . . . to proclaim release to the captives and recovery of sight to the blind, to let the oppressed go free, to proclaim the year of the Lord's favor"?[5] Given our own specific gifts, what might that look like?

Entering into the Triduum
At the Evening Mass of the Lord's Supper:
Holy Thursday Night

Lent is over. I am now always profoundly moved, often to tears, by the entrance into this annual celebration on Holy Thursday evening: "We should glory in the cross of our Lord Jesus Christ, for he is our salvation, our life

---

3. Buechner, *Wishful Thinking*, 39.

4. Buechner, *Wishful Thinking*, 39. Please note his use of male language only for God, common in those days (the 1970s).

5. Luke 4:18b–19, from the inaugural address of Jesus.

and our resurrection; through him we are saved and made free."[6] As the music begins, I am expectant. Awaiting the presentation, once more, of the recently blessed church oils, to be poured out on our ministries. Awaiting the intimately tender washing of the feet. Awaiting the procession with the Body and Blood of Christ around the church . . . with the dimming of lights and stripping of the altar that usher us into silence, reflection, and maybe visitation of other churches. Without fail, I experience a merging of past, present and future: fond childhood memories of visiting several churches . . . passionate love of the liturgy, become bone of my bone and flesh of my flesh . . . and rekindled desire to follow Jesus, wherever he will lead.

A Preaching Word for Holy Thursday Evening

"Gloria, you can ask me to do anything. But, don't *ever* ask me again to have my feet washed!" Such was the firm statement of a man I treasured. An artist. A man who continually created beautiful banners for the church. A man who simply insisted, "God gave me these gifts, and I'm just giving them back." All this he gave, gladly. But, having his feet washed again on Holy Thursday night? No thanks!

He's not alone. I remember, early on in parish ministry, the struggle to recruit people to be part of this tender, intimate tradition. What's the difficulty here? I wonder. Is it simply about inconvenience, as it was for my friend? Struggling to put a sock back on a foot that's still damp. Or, does it go deeper than that? Does it perhaps have to do with making visible a not-so-handsome part of our anatomy? The corns, calluses, and imperfections we'd all just as soon cover up? Does it even have to do with unveiling some other blemishes we usually try to hide? Like the taunting whispers we lug around from ancient wounds. Or the trepidations that keep us from naming and stepping out into our truth. To put it another way, does it perhaps have to do with becoming more vulnerable to one another, revealing ourselves just as we are, warts and all? Maybe.

And yet, isn't there something even *more* challenging about this business of foot washing?[7] Why was Peter so *scandalized* by

6. These are the words I recall from a sacramentary (or community prayer book), from the Introductory Rites to the Evening Mass of the Lord's Supper, taken from Gal 6:14.

7. I was influenced in this line of thinking by Schneiders, *Written That You May*

the actions of Jesus? How on earth could *Jesus*—his Teacher and Lord—wash *his* feet? Oh, Peter knew Jesus was serious about serving. But, did his gut intuit the unthinkable? That this service of Jesus had *nothing* to do with expectations placed upon "inferior" ones. This service had *nothing* to do with arguments over "who's the greatest." This service had *nothing* to do with keeping score, even with good intentions that could go awry, as in "after all I've done for you!" This service had *nothing* to do with human divisions and inequalities. No. On the contrary, foot washing had *everything* to do with the heart. With friendship. Mutual love for the other, for *every* other. No exceptions. Even for women. Even for slaves—*anyone* perceived as "less than." Had Jesus just turned his world upside down? Did Jesus *really* mean "love one another as I have loved you"?[8] Was Peter ready for this? Are we?

Yet Jesus is very clear. Such activity is the *centerpiece* of his actions at the Last Supper. The *centerpiece*, in fact, of his entire life's ministry. The centerpiece, then, of communion among friends around his table. "Do you know what I have done to you?"[9] That question of Jesus searches our hearts, as well. Are we *really* to serve every other? Without judgment? Without pretense? Without "lording it over" anyone? Not just the ones we like, but the ones we don't like. The cranky ones. The ones with whom we disagree. The ones we find hard to respect. Could it be that Jesus means to unveil our humanity, as well as our feet? Our limits. Our weaknesses. Our vulnerability. Ultimately, our need for the heart of God alone. Yes! And, yes again! Jesus is very clear about all this.

Thus it has been, for disciple after disciple, age after age. For some it has meant pouring oneself out tenderly. Like my Aunt Anna. The family saint. She was the one who lived with her husband and two young sons in an apartment over her aging and ailing parents, just to make sure their needs were met. She was the one who happily toiled, week in and week out at the parish pantry. She was the one who set Thanksgiving dinner before anyone in her family who needed a place at the table. Like a sister, who suffered from mental illness. Another sister, widowed at a

Believe, 149–79.

8. John 15:12; these words of Jesus follow his action of foot washing in John 13:1–15, a centerpiece of the Last Supper, only found in John's Gospel.

9. John 13:12b.

young age. A grandson, fresh out of college, steadfastly seeking a teaching position. Or anyone else.

For others it has meant pouring oneself out courageously, knowing full well what lies just around the corner. I'm mindful of Jean Donovan, one of four American church women killed in El Salvador on December 2, 1980. The women lived among people they cherished in the midst of a brutal civil war. They each agonized, just like Jesus in the garden. And they each chose to stay. As Jean put it, "The Peace Corps left today, and my heart sank low. The danger is extreme and they are right to leave. Now I must assess my own position, because I am not up for suicide. Several times I have decided to leave. I almost could except for the children, the poor bruised victims of adult lunacy. Who would care for them? Whose heart would be so staunch as to favor the reasonable thing in a sea of their tears and loneliness? Not mine, dear friend, not mine."[10]

As for my friend, the artist, while he remained uncomfortable with having his feet washed, he'd become generous in pouring out all the gifts that God had showered upon him. Indeed, this man of bushy eyebrows and welcoming smile had come to know Jesus well. The One who washes our feet . . . *all* feet, without exception. And sends us out to do the same. Even if it's inconvenient. Or really tough. Or asks something new—even shocking—of us. Even if it stretches us, mightily, into Jesus-love, the love that welcomes and serves everyone, without exception. "Do you know what I have done to you?" How does each of us—*today's* disciples of Jesus—respond to that all important question?

Through Good Friday and the Silence of Holy Saturday . . .

Question: why is this Friday called "Good"? The answers may be as varied as the people who offer them. What do *you* say?

The official church responds with the passion account from John's Gospel, different from the three Synoptics in so many ways. Jesus is majestic, even in and through the horror of it all. He knows what's coming. He's already experienced his "agony in the garden."[11] Not alone, with a few

10. Brett and Brett, *Murdered in Central America*, 252; this is part of a letter of Jean Donovan to a friend.

11. See John 12:27–36.

drowsy disciples, but with a crowd of people, who still don't "get it." His words set the stage for the passion itself:

> "Now my soul is troubled. And what should I say—'Father, save me from this hour'? No, it is for this reason that I have come to this hour. Father, glorify your name." Then a voice came from heaven, "I have glorified it, and I will glorify it again." The crowd standing there heard it and said that it was thunder. Others said, "An angel has spoken to him." Jesus answered, "This voice has come for your sake, not for mine. Now is the judgment of this world; now the ruler of this world will be driven out. And I, when I am lifted up from the earth, will draw all people to myself."[12]

In fact, Jesus even begins this drawing to himself during his passion. From the cross, he begins forming the infant Church, the community of his mother and his "beloved disciple."[13]

> When Jesus saw his mother and the disciple whom he loved standing beside her, he said to his mother, "Woman, here is your son." Then he said to the disciple, "Here is your mother." And from that hour the disciple took her into his own home.[14]

Exhaling his final breath a few moments later, Jesus utters, "It is finished."[15] His work in the flesh is done. His spirit is now poured out, along with his blood and water, as "one of the soldiers pierced his side with a spear."[16] *This* solemn moment is the birthing of the sacramental Church of baptism and Eucharist, according to John.

With the death of Jesus, we enter into the darkness of Good Friday night. Often within a solemn Tenebrae service. A service in which gifted, well-prepared lay people can preside and preach. There is Scripture . . . silence . . . music . . . increasing darkness as one candle after another is extinguished. Until finally, just one—only one—is relighted. And we, the Church, wait, in silence. One in our own personal grieving, yearning, and hoping against hope for more.

12. John 12:27–32.

13. Who is this? We cannot be sure. A disciple deeply loved by Jesus. Maybe all of us, who are "beloved" of Jesus.

14. John 19:26–27.

15. John 19:30.

16. John 19:34.

To the Easter Vigil, the High Point of the Church Year

I come eagerly, with anticipation. *We* come. We come as Church, the people of God, each with our own story. For some, there's an eagerness to celebrate. Is a loved one entering fully into the life of the Church? Or, is there a new love to share? For others, there's a heaviness of heart, for the love of their life is no more. We come, the multiplicity of God's people.

And we begin, as we must, in the hush of darkness, not unlike the moment before Creation's dawn itself. We huddle outside, ready to light the Easter fire once again. From this fire, we light the imposing candle of the Risen Christ—the One who walks with us, among us, and within us at every moment—holding it aloft for all to see. As we light our own candles from this ultimate Source of Light, the light slowly, surely spreads, lending an ever increasing soft glow to the pervading darkness, choreographed but never totally adhering to the script. Upon entering church, we join our voices to those of our first-century Christian ancestors, in singing the "Exsultet." Is it possible that we are now silently companioned by others who have gone before us? So many of us now gently stroked by Christ; so many of us now enfolded in Christ, so many of us now becoming clothed in light. Perhaps. Just perhaps.

On this night that is different from every other night, we continue to pull out all the stops in honor of our Risen Christ. Lift high the incense, like prayers rising before the Living God. Lift high our voices, in sung praise. Tell our stories from ages past, the same stories we've heard all along. Yes, *tell* them! Some by heart, surely! Some enhanced with liturgical dance, video, and/or music so as to lift them into whole new realms. The Hebrew Scripture passages take us from "in the beginning" . . . to the exodus event . . . to the dustbin of exile . . . to the prophetic, heretofore unimagined hopes that point beyond that profound struggle. The exodus event (the Third Reading) *must* be told, for it has formed the identity of the Israelites as God's people, God's special treasure. And finally, with lights up full and the thrill of Alleluias resounding, the Easter Gospel of the Risen Jesus is proclaimed! And yet, there's even more! Call forth the saints from ages past, so that our assembly is crowded with energy beyond our seeing. Reclaim our baptismal bond with God's Holy Spirit, by renewing our own promises. Immerse adults and children into the font of new life, abundantly anoint their heads with the gleaming oil of chrism (ah, the sweet smell of strength), and then offer them the eucharistic Feast for the very first time. Do this with all the lavishness we can muster; for God has never held back even an ounce of divine love! Amen! Alleluia!

But a Question Has Emerged in Me: Shall We Update the Readings for the Easter Vigil?

Yes, I *love* the liturgy of the Roman Catholic Church! I *love* the magnificence of the Easter Vigil, the ultimate celebration of our entire Church year! But, I have a question. And I'm not alone in asking: is it time to update the readings for this liturgy? On March 5, 2019, *U.S. Catholic* published an article by Jean P. Kelly on that very same question. In a follow-up survey, 84 percent of those who responded agreed that the readings should be updated, and 85 percent agreed that more women should be included. Here are my thoughts on all this.

Our lectionary, assembled out of the loving turbulence of the Second Vatican Council, is now over fifty years old. Think of the changes that have occurred in that time! Changes in society . . . changes in women's roles in society . . . changes in our church itself. Even in 1963, Pope John XXIII named the change in women's roles as one of three significant transformations in his day. "Women are gaining an increasing awareness of their natural dignity. Far from being content with a purely passive role or allowing themselves to be regarded as a kind of instrument, they are demanding both in domestic and in public life the rights and duties which belong to them as human persons."[17] In our day, some fifty-seven years later, we can also say this: women have been "demanding" recognition of their human dignity in the Church, as well.

So, then, I can't help but ask: where are women in the readings? Women of faith, women of life-giving courage, strength, healing, and hope? I know they were there, at the cross and the empty tomb. All the Gospels say so. I also know, for a fact, that one of them, Mary of Magdala, was first to experience the risen Christ, first to be sent by him as apostle to the apostles . . . and first to proclaim the Easter gospel. For John the Evangelist tells us so.

Why, then, do the women remain so silent in our lectionary . . . so hidden . . . beginning with the salvation history of our Hebrew ancestors in faith. There's no mention of the courageous Hebrew midwives Shiphrah and Puah, our first models of nonviolent resistance to oppression.[18] Or the women surrounding the birth of Moses, who conspired to save his very life, thus making possible his ministry of liberation.[19] Or Ruth, great-grandmother of King David, who modeled for us the *hesed*, the

---

17. John XXIII, "*Pacem in Terris*," 134.

18. See Exod 1:8–22.

19. See Exod 2:1–10.

extraordinarily ever-faithful-love of our God for us.[20] Remember her words to her grieving mother-in-law Naomi? "Do not press me to leave you or to turn back from following you! Where you go, I will go; where you lodge, I will lodge; your people shall be my people, and your God, my God."[21] The list goes on and on. Why, even on Easter Sunday, our Catholic lectionary stops short of the centerpiece of the Easter gospel, the sending of Mary of Magdala by the risen Jesus to proclaim the good news: "I have seen the Lord!"[22] Her cry is none other than Easter's earthquake, Easter's victorious shout! What's to be done? How can it become a drama in which we *all* play a part, women as well as men?

On this night of all nights, God's word must be a saving word. A life-giving word. A challenging, yet comforting word. Indeed, the exodus event—that ultimate formation event for our ancestors in faith—*must* be told and told well! Just recently I heard it powerfully proclaimed in word, punctuated in several places by an energetic sung refrain![23] But there's another account of this great event, as found in the Book of Wisdom, 10:15–21. Written during the first century BCE by Jewish people living in Alexandria and yet unknown to most people, this version tells the story through Wisdom's eyes and heart. Listen!

> A holy people and blameless race wisdom delivered from a nation of oppressors. She entered the soul of a servant of the Lord, and withstood dread kings with wonders and signs. She gave to holy people the rewards of their labors; she guided them along a marvelous way, and became a shelter to them by day and a starry flame through the night. She brought them over the Red Sea, and led them through deep waters; but she drowned their enemies, and cast them up from the depth of the sea.[24]

Would that selection perk up ears that have become dulled? Would it help create new hearts, open to the God beyond our imagining? Might it be offered as an alternative to the Exodus reading?

---

20. See the book of Ruth.

21. Ruth 1:16.

22. John 20:18.

23. It was the 2019 Easter Vigil on videotape from Old St. Patrick's Church in downtown Chicago.

24. Wis 10:15–19. This is part of the Apocrypha, the added Scriptures concluding the Old Testament. While it is among the Catholic deuterocanonical books (thus part of the Catholic Bible), our Protestant brothers and sisters do not accept these books, for they were originally written in Greek rather than Hebrew.

Finally, I *must* name my profound concern about the Second Reading, Gen 22:1–19. Yes, this reading weighs heavily on me. For it recounts Abraham's willingness to prove his love for God by *killing his son Isaac in sacrifice!* Yes, I know: human sacrifice was common enough in that day. But still! After all the years of journeying with this God, how on earth could Abraham have conceived of such a thing! Furthermore, where was *Sarah* in all this? We don't know. We only know this: five verses beyond this story, Sarah died. Why? From a broken heart? From the anguish of imagining Abraham actually killing their son of laughter? (Indeed, the name Isaac means laughter.) *Her* only child? (Recall that Abraham had another son, Ishmael, born of Hagar.) Yes, other people offered their children to other gods, but the God of Israel was different. *Theirs* was a God of life! Always! At all times!

But, doesn't this story smack of a punishing god, who only relents at the last moment? Doesn't this story raise for us all the ultimate questions of our very lives? Who is God? Who are we in relationship to God? Where was God in the midst of the most depraved human suffering? In the crucifixion of Jesus? During the holocaust? Where is God in our tough times?

People of faith and good will have wrestled mightily over the centuries with those questions. Yet we are human. Limited. Sinful. Surely, even at our best, we are lacking in the pure love we ascribe only to God. How, then, can one describe the depths of God's love? A love that shatters death itself with the force of resurrection! People of holiness and wisdom have continually tried. Like St. Anselm, eleventh-century theologian and Doctor of the Church, whose words prevailed throughout much of the second millennium. In short, he professed that Jesus died to save us/redeem us from our sins. In other words, God's merciful love in Jesus paid the price/the penalty of human sin. (But, do I hear whispers of "satisfying" a punishing God?)

There have been other strains in the tradition of God's love song that I find more satisfying. Enter St. Francis of Assisi (1181/82 to 1226) and his followers. For Franciscans, even if "Adam and Eve" had never sinned, Christ *had* to come. He *had* to reveal the depths of God's love, not just for humanity, but for all of creation itself. Thirteenth-century Franciscan theologian John Duns Scotus envisioned Christ as Our-Companion-on-the-Way-of-Pure-Love, both now and forevermore. In light of these and ongoing theological and scientific developments, theologian Elizabeth Johnson can *now* declare: "*God is unfathomable love; love seeks union with the beloved;* this union occurs in the incarnation when the divine Word enters into personal union with the created world in Jesus Christ."[25] In doing so, Christ "carries the

25. Johnson, *Ask the Beasts*, 226; my emphasis.

whole creation toward its destiny. His resurrection is the beginning of the resurrection of all flesh."[26] *All* flesh, *all* creation. We can hear God's joy in tinkling brooks, absorb God's cries of pain in every polluted stream. For God sobs with us, rejoices with us, walks with us and our created world through every ecstasy and every degradation. Now, in light of the pandemic, we know that a woman in Wuhan is my sister, a man in Uganda is my brother. We know that Christ is forever with us . . . *and* beyond us!

So, then, what do *we* say? What does resurrection mean to *us*? When have *we* experienced resurrection? Oh, not the ultimate event. For, as Elizabeth Johnson suggests, "a seed is unrecognizable in the mature plant into which it sprouts."[27] But surely the tiny glimmers of resurrection abound, nonetheless. Like a sunset or landscape that stuns the imagination. The comfort of a beloved pet. Or a gaze of pure delight. A tender touch, powerful enough to heal a wounded soul. Or, a direct challenge to become more the person that God has created: to speak our deepest truths in love and then act upon them. In short, to become healers of our world, like the "field hospital" that Pope Francis envisions for us. If so, then the God of our lives is *never* a god of punishment. No, the God of our lives is *always* a God of Pure Love, no matter what.

Well, then, what Scripture story might we tell instead? What story conveys the sacrificial love that shines through the letting go of something/someone precious for a greater good? Hannah's story, as told in the First Book of Samuel, comes to mind for me.[28] Now *here* was a woman whose womb cried out for a child. Year after long year, she remained barren. To make matters worse, even though her husband Elkanah repeatedly assured Hannah of his love, he'd been given several children by his other wife, Peninnah. *Finally*, on their yearly trek to worship at Shiloh, Hannah prayed fervently to God for a child, vowing to consecrate this child forever to God's service in response. Now, as the priest Eli was watching her pray, watching her silently moving her lips, he thought she was drunk! But Hannah insisted otherwise. No! She was only pouring out her soul to their God! Eli recognized that truth and blessed her. Indeed, Hannah would be lifted up as a model of prayer in the rabbinic tradition. In short, her prayer was answered, and she was true to her word. After she had weaned her son—Samuel, the great and last judge of Israel—she handed him over to Eli's keeping, as a gift "to the Lord." What follows, then, is her prayer of thanksgiving, the basis of Mary's Magnificat.

26. Johnson, *Ask the Beasts*, 227.

27. See Johnson, *Ask the Beasts*, 207, and 1 Cor 15:35–49.

28. See 1 Sam 1:21—2:10.

Now, *here* is a handing over that gives life, in so many ways. *Here* is a handing over that birthed a hymn of praise to God, generation after generation, from Hannah to her children and her children's children, all the way to Ann, to Mary, to Jesus, to all of us today. *Here* is a handing over that honors and claims our God as the ultimate Source of life, as Lover-of-Us-All.

Celebrating Easter Joy with Mary of Magdala

All four Gospels honor Mary of Magdala as the very first witness to the resurrection of Jesus. So it is that we re-member her in a unique way, claiming her as apostle to the apostles.

A POETIC RE-MEMBERING

Note: A painting by Gian Girolamo Savoldo (active 1506 to 1548) entitled "Mary Magdalene," circa 1530, inspired these words in me.

The painting hangs in the National Gallery in London.

The sky is smudged . . .

receding from pitch black midnight . . . to pre-dawn gray . . .

and a woman waits, soulfully lamenting, weeping inconsolably,

cloaked in silver, reflecting the Son,

for Love holds her fast to the spot.

But, what is *this*? The tomb is *empty*!

Where has her beloved *gone*? Who has taken him from the tomb?

Now frantic . . . until . . .

Someone breaks through her anguished reverie.

Someone addresses discipleship words to her,

"Woman, whom are you looking for?"[29]

His logical question no balm for her severed soul.

Is it the *gardener*? Has *he* removed the body of her beloved?

But then . . .

    She hears the sound of her name,

        tenderly wrapped in love, once again . . .

29. John 20:15.

by the very same voice

that had hurled seven demons from her soul;

by the very same voice

that had shepherded her into wholeness.

This time, joy propels her forward . . .

banishing her throbbing, jagged pain.

And yet . . . his hand cautions: *Wait!*

His voice commands attention: "Do not hold onto me,"[30]

For *nothing* is the same!

If Resurrection is anything, it is Love-Beyond-Imagining . . .

Love, bursting open *all* our puny human expectations . . .

Challenging us . . . transforming us . . . empowering us . . .

into our God-gifted identity . . . into *courage*!

Propelling us forward with the *ultimate* good news:

"I have seen the Lord!"[31]

Yes, *she* is the first disciple of the Risen One,

Her Beloved,

And *she*—apostle to the apostles—is sent by *him*,

in the half-light of the smudged sky

to proclaim the Easter gospel.

He has chosen well! There is no mistake!

For a great new day is dawning!

Go! Tell the others!

But, the sky is still smudged,

as has been her reputation, generation after generation,

age after age.

Yes, the writers of the Easter good news

have left her out once again!

Ignored her . . . considered her unimportant . . .

this Mary of Magdala, apostle to the apostles.

For her story—"I have seen the Lord!"—

the *full* proclamation of the Easter story

30. John 20:17.
31. John 20:18.

isn't even *told* on Easter Sunday!

So, if Jesus *is* truly risen to new life

and a grand new day *is* dawning,

how do *we* celebrate this resurrection challenge

beyond any fear of reprisal?

Who *else* must be raised up

from the ash heap of rejection

under the still-smudged skies of exclusion?

Who *else* must we stand with . . . toward full human dignity?

Whose dreams have withered . . . almost unto death?

Whose visions have been squashed . . . hammered . . . bludgeoned?

To whom must *we* urgently proclaim the word of Easter,

"I have seen the Lord!!"

An Imagined Conversation with Mary of Magdala: Apostle to the Apostles, First Proclaimer of Easter Good News

Gloria: I've had quite the conversation this week with *you*, Mary of Magdala! It's gone something like this: "OK, Mary, I've researched you. Even though there's precious little to be found about you, especially after the resurrection. I've lived with you. Prayed with you. Written about you. Become angry on your behalf when the hierarchy of the Catholic Church I love refuses to tell your story . . . Jesus' story . . . the resurrection story . . . on Easter Sunday, of all things! At least, in this country. But, fortunately for you and Christ and for us all, John has written that story in his Gospel: your encounter with the risen Jesus, as the very first apostle of Easter. The Canadians tell it on Easter. So, now, what word do you have for us today, here and now?"

And I heard *nothing*. Until I began to remember the weeping. The agony. The loss. I was a brand-new teacher back then. And I will never forget that November afternoon. We heard the news over the PA system. President Kennedy had just been shot. School was immediately dismissed. As we tried to make sense of the senseless, the enormity of the loss, many of us simply gathered.

First, just to walk around the outside of the White House (yes, I lived and taught in Arlington at the time). Then to stand for hours . . . patiently . . . with people from all over the country . . . just to walk past the tomb . . . his body in the Capitol rotunda. The point here is *not* to compare John Kennedy with Jesus. Absolutely not! Rather, the point is about coming to terms—*somehow*—with profound loss. Of remembering that such a "coming to terms" is a *process*. A *long* process. And the answers don't come easily.

Mary: Oh, yes, how true! For me, the answers erupted with tears. Heartbroken tears. Overflowing tears. Necessary tears. Until words broke in: "Woman, why are you weeping?"[32] I wanted to say, "What's the *matter* with you!? Don't you understand the agony of love, now gone? After all, dead is dead! And, dead is bad enough. But there's even more! Someone must have stolen his body! All I want to do, all I *need* to do, is this: stay close by. Have a little more time with his dead body. Remember how it was. Draw strength from how things were."

Gloria: Oh, Mary, yes. What grief for you! For *you* actually knew Jesus in the flesh so profoundly! I can't *begin* to imagine your loss! And yet, deep down, you and I both know. That's *not* enough for Jesus. That's *not* enough for God. That's *not* what Easter is all about!

Mary: Yes, you *do* understand! For suddenly, without warning, I heard the sound of my name, "Mary!"[33] *That's* when I *turned*. *That's* when I *saw*. *That's* when I *knew*. Jesus was no longer to be found in a dead body. No! Love itself had *burst* the bounds of all human understanding, even the bounds of death itself. Love itself had birthed a *new* body! But how? And why? And where would it take me?

All I knew was this: the Love that now propelled my feet, my heart, and my tongue back to the others was the very same Love that had once peered into the depths of my soul. And taken delight in what was there. It was the very same Love that had snatched my seven demons from death's grip. And restored my very soul to new life . . . courage . . . conviction . . . and truth. Did it matter that the men would *never* want to hear the good news

32. John 20:13, 15.
33. John 20:16.

from a woman? Oh, no! For I had *heard* and I had *seen*. And I would *never* stop proclaiming, "I have seen the Lord!"

Gloria: Thank God for you, Mary! Thank God for such radical love! The kind that *never* gives up on us, *any* of us. That *empowers* us, even *commands* us to imagine beyond the narrow confines of any grave, any loss, any injustice, any wrong that *must* be righted.

We never knew Jesus in the flesh. But as his followers, we, the body of Christ, experience our own challenges, day in and day out. Conflict on every side. Name calling. Bullying. The degradation of immigrants. Yes, we *know* their degradation, for we are their children. So we also know their persistence. Yes, we *insist* on building a Church of wide-open doors wherever those doors have been slammed shut. And in these days of COVID-19, we are learning much more. To stay sheltered for the good of all people. To gratefully honor first responders willing to risk their lives for the sake of those seriously ill. In all this, and more, we know we can *count* on Easter Love as a living, breathing, palpable Love meant precisely to walk with us, work with us, heal, forgive, and continually strengthen us. To advocate for anyone gasping for life. Mary, you have given your witness to the world. Now that witness is up to us!

AN IMAGINED INTERVIEW WITH
SR. (MARY) THEA BOWMAN, FSPA:
TWENTIETH-CENTURY PREACHER EXTRAORDINAIRE

Sr. Thea: "*Oh, no*, I don't preach! I witness. I testify. I share the good news of the Lord Jesus Christ. The priests can preach. You know women don't preach in the Catholic Church."[34]

Gloria: Well, Sr. Thea, I really hesitate to contradict you, but I'll say this: you surely could preach! So powerfully, so convincingly, and always in the Spirit of Jesus Christ! Profoundly inspiring so many, for that's what good preaching is all about. And, I know you haven't seen it, but women now can and do preach in the Catholic Church. At least here and there. Until the day comes when called, gifted, and prepared women can do this *everywhere*!

34. Nutt, *Thea Bowman: In My Own Words*, 96.

Tell us then, Sr. Thea: who are you? The granddaughter of a slave, I understand, born on December 29, 1937, to Dr. Theon and Mary Esther Bowman in Mississippi. Please tell us more.

Sr. Thea: Yes, I was so fortunate. I loved my parents! And they loved me! They were both well educated, my mother a teacher, the *daughter* of a teacher. My father a doctor, who gave up a promising career in New York to help heal the folks right here in Mississippi. They named me Bertha, after my aunt. An only child, "I'm what they used to call an 'old folks' child. When I was growing up, my parents—especially my mother—made a concerted effort to keep me in touch with the elders. She wanted me to hear from them. She wanted me to learn the old songs and the old stories. She wanted me to learn from their lips about slavery and what they had been through."[35] Why, did you know that slaves—in order to draw strength to deal with the horror and brutality of slavery—would sometimes, late at night, go deep into the woods to pray? Into "hush harbors," they called them, led by coded signs: like the hymn "Steal Away" or "Go Down, Moses."[36]

Gloria: You never forgot the values they taught you. Please tell us more.

Sr. Thea: My parents insisted on compassion and service to others. Faith in Jesus. Faith in our God, who "made a way where there is no way."[37] Hearing and learning Bible stories. (My father was Methodist, my mother Episcopalian.) At a very early age, I was learning what would eventually become my hallmark: "bringing faith alive through preaching, teaching, singing and praising."[38] The importance of education. *And* nonviolence. *Never* returning insult for insult. As my mother told me, "Returning insults makes you small like they are."[39] Oh, and one more thing, that didn't quite work (*said with a chuckle*): "My mother wanted me to be sweet and cultured; she wanted a child who was going to be

35. "Sr. Thea: Her Own Story," cited by Nutt, *Thea Bowman: In My Own Words*, 2.

36. Nutt, *Thea Bowman: Faithful and Free*, 10–11.

37. I would learn, later on, that this became a hallmark of so-called womanist theology.

38. Nutt, *Thea Bowman: Faithful and Free*, 17.

39. "Sr. Thea: Her Own Story," cited by Nutt, *Thea Bowman: In My Own Words*, viii.

a little lady, who would sit right and talk right, but instead she got a little 'rowdy'!"[40] I was *always* respectful, but I spoke my mind!

Gloria: You became Catholic at the age of nine. Before your parents! How did that happen?

Sr. Thea: As you may know, the public schools in Canton, where I lived, were like most public schools for "Negroes." Few resources. Poorly paid teachers, often poorly trained. But when I was only four, some Trinitarian brothers came to town, followed shortly by some sisters. Here's what they saw: we were lagging way behind in school! So they opened the Holy Child Jesus Mission, a school and church. Then they begged the Franciscan Sisters of Perpetual Adoration (FSPA), from La Crosse, Wisconsin, to come teach in Canton. The sisters came, and my parents made sure I went to school there. How we loved our teachers! For we knew they loved us first! Why did I become Catholic? Because of the teachers, of course. And also, the "personal witness of the priests, sisters, and laity at Holy Child Jesus" drew me in.[41] I was conditionally baptized on June 1, 1947, since the baptismal records of my Episcopal baptism were not to be found. Several years later, my parents would also become Catholic.

Gloria: Yes, I can see why you became Catholic. I'm also told that you played nun. Prayed the rosary. By age fourteen, you even convinced your dear friend Flonzie (then eleven) to become a Franciscan sister with you. But, your parents were opposed at first, weren't they? Of course, they were no match for your indomitable spirit! Can you tell us a little bit about heading off to Wisconsin, some nine hundred miles away? Where the food was different, for these sisters were originally from Germany. Where the climate was different: brrrr! Where almost *everything* was different.

Sr. Thea: Oh, yes. I was so determined to become a Franciscan sister that I went on a hunger strike! My parents, of course, loving me as they did, could not abide my going hungry. So, off I went, to the frigid North, at least during the winter. It was 1953, and it would take me eight years to complete the process. Of course, I stood out physically, for I was the "first black aspiring

---

40. "Sr. Thea: Her Own Story," cited by Nutt, *Thea Bowman: In My Own Words*, 2.
41. Nutt, *Thea Bowman: Faithful and Free*, 19.

sister to enter the convent in La Crosse."[42] But most of the sisters welcomed me in, despite some racist insults from others. Thus began my lessons in survival. I recognized my God-given gifts, to be used for the good of others. School came easily. I loved words. And appreciated the mission of my religious order: "We are a community of vowed Franciscan women centered in Eucharist, committed to be loving presence through prayer, witness and service."[43] Yes, I flourished as a postulant at Viterbo College, especially in the fine arts classes.

Gloria: We know you now as Sr. Thea Bowman, not Bertha Bowman. How did you receive this name you instantly loved so much?

Sr. Thea: The date was August 12, 1956. A date emblazoned on my heart! I had now officially entered the novitiate; this meant that we were given a saint's name, usually preceded by the name Mary. How thrilled I was to become known as Sr. Mary Thea Bowman! For it was a name meaning "of God," as well as being the feminine of my father's name, Theon.

Gloria: So it was that upon completion of your formation, you were sent back home, in 1961, to teach school in Canton, Mississippi. It must have been a thrill and also an enormous challenge, entering into the decade of the civil rights movement.

Sr. Thea: I was very aware of the turbulence. "When I was riding with the white nuns, I would duck down in the car when we passed white people in the streets or on the roads—and especially when we passed the white police."[44] But I was always intent on doing my own little bit, at first by simply teaching high school students. How to excite them to learn? I formed a choir, and after a few years this choir of fifty was ready to record *The Voice of Negro America*. They felt what I knew to be true: I loved teaching! I loved the kids! I knew how to encourage and inspire them. Most of all, I knew this: "It is so important that they learn to value themselves before the world has had a chance to beat

42. Nutt, *Thea Bowman: Faithful and Free*, 31.

43. Nutt, *Thea Bowman: Faithful and Free*, 36.

44. Margaret Walker and Thea Bowman, "God Touched My Life: The Inspiring Autobiography of the Nun Who Brought Song, Celebration, and Soul to the World," unpublished manuscript, Thea Bowman Collection, FSPA Archives; cited in C. Smith and Feister, *Thea's Song*, 90; also cited by Nutt, *Thea Bowman: Faithful and Free*, 44.

them down."[45] But there was always more to learn. In July of 1965 I earned my BA in English from Viterbo College: another step along the way.

Gloria: You loved to learn! You continued to earn degrees in English at Catholic University of America in Washington, DC, from 1966 to 1972, becoming one more "doctor" in the Bowman family, this time in English. Teaching and learning: for you they went together. As early as 1968, already recognized as a powerful speaker, you were invited to speak often, this time at Howard University.

Sr. Thea: Yes, at times like this, my heart's desire ignited the words: "Our young people have risked their lives to attend meetings, to march, to boycott, to demonstrate, to sit in. These things are useful and good. But I'm asking our young people for something better and something bigger. How many of you the educated, the elite, are willing to prepare yourselves to lead? To write for your people? To speak for your people? To represent us into the courtroom? To see that justice is done? . . . Will you lead us to the promised land?"[46]

Gloria: You continued to grow in helping your people know and believe, little bit by little bit, that "Black is Beautiful!" Please say more about this.

Sr. Thea: I came along at a good time. The National Black Sisters' Conference met for the first time in August 1968, and I was there. Being among such committed, like-minded women only nurtured my resolve "to be a catalyst for the voiceless, neglected, and unheard."[47] Through all my God-given gifts of teaching, preaching, singing, and more. After I returned home to Canton in 1978, my diocesan bishop, Joseph Brunini, often called on me. Deeply committed to ecumenical and interfaith relations in the midst of racial tensions and poverty, he formed an alliance with his successor, Bishop William Houck, to address the issues of Black Catholics. Both sought me out to advise—and then lead—the new Diocesan Office for Intercultural Awareness. I

---

45. Interview of Thea Bowman by Joseph Smith, *Smith and Company*, WPTV Milwaukee.Public Broadcasting Service; cited by Nutt, *Thea Bowman: Faithful and Free*, 49.

46. C. Smith and Feister, *Thea's Song: The Life of Thea Bowman*, 108–9; cited by Nutt, *Thea Bowman: Faithful and Free*, 59.

47. Nutt, *Thea Bowman: Faithful and Free*, 58.

worked to defuse tensions, to make spectators into participants, to put people at ease with my folksy nature, but to always tell my "true truth."[48]

Gloria: I was taken with your ability to become bilingual, as you put it. Please explain.

Sr. Thea: "I learned survival. I'm from Mississippi, and people who did not learn to contain their anger and frustration did not live long. You learn very early on how to wear the mask so that if I had to work with you and I felt—not that I knew—that you were racist in your heart, I learned to guard my manner, to guard my speech, even to guard my thoughts, my feelings, passions, and emotion. I did that not because I hated you, but because I had to survive . . . I walk in a number of different communities . . . When I come into the world of academe, or when I come into the world of business, or when I come into the world of politics or statesmanship, or into the world of international conversation, I have to be bilingual, bicultural. I have to be able to talk your talk and talk it better than you can, if I am going to be accepted and respected by many people in your society."[49]

Gloria: You also grew in being your true self: joyful, bold, empathetic and compassionate, telling your "true truth," simply living "Black is Beautiful." Your second home—where you taught from 1982 until 1988—became the Institute for Black Catholic Studies at Xavier University of Louisiana, the only historically black and Catholic university in the country.

But then, in 1984, you had a tough year. You were diagnosed with breast cancer in the spring of that year. Furthermore, your mother's health had been declining for several years. Until finally, death claimed her in November. Simply grief-stricken, your father suffered a stroke and died the following month. But you knew, as you often said, that they were in a better place.

Sr. Thea: Yes, "through it all, rightly, or wrongly, God knows, I've tried to walk and work on as if my world was steady."[50]

48. Nutt, *Thea Bowman: Faithful and Free*, 70. She would use that phrase, her "true truth," often.

49. Interview of Thea Bowman by Joseph Smith, *Smith and Company*, WPTV Milwaukee Public Broadcasting Service; cited by Nutt, *Thea Bowman: Faithful and Free*, 70–71.

50. Thea Bowman Collection, FSPA Archives; cited in C. Smith and Feister, *Thea's*

Gloria: Walk on, you did! You gave a talk at the May 21–24, 1987, National Black Catholic Conference that seemed to sum up everything you had become.

Sr. Thea: I remember it well. "When we know who we are and claim the history, we claim the struggle, the pain, the challenge, the purpose, the journey, and the dream. We are who we are and whose we are because of all our journeys, and the children that belong to our communities are enriched because of a pluralism that reflects life in a world that is pluralistic. Do we know all we can know, of ourselves, of our history, of our arts, and of our experience, of our goals and of our values, the full range of what has made us a people? When we know and understand, then we can do what we need to do to help ourselves."[51]

Gloria: You always proclaimed yourself to be a teacher, above all else. You simply loved teaching English and preaching. But I chuckled and felt like shouting "Amen, Sister!" when I saw the comment you often made to students in your preaching course.

Sr. Thea: I'm guessing it's this: "How am I supposed to believe what you are saying if you don't believe it yourself? Preach with confidence and conviction, or sit down!" (Yes, I can see by your smile, that's the one!)

Gloria: Sr. Thea, I have been profoundly moved by your talk to the U.S. Catholic bishops on June 17, 1989. By then, you were frail, in a wheelchair. In severe pain, for your cancer had spread to your bones. And yet your indomitable spirit resounded, yet one more time, about the "true truth" of what it means to be black and Catholic. Not only that, you brought the bishops together in a whole new way. Remember?

Sr. Thea: I do, indeed! "Now bishops, I'm going to ask you-all to do something. Cross your right hand over your left hand. You've got to move together to do that. All right now, walk with me. See, in the old days, you had to tighten up so that when the bullets would come, so that when the tear gas would come, so that when the dogs would come, so that when the horses would come, so that when the tanks would come brothers and sisters would not

Song, 185–87; also cited by Nutt, *Thea Bowman: Faithful and Free*, 91.

51. Thea Bowman, "Black History and Culture," *U.S. Catholic Historian*, 309; cited by Nutt, *Thea Bowman: Faithful and Free*, 104.

be separated from one another. And you remember what they did with the clergy and the bishops in those old days, where they'd put them? Right up front, to lead the people in solidarity with our brothers and sisters in the church who suffer in South Africa, who suffer in Poland, who suffer in Ireland, who suffer in Nicaragua, in Guatemala, in Northern Ireland, all over the world."[52]

Gloria: You concluded with a heartfelt, heartrending rendition of "We Shall Overcome." And I've been told that everyone tearfully joined in, before giving you sustained applause.

How fitting, then, during this Holy Week, to conclude this interview with your very own words. These were your last printed words, dictated from your deathbed.

Sr. Thea: "Let us resolve to make this week holy by sharing holy peace and joy with the needy, the alienated, the lonely, the sick and afflicted, the untouchable. Let us unite our sufferings, inconveniences and annoyances with the suffering of Jesus. Let us stretch ourselves, going beyond our comfort zones to unite ourselves with Christ's redemptive work when we reconcile, when we make peace, when we share the good news that God is in our lives, when we reflect to our brothers and sisters God's healing, God's forgiveness, God's unconditional love.

"Let us be practical, reaching out across the boundaries of race and class and status to help somebody, to encourage and affirm somebody, offering to the young an incentive to learn and grow, offering to the downtrodden resources to help themselves. ... During this Holy Week when Jesus gave his life for love, let us truly love one another."[53]

Sr. Thea Bowman died to this life and entered eternal life on March 30, 1990, at 5:20 a.m.

52. Bowman, "To Be Black and Catholic"; cited by Nutt, *Thea Bowman: Faithful and Free*, 111–12.

53. Thea Bowman, "How to Celebrate Holy Week," printed after her death in *Mississippi Today*, April 6, 1990; cited by Nutt, *Thea Bowman: Faithful and Free*, 116–17.

5

Eastertime: Easter Sunday through Pentecost

Easter Is More than a Day: Rather, Easter Is an Entire Season

Easter life erupts from deep within,
Forcefully ejecting anything in its path,
Transforming even gigantic rock
Into pebble-sized matter.
So it has *been*, from the beginning.
So it is *now*, and forevermore!
    With Easter life,
There is no repression . . .
No stifling control . . .
No fear-based, shame-based pressure . . .
No domination of any kind.
For the Source of Easter life is pure Love!
    I know,
For resurrection dawned
Through God-like unconditional love,
Transforming my silent, stilted soul
Into Voice! Identity, of God's making . . .
Accompanied by my own long-laboring efforts.
    So it is
That I spend my precious days
In grateful celebration of such transformation . . .

And in purposeful, intentional challenge
(On my better days)
To any system . . . especially ecclesial . . .
That would dominate, repress, and control.
   For Easter life dawns from deep within,
From tenderly transformed hearts . . .
And souls plumped by God with courage.
It is total gift, ours for the taking . . .
Ours for the co-creating
Of God's treasured world.

In my part of the world, the Easter season coincides with springtime. However, it can snow one day, as it has been known to do during the Easter Vigil, and embrace us with enough warmth the next to penetrate and heal the most broken heart. How serendipitous that nature should herald the Paschal Mystery we celebrate at this time of the year!

I never cease to be amazed at little shoots of green pushing through the hard ground, soon to become fragrant lily of the valley. And seemingly dead-as-a-doornail trees, looking like forlorn stick figures, slowly blossom out into lacey, reddish pink, graceful redbud trees. It always gives me hope that *anything* in life can be healed, that the dying and rising of Jesus Christ is for each of us, as well.

So it is that the Church celebrates this emergent, ever-pulsating life for seven full Sundays of Easter, concluding with the Holy Spirit's breakthrough on Pentecost (fifty days after Easter). For Christ's Spirit overflows all bounds, like a deluge of Love, Healing, Truth, Courage, Mission, and Life-beyond-All-Telling. In all three cycles, our First Reading recounts stories of the early Church, as found in the Acts of the Apostles. And our Gospel stories are most often taken from John, the last of the canonical Gospels, offering us a variety of that community's resurrection accounts. The only exception comes on the Third Sunday of Easter in Cycles A and B, with Luke's account of the two disciples on the road to Emmaus and their return to Jerusalem.

What, Then, Is Resurrection?

Nobody saw Jesus rise from the dead. The women were first to see the evidence: an empty tomb and resurrection appearances. But, how to describe what was seen? In this, they and we are tongue-tied. Word-deprived.

Grasping at straws to express the "disconnect" between human expectations and an unfathomable reality.

But try we must. For in ways beyond our understanding, we are seeded with divinity. So we probe. We question. *Was it something that changed Jesus? Clearly, yes! And also, wasn't it something that transformed his disciples? Once again, clearly, yes.* But, how can this profound Mystery be put into words? *Here* is how Edward Schillebeeckx, twentieth-century theologian of giant proportions, says it.[1] Resurrection is a *process*, he maintains, a three-part process, most fully expressed by John the Evangelist. The process begins with Jesus' "descent" from God's fullness into flesh . . . continues with his saving mission of creating siblings to go and do as he did . . . and climaxes in his earthly death/"glorification" on the cross. At this very moment, when his life ends—given for God—the life of the Church is about to begin.

How can this be? Listen to John the Evangelist. "Standing near the foot of the cross of Jesus were his mother, and his mother's sister, Mary the wife of Clopas, and Mary Magdalene. When Jesus saw his mother and the disciple whom he loved standing beside her, he said to his mother, 'Woman, here is your son.' Then he said to the disciple, 'Here is your mother.' And from that hour the disciple took her into his own home."[2] In other words, the "glorifying" ministry of Jesus in the flesh—that is, giving glory and praise to God— has been passed into the "glorifying" ministry of the Church.

However, we are not there yet. For the process continues, says Schillebeeckx, when Jesus "ascends to the Father," into full "glorification" in the Father—into their full union in love. It is from *this* place that Jesus can send his empowering "Easter gift" of the Spirit onto the believing Church. This Spirit, serving as both helper and advocate, keeps the Church on track, in the truth. Not only back then, but on and on and on, right into this present moment, and beyond.

So it is that the first disciples, along with today's disciples, are siblings of Jesus. That's *us*, folks. Daughters and sons of the same Father. Capable of living out what Jesus had promised in his Last Supper: "Very truly, I tell you, the one who believes in me will also do the works that I do and, in fact, will do greater works that these, because I am going to the Father. I will do whatever you ask in my name, so that the Father may be glorified in the Son."[3] "I will not leave you orphaned; I am coming to you. . . . On that day

---

1. See Schillebeeckx, *Christ*, esp. 416–27, which I have summarized; this book is translated from the Dutch into English by John Bowden.

2. John 19:25b–27.

3. John 14:12–13.

you will know that I am in the Father, and you in me, and I in you."[4] "The Advocate, the Holy Spirit, whom the Father will send in my name, will teach you everything, and remind you of all that I have said to you."[5]

In short, resurrection is what happened to Jesus, though that still remains beyond our comprehension. As we all know, Jesus appeared to the first disciples, beginning with the women. For many, he looked different than before. Recall that Mary of Magdala thought he was the gardener. And yet, the evidence of continuity between the Jesus of history and the Christ of faith has always been there. Whether it was the sound of that same dear familiar voice calling Mary by name[6] . . . or the sight of the Wounded Healer, forever branded with the scars of love[7] . . . the message is the same. The moaning, keening lament, "He's dead!" is transformed into joyful explosion, "No, he's alive!" Mary's great cry of Easter—"I have seen the Lord!"[8]—says it all. And he returns, again and again and again, never giving up on any of us.

At the same time, resurrection is also what happened to his disciples, from way back then up 'til now. Paralyzing fear—whether of disciples back then huddled behind locked doors, or disciples today shrinking from speaking aloud what we *know* to be true, anxiously stressing over illness, the coronavirus pandemic, our own diminishment due to aging, and so much more—*can* become Spirit-driven voice. Near despair of the two disciples on the road to Emmaus—"we had hoped"[9]—*can* become new sight and restoration to community.

We know their story well, for they are us.[10] Very possibly a husband and wife, they were totally downcast, unbearably distressed at Jesus' death on the cross. They gave up. Headed back home. That is, until a "stranger" joined them, though their "eyes were kept from recognizing him."[11] And yet, there was *something* about him. After a very long day's trudge on the road, they simply couldn't abandon him. Wouldn't he come in? Have supper? Stay with them? Suddenly, in the breaking of the bread, they saw! Jesus was right *there*! And then gone, in a flash! But they vividly remembered: "Were not our hearts burning within us while he was talking to us

4. John 14:18, 20.

5. John 14:26.

6. John 20:16.

7. John 20:19–27.

8. John 20:18.

9. Luke 24:21.

10. Luke 24:13–35; this is always the Gospel given for Easter Sunday afternoon, though I doubt that *anyone* hears it then! It's also the Gospel for the Third Sunday of Easter, Cycle A, and is referenced in Cycle B's Gospel for that same Sunday.

11. Luke 24:16.

on the road, while he was opening the scriptures to us?"[12] Didn't they, in effect, experience the essence of Eucharist? The *Word of God: in preaching* that can stir the soul, bend the heart, and alter one's path in life. Followed by *Jesus, the Christ, alive in the Breaking of the Bread.* In short, yes. Oh, it was just a glimpse. But they *knew*—without a doubt—that he was there. With them. Don't we simply yearn for that now?

I know for a fact that inspiring preaching can and does happen! I remember attending my first preaching workshop, back in 1983. The preacher, Dominican Sr. Joan Delaplane,[13] told the story of the man healed by Jesus at the pool of Bethsaida. She "became" the man, who said something like this. "Do you want to be healed? Oh, you might think that's an easy one to answer. But I wasn't so sure. After all, my life now would be totally different! I'd have to get up and work!" As she continued, I only knew *this*: she had lit a fire in my belly! I simply *had* to learn how to do this!

Back to the risen Jesus. Did he really *look* different? Yes, it seems so. And also . . . did *they*, those first disciples, begin to *see* differently? With Gospel eyes? With intense penetration, beyond the confines of culture and human expectations? Hasn't that been a very long, weary, ongoing struggle for *every* generation? Down to this very day. Even for Paul, that passionate evangelist for Christ. Clearly, he had come to embrace women as coworkers (like Prisca) and apostles (like Junia, "prominent among the apostles"); he also named Phoebe a deacon.[14] And yet, he left Mary of Magdala off his list of the first witnesses to the resurrection.[15] Is this because he received it this way from the Jerusalem community, where patriarchy (male dominance) was an accepted way of life? And yet, didn't his experience of working with women teach him about women's full discipleship, alongside men? It seems so. And yet, we, the Church, are still working on this!

God's First Words of Easter:
"Do Not Be Afraid"

Fear stalks the earth, seeking its prey. Always has, always will. Especially at times of total disconnect . . . of events beyond imagining. Slinking up to the

---

12. Luke 24:32.

13. Sr. Joan is professor emerita of homiletics at Aquinas Institute of Theology in St. Louis; she taught there for twenty-five years and in 2001 received the school's Treat Preaching Award for building up the Catholic community.

14. Rom 16:1–7, written about the year 58.

15. 1 Cor 15:3–9, written in the early 50s.

discomforted, it purrs, "Oh, best to be quiet. Don't rock the boat. You might get into trouble." Sound familiar?

> Fear: Midnight stalker.
> Disturber of dreams.
> Agitator of peace.
> Root of all war: blaming ... shaming ... bullying ...
> bitterness and anger.
> Separating and dividing one from another, honestly revealing
> Our very own flaws, warts, weaknesses, and backsliding.
> But God persistently, insistently proclaims
> > "No! Do not be afraid!"
> To person after person, generation after generation,
> Over and over and over again.
> Do not be afraid to gaze into your heart,
> To claim and then reveal your own bruised goodness.
> Do not be afraid to see yourself in the other, *any* other,
> > on every margin.
> Do not be afraid to see the seed of goodness
> > *even* in that pompous, self-important man
> Who makes every herculean effort
> > to shield his own torn vulnerability from the entire world.
> Do not be afraid to *listen* to the other ...
> > enter into relationship with the other ... *every* other.
> Do not be afraid to listen to the whispers of God deep within.
> Do not be afraid, *do not be afraid!*

It's so easy to play it safe, isn't it? To go along with the crowd. To remain silent, even though one's insides are fairly *bursting* to speak the truth that's buried there. It's so easy to pretend one hasn't seen. To pretend one hasn't heard. To try to please others. To try to fit into a system that simply won't budge. Just for security. Or status. Or comfort. Or complacency. It's so easy to give into fear of any kind. Or so it seems. At first.

Yet, the truth is, it's *not* so easy. It's *not* the gospel. It's *not* the way of Jesus. It's *not* what he has in mind for any of us who follow him. The truth is: it diminishes everyone. Makes puny the human heart, mind and spirit. Leads to death rather than life. The truth is: it even—and especially—diminishes the power of God!

Perhaps *that* is why the first words proclaimed at Easter to "Mary Magdalene and the other Mary" were these: "Do not be afraid."[16] Words spoken, over and over, time and time again, by God, or God's messengers, to people chosen to do God's work. Words spoken to Abraham, by then withered in age, with not a child in sight, despite the promises of God. "Do not be afraid, Abram. . . . Look toward heaven and count the stars, if you are able to count them. . . . So shall your descendants be."[17] Words spoken to the broken, enslaved people of Israel through Moses: "Do not be afraid, stand firm, and see the deliverance that the Lord will accomplish for you today."[18] Words tenderly spoken through the prophet Isaiah to a disconsolate people "stuck" in exile in Babylon, "Do not fear, for I have redeemed you; I have called you by name, you are mine."[19] Words spoken to a "perplexed" Mary, at her annunciation, by Gabriel. "Do not be afraid, Mary, for you have found favor with God."[20] Words spoken by Jesus to his first disciples, during his ministry: "Do not be afraid, little flock, for it is your Father's good pleasure to give you the kingdom."[21] Words we *all* need to hear, at one time or another, if we're honest.

There are women, age after age, as numerous as the stars in heaven, who have stood firm, despite great fear. Who have proclaimed their own truth: that the earth cries out for healing . . . that women are every bit as gifted and capable as men . . . that every single person of every single color and every single religion on the face of this globe is loved by God and worthy of dignity and respect. We know these women. Some of them personally. And/or by reputation.

Who, then, to explore? In days gone by, in the beginning days of the Church, surely there are Prisca, Junia, and Phoebe, friends and coworkers of Paul, always subject to persecution. Alongside Lydia, leader of Paul's community of joy in Philippi. Who comes to mind for you today? Consider women religious, represented by the Leadership Conference of Women Religious, under the duress of a Vatican investigation. In particular, I focus on one of their prophets, Sandra M. Schneiders, IHM. Finally, there's a great woman of courage from my neck of the woods, one who has been an enormous inspiration to me and so many others: Ann Kurz.

16. Matt 28:1, 5.
17. Gen 15:1, 5.
18. Exod 14:13.
19. Isa 43:1c, d.
20. Luke 1:30.
21. Luke 12:32.

Women Leaders of the Early Church
Respond to God's Voice

Is it even *possible* to imagine the beginning? Jesus: crucified . . . done for! The end of so many hopes, dreams, and how it might have been. "We had hoped."[22] But no! He's alive! In a whole new way! Infusing his first follow-ers . . . and later followers . . . one at a time . . . with courage and life they had never before known! Saul, the persecutor, was transformed into Paul, Christ's missionary, who traveled over ten thousand miles around the Medi-terranean for the sake of the gospel. Communities took root; many of them tiny households of no more than fifty people each. Always, always, under threat of persecution. Imprisonment. Even loss of life itself. Who were some of these brave people? How might they tell their stories?

In the spring of 1995, during a course on "Women in the Pauline Lit-erature," I encountered Prisca, Junia, and Phoebe, friends of Paul, mission-aries deeply rooted in their faith. Because I loved parish ministry myself, I could almost see their faces, hear their voices, and know the depths of their passion. As part of a paper for this course, I imagined a conversa-tion between Prisca and Phoebe, with mention of Junia, and then spent a couple of years—with two colleagues—bringing their stories to life in over thirty parishes in our diocese. (I was always Prisca, who occupies a special place in my heart.) Responses often ranged from "I never knew any of this!" to "Wow, think about the great women leaders at the very dawn of Christianity!" or "Whatever happened to women down through the centuries?" *This* we know. These women were much admired and re-spected by Paul, as he noted in his Letter to the Romans (16:1–7). So, then, imagine being in their presence. Listening to their stories. Taking them in. Pondering their contributions to women's ministry today. Then consider: what hope do these women offer us today?

An Imagined Conversation between Prisca and Phoebe

The year is 58. The place: ancient Rome, in the house church of Prisca and Aquila.

Welcome by Prisca: Welcome, everyone, to the home I share with my husband, Aquila, where forty or fifty of us gather early every Sunday morning, the First Day of the Week. Resurrection Day. We come together to pray the psalms—we're Jewish, you know—tell

22. See Luke 24:21, words of one of the two disciples on the road to Emmaus.

the stories of Jesus, pray for one another and those who are ill, and break the Bread and share the Cup of Jesus. Without fail, every time we do this, we *know* that Christ is present . . . with us . . . alive in our midst. We do this very early in the morning, since Sunday is a workday here in the Roman Empire. We do this to gather strength for the week ahead, knowing full well that we are constantly under threat of persecution. Aquila and I are successful tent makers, as well as preachers and teachers of the Way. While each weekly gathering is nourishing and life-giving, *this* one is more exciting than usual because Phoebe, one of our dear friends in ministry, has just arrived with a letter from Paul.

So, come on in. Make yourselves at home. Greet one another, especially the folks you may not already know. And, listen in on our conversation. After listening to us, you might want to ask us some questions or share some observations. Shall we begin?

Prisca: Phoebe, how wonderful to see you again! How good to have an opportunity to catch up! There are some newcomers with us today, too, that I want you to meet. I see that you have a letter from Paul, our dear friend. Would you read a little of it to us?

Phoebe: Of course! (*She reads Romans 16:1–7.*)

> I commend to you our sister Phoebe, a deacon of the church at Cenchreae, so that you may welcome her in the Lord as is fitting for the saints, and help her in whatever she may require from you, for she has been a benefactor of many and of myself as well.
> Greet Prisca and Aquila, who work with me in Christ Jesus, and who risked their necks for my life, to whom not only I give thanks, but also all the churches of the Gentiles. Greet also the church in their house. Greet my beloved Epaenetus, who was the first convert in Asia for Christ. Greet Mary, who has worked very hard among you. Greet Andronicus and Junia, my relatives who were in prison with me; they are prominent among the apostles, and they were in Christ before I was.

Prisca: Oh, thank you, Phoebe! It's always so good to hear from Paul, as well! Remember when you and I first met, right after Aquila and I left Corinth with Paul, on our way to Ephesus? Paul was recommitting himself to our Lord in a special way and needed to stop in Cenchreae, the community you serve. I knew as soon as I met you that you are a soul mate! On fire with Christ! Compelled to preach! It's made all the difference in life, hasn't it? Even when times are tough, there's *joy*! That's so hard to *explain*. But you know what I mean, don't you?

Phoebe: Oh, yes! And, it's so good to see you again, too! I was *thrilled* when Paul asked me to deliver this letter to you and the Church in your house. How does it feel to be back in Rome?

Prisca: It *is* home, Phoebe! And it's so good to be back here! Though things have changed quite a bit since we left nine years ago. It's so busy now! And noisy! But, this is where we first met Christ. What tender, fond memories Aquila and I have of those early days! The preaching of others, turning our hearts to Jesus! Then, the early prayer gatherings in *our* house! It was almost like a honeymoon time. Although I must admit, there was turmoil back then, too. There were Jews like us who turned to Jesus, who *knew* without a doubt that we had found in him the long-awaited Messiah. Alongside those who simply *couldn't* believe. Confusion reigned in the synagogues. Even disorder. Until Emperor Claudius finally sent *all* of us packing, turning our lives upside down! Ah, but so much good has come out of it. At first Aquila and I agonized: Where would we go? What would we do? Until suddenly, we knew! We were tentmakers, and Corinth was beckoning to us. Every May and June, right outside Corinth, there are the Isthmian Games at the sanctuary of Poseidon. Surely people would need our services *there*! Indeed, they did. Wouldn't you know that God would have even more surprises in store for us, as well? *Wonderful* surprises. For that was where we first met Paul. And, that was where we first worked together with *you*. As you well know, there was *never* a dull moment after that!

Phoebe: Right you are! Paul seems to have a knack for getting himself into trouble, doesn't he? (*with a chuckle*) Of course, I've been really fortunate, having wealth in my own right and the people-connections that come with it. Believe me, I'm no stranger to the legal system or the local rulers. Paul has found my connections useful on more than one occasion. But I so admire his passion for the gospel! And his ability to strategize on how best to use people's gifts on behalf of the good news.

Prisca: Yes, Phoebe, I know just what you mean! Did you know that Paul urged us to go to Ephesus with him because he trusted our ability to preach? He even asked us to teach Apollos, a very bright young man from Alexandria. For he knew that Apollos would benefit from our wisdom. Age can have its benefits, you know. (*with a laugh*) And Paul knew that Ephesus would be just the place for another house church . . . halfway between Corinth and Galatia . . . where he could keep an ear tuned in to both communities. He surely needed to do just that!

Phoebe: It sounds just like him, Prisca. But, tell me, I heard that trouble was brewing when you first arrived. That you and Aquila even saved Paul's life.

Prisca: I suppose you could say that. As you know, Paul usually begins preaching in a new place at the local synagogue. However, the day he arrived, he was drawn to the outdoor amphitheater, built in honor of the goddess Artemis. The next thing we knew, the silversmith Demetrius was starting a riot on the spot! Now, Paul doesn't always listen to us, but he did that day, thank God! And we were able to get Paul out of that mess. Afterward, I just wondered if Demetrius was afraid of losing some of his trade, making all those trinkets in honor of the goddess.

But, tell me, Phoebe, I know that Paul calls you a deacon, the leader of your community. How are things going with you?

Phoebe: Well, you know how much I love to preach the good news! And God has given me so many gifts to pastor the people. How I love to see people grow in their faith! A little encouragement here, bringing out the gifts in people there, and offering welcome at all times, turning nobody away. And always, always, keeping the vision of Jesus right in front of our eyes: creating a space where people can truly be brother and sister to each other, reaching out to *anyone* in need. It *is* exciting, isn't it! And simply amazing to see how the community grows and flourishes.

Prisca: Yes, it certainly is! Even with the nearly constant threat of persecution. You know, that reminds me of another friend of Paul's, a woman named Junia. Do you know her? She and her husband Andronicus are Paul's relatives, in fact, and members of the original Jerusalem community! And they *both* love to preach, too. They've gone on missionary tours with him, wherever needed. In fact, Paul told me that they've even gone to prison with him, for the sake of the gospel. In his eyes, they are certainly "prominent among the apostles."[23] I hope that people everywhere will always be inspired by their example! Now tell me, Phoebe, I know Paul well enough to know that you're not simply here on a visit of friendship. Paul must have something in mind, to send you here with a letter.

Phoebe: Right you are, Prisca! Paul sent me here because he knew you'd accept me. And trust me to interpret his letter to you. He's on his way to Jerusalem right now with a collection from the gentile churches for that original community. It's so important to stay connected to Jerusalem, to foster trust among all of us who follow Jesus, whether Jew or gentile. But, this is only his first stop. His hope and dream is to come here, to Rome, and stay for a short time before setting out on a totally new missionary activity. He's looking west, this time. To Hispania (modern-day Spain and Portugal). A whole new world to evangelize!

Prisca: How exciting! Tell me more!

Phoebe: It *is* exciting. But he knows this territory is really different from what he's used to. Hardly anyone there speaks Greek! Not only that, there are so many different dialects! And so few Jewish people! Which means, practically no synagogues as bases for preaching. The only cities are in the northeastern province of Baetica, so, of course, that would be the place to start. But we need money and government and diplomatic connections and translators and, of course, missionaries willing to spread the good news.

Prisca: I'm sure that Junia and Andronicus would be interested in being missionaries! As for Aquila and me, we're just settling into our new house church here, and that needs so much tending right now. But, have no fear, Phoebe. Our community will support you in whatever ways we can. The word *will* be taken west. You'll see. (And so it was!)

23. Rom 16:7.

Lydia, a Leader of the Church in Philippi,
Responds to God

On the Fourth Sunday of Easter, we always celebrate Jesus, the Good Shepherd. There's *one* woman who heard the Good Shepherd's voice . . . through Paul. One virtually unknown woman whose story is *never* told on *any* Sunday in our three-year cycle. Another courageous leader of the early Church. That one is Lydia, leader of Paul's community of joy, in Philippi.

Her story in Scripture is brief (Acts 16:11–15, 40) but intriguing, leaving us with more questions than answers. Scholars today are rummaging, probing, digging deep beneath the sparse words for ancient whispers and signs of her life. On this much they agree: she was Paul's first European convert. A gentile "worshiper of God" from the city of Thyatira (in Lydia, the western part of present-day Turkey), she met regularly with Jewish women in Philippi for prayer. Profoundly moved by Paul's words, in that setting, she begged him to baptize her and her household (probably workers associated with her trade). Then, urging Paul to "come and stay" at her home—a metaphor for eucharistic community, as Luke tells it—she became leader of this faith community.[24] As such, she was the recipient of Paul's Letter to the Philippians, his favorite, tenderhearted community of joy. Was she wealthy? Probably not, though only the wealthy could purchase her much-desired product, purple cloth. But, no. According to most recent scholarship, she was most likely a freed slave, named after her place of origin—Lydia—for its expertise in purple dye.[25] She was also a woman of grit, perseverance, and unwavering courage, following the call upon her heart, despite the very real possibility of persecution.[26]

Her story begins as Paul is urged in a dream to go west, to Philippi. Listen, then, as Lydia might tell us her story.

> It's Sunday morning, still early . . . and quiet now. The folks have just left my house after our weekly prayer service. How I relish each gathering . . . and also the quiet that follows. It allows me to absorb everything that's taken place. You see, soon I must head off to work, for Sunday's a workday here in the Roman Empire.

24. Luke, author of his Gospel and Acts, uses this phrase in only one other place: on the road to Emmaus, as the two travelers urge Jesus to "stay with us," upon arriving at their house. What transpired was a eucharistic celebration, as they recognized the risen Jesus in the breaking of the bread (Luke 24:29–30). Also, see Acts 16:40, which refers to the faith community gathered in Lydia's home.

25. For more information, see Ulterino, *Walking with Wisdom's Daughters*, 70–73.

26. See Acts 16:16–40.

And I'm "a dealer in purple cloth."[27] But today was *most* special. For this morning I shared with our folks—maybe fifty of us today—a letter I had just received from Paul. Paul began, "I thank my God every time I remember you, constantly praying with joy in every one of my prayers for all of you, because of your sharing in the gospel from the first day until now."[28]

"Every time I remember you . . . from the first day until now." . . . *I* remember . . . *my* first day. My *new* day. It all began back in the region of Lydia, where I was born and grew up, in what *you* would call western Turkey. I was young and healthy, crusty in a determined kind of way, but gentle with folks, at the same time. I was still a slave back then, my family being so very poor. But I thought I could do *anything*! Yes! I *would* purchase my freedom. I *would* be set free! So I worked very hard at my trade; in all honesty, I can claim to be very good at it. In fact, folks with money were willing to pay a great deal for this purple cloth. It spoke to them of richness . . . and royalty. Truth be told, though, they wanted nothing to do with *me* . . . or anyone else who makes this precious cloth. For it takes urine, mixed with the roots of vegetables, to make the dye. Yes, it's *smelly*! The whole *place* smells! But I'm not complaining. For I did earn enough to buy my freedom . . . and head west . . . with my entire household. We ended up right here, in this bustling Roman town of Philippi, on the trade route to Rome.

You may be thinking: oh, *she's* only interested in work. But no. There's much more. Something . . . Someone . . . kept on calling to me. It's hard to explain. Not a voice, exactly, or even a nudge. It was more like a magnet drawing me, though I was never quite sure where it would lead. But, in time, I began to trust it more and more. In the end, my search brought me to worship every Sabbath with a group of Jewish women. They gathered right here on the water, which they needed for all their ritual cleansings. And I found it good . . . even healing. . . . somehow, though, it was not quite right, not quite my heart's desire. Then one day two men joined us: an older one named Silas and a man named Paul. Paul did all the talking that day . . . as he *always* does, I discovered. Afterward, I chuckled to myself, "He simply couldn't help himself!" For he was *brimming over* with passion for Jesus Christ. How he *ignited* my heart with his fire! It took no time at all before I could say, "Yes! *This* is the One who's been calling to me! *This* is the One I've been searching

27. Acts 16:14.
28. Phil 1:3–4.

for!" So I *pleaded* with Paul, "Come, baptize me . . . and my entire household into Jesus Christ!" And he did. How will I ever forget being drenched in God's love! The next thing I knew I was urging Paul, "If you have judged me to be faithful to the Lord, come and stay at my home."[29] Once again, he came. So it was that I eagerly learned, soaking up everything he had to offer. He told me of his life-changing experience on the road to Damascus. He told me of the courage it took to face so many of his Jewish kin, still fearful of his intense persecution. He told me of the trust that was sinking ever more deeply into him, trust in the God of Jesus Christ. Gradually, I began to absorb the depth of his believing—until *I* could preach myself, in the power of the Spirit, and draw people in. Thus began our gathering for prayer: my telling the stories of Jesus, before leading us all in the Breaking of the Bread and the Drinking from the Cup. Without a doubt, Christ was *here*, filling us and comforting us. Challenging us and strengthening us for the week ahead. For there are always people ready to hate us . . . persecute us . . . jail us . . . even kill us. But the power of our gathering is *always* stronger than our fear.

Ah, what joy to remember all this, just as Paul remembers us. In his letter he went on to say, "I am confident of this, that the one who began a good work among you will bring it to completion by the day of Christ Jesus."[30] Oh yes, how true! For I have found the Love of my life!"

Where and how does her story live in you?

Resurrection Today: Contemporary Women Prophetically Respond to God

Indeed, nobody saw Jesus rise from the dead. Not back then, and not now. Like our ancestors in faith, we know fear. Like them, we wrestle with God's compelling call: "Do not be afraid." Like them, we are urged to lift up our own voices, according to our own particular gifts. Those who respond give birth to courage and hope for us all. Here are two such women.

29. Acts 16:15. The only other time this phrase is found in Scripture, urging someone to "stay at my home," is in Luke 24:29, when the two disciples on the road to Emmaus urged Jesus to stay at their home. In both instances, a eucharistic meal follows.

30. Phil 1:6.

The Prophetic Voice of Sandra M. Schneiders, IHM[31]

Who *is* this woman? A Scripture scholar of giant proportions, she was trained by the recognized expert on John's Gospel, Father Raymond Brown. And she has brought a feminist mind and heart to bear on her work. Indeed, her book on John's Gospel, *Written That You May Believe: Encountering Jesus in the Fourth Gospel*, has become an epiphany to many, myself included. However, *here* I focus on her ministry in another regard: her response to the recent Vatican investigation of women religious in this country.

It was early in the year 2009. And the abrupt announcement was unsettling, disturbing, even threatening. Women's religious communities in the United States were about to be investigated. Why, exactly? It seems that in September 2008, a small group of conservative women religious (representing about 5 percent of the total communities in this country) held a conference at Stonehill College in Massachusetts. In their view, the vast majority of women religious were on the wrong track. And the cry "Investigate them!" was raised. As it happened, Cardinal Rode, the highest-ranking overseer of religious life in Rome, had been invited and was in attendance. Without consulting anyone—bishops, other religious, lay people—he ordered an investigation of all the *women's* religious orders *and* the Leadership Conference of Women Religious, which represents 80 percent of sisters' communities in this country.

Many were simply stunned! Not only women religious, but myriads of folks who had been touched by their good works over the years. Consider, for example, the exhibit at Ellis Island, "Women & Spirit: Catholic Sisters in America." Consider the pioneer spirit that brought so many from Europe to this country in the nineteenth century to teach . . . to found hospitals . . . to care for the wounded during the Civil War. Consider their prophetic work on into the twentieth century: walking the road to Selma to protest segregation . . . walking the Way of the Cross with the marginalized folks they loved in El Salvador (like Jean Donovan, alongside Sisters Maura Clarke, Dorothy Kazel, and Ita Ford) . . . defending the rights of native peoples in Brazil exploited by land-grabbers (in the persons of Sr. Dorothy Stang and her colleagues)

31. Sr. Schneiders is professor of New Testament and spirituality at the Jesuit School of Theology at Berkeley. She dedicated the book mentioned above to her "teachers and friends," Raymond E. Brown, SS, and Edward J. Malatesta, SJ.

... feeding the hungry ... serving as lawyers, doctors, and other advocates ... and on and on and on.

Into this chaos and anguish, a clarion voice emerged, that of Sr. Sandra Schneiders.[32]

In her words, this investigation was all about competing visions of the Second Vatican Council, a "power struggle in the contemporary church between the promoters of the renewal initiated by Vatican II and a program of Tridentine restoration."[33] What does this wrestling have to do with women religious? Nothing less than this, she asserts. Who is the God they know and follow? Who is the God they serve? Will they be a "work force" for the hierarchy ... or "a charismatic ministry in response to God's call and human need"?[34] Placed in that context, the response becomes clear. Religious life, at its core, is prophetic. As prophets, women religious do what Jesus did: they tell "the absolute future of God, what Jesus called 'The Reign of God,' into the present."[35] Just like Jesus, just like prophets of old, they cock one ear to God and the other ear to the lives of their people. They know, as Jesus did, that God is *Compassion* ... and that God's *passion* is justice ... or "God's dream for humanity."[36] Their lives bear witness to and serve this God, who "makes no appeal to coercive power."[37]

What did Jesus teach us about prophetic ministry?[38]

℣ It is rooted in prayer and intimacy with God.

℣ It requires courage to question religious authorities—the hierarchy today—when their lives do not measure up to the gospel. Their status alone does not guarantee that they speak on God's behalf.

℣ It requires freedom from attachments.

---

32. Sr. Schneiders wrote a series of five articles on the meaning of religious life today, which appeared in the *National Catholic Reporter*, in January 2010.

33. This quote is from Sr. Schneider's introduction/part 1 of her articles.

34. This significant question is posed and answered in Sr. Schneider's part 2, "Call, Response and Task of Prophetc Action."

35. Sr. Schneiders proposed this theme of prophetic action in part 2, "Call, Response."

36. Here she quotes Marcus Borg, in ch. 7 of his book *Jesus*.

37. Again, she quotes from Marcus Borg.

38. The answer to this question forms the basis of part 3.

ꙮ It requires continual discernment through attentive listening to God.

ꙮ There is an integrity . . . or coherence . . . between the prophet's message and life.

ꙮ If there is a conflict between faithfulness to God and faithfulness to the hierarchy, one must first obey God.

Truthfully, is it *not* possible to imagine that *some* church officials *might* have felt threatened? In part 4 of her series of articles, then, Sr. Schneiders continues to drive home her point. She reminds us about the origins of religious life in this country: that religious life was founded by strong, independent women, who only gradually . . . by the early twentieth century . . . came under hierarchical control. But, the undulating waves let loose by the Second Vatican Council caused women religious to plumb their depths, and their mission in today's world. They concluded: Vatican II requires an ecclesiology (way of being Church together) of equal discipleship, rather than blind obedience to church authority. As Schneiders maintains, the Church is *not* "a fortress of truth and moral righteousness in a sea of wickedness"; rather, it *is* "the suffering Body of Christ in solidarity with all that is human, as real people, individually and as a race, struggle toward the light of the Resurrection."[39]

Finally, she assures us that the path will never be easy, just as Jesus discovered. But she inspires us all with these words. "Religious cannot expect to experience Jesus' resurrection if we are unwilling to share his passion. And we do not always have the luxury of choosing whether we will suffer at the hands of secular powers or of the Church's power structure."[40] So, what are women religious to do? They must "pray their way, personally and corporately, into a peaceful and courageous acceptance that the tension between institutional authority and prophetic ministry is and will always be part of the life of the Body of Christ . . . because it was structurally intrinsic to Jesus' own prophetic life and ministry." And they must pray knowing, as Paul did, that God's "grace is sufficient for you, for power is made perfect in weakness."[41]

39. This is at the heart of part 4.
40. This is her opening statement of part 5.
41. Her closing, based upon 2 Cor 12:9.

Their prayers, and her prophetic wisdom, prevailed in the end, though not without some bumps along the way. Indeed, she and the leaders of the Leadership Council of Women Religious have prayed their way through conversations with Vatican officials, now influenced by the desire of Pope Francis to listen and resolve tensions, wherever possible.

The Prophetic Voice of Ann Kurz:
Living with Cerebral Palsy

Ann would come into church on her walker, always followed by her assistant. Bright. Friendly. Capable. A ready smile on her face. Those were my first impressions. I couldn't help but wonder: who *is* she? Then I came to know her, little by little. Her profound faith, her ability to write so beautifully, her thoughts more than well worth the close attention necessary to hear and understand them. In fact, she has a responsible position at one of Rochester's largest employers, and she's one of a small group who prepare the Prayers of the Faithful for Sunday Mass. As I was pondering, then, on selecting another contemporary courageous woman, I knew she *had* to be the one. What follows is her story, told in answer to my questions.

1. What was most helpful to you from the beginning, especially in terms of your parents' love?

> What was most helpful from the beginning was my parents' decision to have other children (I'm the oldest of five). My sister Lyn was born 363 days after me. My mom said that during the first year of my life, she was very protective of me—probably because the doctors warned her not to be surprised if she found me dead in my crib someday. However, as Lyn developed and prospered despite falls, bumps, and bruises, Mom and Dad questioned why they needed to be so cautious with me, so they loosened their guard with me. Their letting me live and grow freely gave me the opportunity to learn how to "keep up" with my siblings, to learn how to interact with people and the world around me. It gave me the opportunity to experience life to my fullest, to make the most of my abilities.
>
> Somehow, Mom and Dad determined that they had to allow me to be their guide as I grew up. People often approach my mom to say that she had done such a good job with me, and Mom will readily admit to those people that I really led them to where I wanted to go, what I wanted to do, and who I wanted

to be. Of course, they guided, taught, and slowed me down, but they loved me enough to let me have choices and determine my own path in life. Mom will say that she and Dad would cringe when I'd announce what I wanted to try to do next, but they were always willing to help me figure out how I might be able to accomplish my goal . . . even if they knew that it would probably not work out (like when I wanted to roller skate).

2. *When did you first become aware of your differences from your siblings and friends? How did you begin to respond?*

People with disabilities are often asked this question, which is difficult to answer. When you're born with a disability, you don't really notice or think that you're different. Like comedienne Geri Jewell jokes, "I don't wake up each morning and think 'Oh, I have cerebral palsy.'" For me, CP is just another characteristic of who I am—I have brown hair, brown eyes, pale skin, CP . . . It's other people who notice the disability and make the distinction that I'm different. In the 1960s, all children with physical disabilities in Rochester were bused into number twenty-nine school in the city to attend special ed for elementary school. When I talk about my friends from my classes at number twenty-nine, people ask me what disability my friends had. More often than not, I don't know because we didn't talk specifically about what disability we had. We were more interested in our favorite TV shows, music, pets, birthday parties, sleepovers—things that most kids talk about.

I do remember when I was about seven or eight, asking Mom why people kept telling me that they didn't understand me. I had never heard myself talk, so I wasn't aware that I had a speech impairment. Mom simply said that because I had CP, I didn't make all my sounds in the same way as other people, and that's why I went to speech therapy. I remember accepting her answer and moving on.

Mom and Dad used any questions that others had about me and my CP as an opportunity to educate and sometimes advocate for me. Questions like "What's wrong with her?" were answered with "Ann has cerebral palsy. Her muscles don't always work the same way as yours do . . ." Or, if an adult seemed to be "dumbing down" their conversation with me or talking to me like I were a young child, Mom and Dad would have pointed out wherever I was in school and listed some of my achievements. They treated questions, stares, and "not quite appropriate" interactions with me as matter of fact. They did not become flustered or upset with others' lack of understanding, and so I learned from them, to live my life without allowing others' questions and negative opinions to interfere with my goals and accomplishments.

That isn't to say that there haven't been times when people's reactions to my CP hasn't bothered me. College and searching for a job were extremely rough. There's been plenty of times when I've cried and questioned how and why people can be so mean. However, to let their insensitivity paralyze or bar me from moving on and striving to meet my goals would just prove them right. A good cry can cleanse my spirit and give me strength to carry on. ("Keep calm and carry on" is one of my mantras.) I definitely don't want to allow anyone to have power over my life—my gift from God. The only way for me to maintain control of my life is to go for my dreams no matter what others think. If people tell me that I can't do something, I'll make it my mission to prove them wrong if that's a goal of mine. (I also like the '50s and '60s song: "Keep Your Eyes on the Prize [Hold On!]")

3. What has provided some of your greatest challenges?

Going away to college comes to mind first. I attended Trinity College (now Trinity University) in Washington, DC. One common family dinnertime discussion was going to college. It was kind of assumed that my siblings and I would all pursue education beyond high school and that we'd live on campus. So, I grew up with that belief that I'd attend college (probably outside Rochester). People always seem to be amazed that my parents and I never questioned whether I'd attend college or not, but attending college was a family expectation that I did not question. Where I'd go became the question. I wanted to get out of the snowy winters as much as possible and far enough away that it would be difficult to call my mom to come help me. I think my mom also wanted me far enough away that she couldn't just drop by either. Besides looking at my parents' alma maters Nazareth and Fisher here, I considered Hofstra U. on Long Island, LaSalle College in Philadelphia, and Trinity in DC. LaSalle was quickly ruled out for numerous reasons. Hofstra was completely accessible, and my parents would have loved for me to go there. But they were all about my disability and I didn't want that. At Trinity, they looked at me. Ann. They saw the whole person, which was definitely what I wanted. I wanted inclusion (Trinity), not segregation (Hofstra). While touring Trinity, I knew in my heart that it was the right school for me. Trinity wasn't accessible but they said they would make it accessible, which they did

. . . slowly! I think they completed all of the ramps by the end of my sophomore year, but at least they followed through!

Physical accommodations aside, Trinity posed some of my biggest challenges socially. My parents' teaching me to just understand that some people would stare at me, say rude things to me, and not accept me did not work well. Inclusion wasn't about letting people cast me aside and put up social barriers. I really needed some advocacy skills to help me show others that I was truly one of them. So, in addition to being away from home, managing a group of classmates who helped me with personal care, and taking a full class load, I had to teach myself to navigate the social arena and figure out when and how to advocate for myself. That was quite challenging and an education in itself.

Searching for a job also proved challenging. I always knew that my CP would pose a barrier to my being hired, but I'd hoped that my success at Trinity and the U of R (University of Rochester) would compensate for what I "lacked" physically. Thus, I wasn't prepared for the blatant discrimination that I experienced. If I mentioned that I had a speech impairment in my cover letter, I never received any replies. If I didn't mention it, I received calls but then they'd hang up when they heard my voice. Interviews were challenging with interviewers struggling to understand me and not knowing what to do when they didn't. I was told that my qualifications were excellent, but I received one rejection after another. I did what I could to network and make myself known. I joined a couple of advocacy groups and volunteered to present at various programs and conferences.

One of these presentations was for a conference sponsored by the NY State Office of Vocational Rehabilitation (OVR), the state agency that was supposedly helping me obtain employment. At the conference, I spoke about my experiences in my job search and what kind of advocacy needed to be done in the business world. After the presentation, there was a small reception, and I happened to walk by the head of OVR just as she stated to the group of people she was with: "Ann will never get a job." I was devastated.

Thankfully, around that same time, United Way asked me to be one of their "film stars" for their annual campaign. The stars' responsibility was to attend various corporate campaign kickoffs and speak about how UW agencies had helped them get to where they were then and what their goals were. Of course, I spoke about how UW agencies had helped me develop physically so that I could attain my degrees and that now I was ready to work. UW thought it would be great exposure to various companies for me, but what they hadn't considered was that I'd be traveling around with Danny Wegman, the chair of that year's campaign. After Danny had heard my talk multiple times, he approached my dad to ask if I'd like to work at Wegmans.[42] Dad told him that he should ask me. Later, Danny asked me, and I said, "Yes."

Wegmans and I approached my employment cautiously. We agreed that we'd give it a year and if either of us were unhappy, we could end the relationship. A year came and went, and there was no looking back. A month ago, I celebrated my twenty-ninth anniversary at Wegmans! I often wonder what the head of OVR would say now if she knew that.

These two stories show that my greatest challenges occur when I'm presented with prejudices that I must overcome to follow my dreams and achieve success. I'm grateful to all who have supported and given me opportunities to succeed.

4. How have you been able to accomplish so much?

5. Where is your faith in the midst of your ongoing growth?

I'm answering numbers four and five together because the answers go hand in hand.

I've always believed that God "gave" me CP for a reason. What that reason is, I'm still discovering. However, I believe God knew that I'd use the gifts that He bestowed on my personhood to somehow make the world a better place. I've very much "sensed" God's presence and support in my life. When I have big decisions to make, such as choosing Trinity and Wegmans, deciding to purchase a house, writing prayers, participating in the Cardinal Mooney/Aquinas Follies, I get a "positive vibe" that affirms for me that this is what God intended for me to do. Is it always easy? Do I always succeed? Do I always make the right choices within my pursuit to live my life the way God intended? No, but I continue to push forward, persevere, and stay determined to accomplish what I set out to do. Whenever I "tackle" something new, that I'm unsure will work or go the way I hope it will, I say a little prayer asking God to help me, to be near me as I attempt to achieve my goal. I feel God's presence, supporting me in, as Gandhi said, "be(ing) the change you wish to see in the world." It doesn't need to be a big, showy change but just a

---

42. Wegmans began as one grocery store in Rochester, NY, and is now a sprawling chain of stores over several states.

drop in the sea. Like in the starfish story, I feel God calling me
to make a difference—no matter how small.

*(A note from Gloria: Ann is—without a doubt—one of the most courageous
people I've ever encountered. She remains an inspiration to so many of us who
know and love her.)*

Pentecost, Conclusion of Eastertime Celebration: A Poetic Reflection

Let the house of Israel say: God's mercy endures forever!
    Pentecost began in the house of Israel, as a bounteous Thanksgiving,
after harvesting their first grain in the Promised Land.
Remembering redemption through the Red Sea,
followed by forty *very* long years, a generation's worth of wandering . . .
through a seemingly endless, directionless, wilderness . . .
they *arrived . . . finally . . .* into the promised land of milk and honey.
What could they possibly offer their eagle-winged God in return?
Surely the first fruits of their grain harvest . . .
and so much *more.*
Their Covenant promises, year in and year out, without fail,
in memory of the Law, given to Moses,
not simply words, powerful as they were, but a way of life,
according to *God's* heart and *God's* vision.
    Let the house of Israel say: God's mercy endures forever!

    Let the redeemed of Christ say: God's mercy endures forever!
In apostolic times, we're given a two-toned tale of Pentecost:
Luke's version stroked in broad, brilliant images,
while John's is couched in tender muted tones of new creation.
But for both, an infant Church is born, back then . . .
        and as often as necessary.
    According to Luke, Pentecost howled in on one fiery day,
tongues of fire, like molten lava of Poured-Out-God,
seeping through the cracks of broken-hearted, whimpering fear . . .
molding those wobbly and weak-kneed disciples
into pillars of strength and ramrods of courage:
women as well as men, one hundred and twenty of them,
gathered together in the Upper Room,
waiting, in prayer, *waiting* for the promised advent of Jesus' Spirit.

When suddenly, this Spirit *whooshed* all over the place . . .
wild, untamed, hot, fiery, driving, passionate Spirit . . .
fueled by love stronger than death . . .
way beyond any human effort to control.
The ultimate miracle was this: Babel was reversed!
Everyone heard "The Other" as kin!
    For John, Jesus is laboring on the cross,
birthing that first Christian community of mother and beloved disciple . . .
together with his mother's sister—Mary, wife of Clopas
        —and the Magdalene.
Then, on Easter night, the Risen Jesus gently appears to disciples
huddled in fear, even terror, behind bolted doors,
his hands and side still bearing love's wounds.
Like God at creation's dawn,
kneeling over and tenderly touching human clay,
he breathes peace . . . healing . . . creation beginning again . . .
and yet again, and again, and again,
reconciling, and commissioning them and *us* to
go forth and do the same.
    Let the redeemed of Christ say: God's mercy endures forever!

Mary, the Mother of Jesus, Remembers Pentecost

Rarely does an image of a middle-aged Mary come to mind. Or an image of Mary at Pentecost. And yet, poet and author Mary Lou Sleevi has captured both images on the cover of her inspiring book *Women of the Word*. Here she is, an older woman now. Wrinkled. With graying hair. Wisdom etched now in her face. Suffering beyond measure etched in those beautiful, haunting eyes. Yes, Mary was there . . . in the Upper Room . . . along with Mary of Magdala and the other "certain women" who followed Jesus from Galilee.[43] Along with the openhearted, yet fallible men. Yes, of course they would follow Jesus! And, yes, they would fail, over and over and over again. But they would never give up trying. All totaled, maybe one hundred twenty followers, waiting on Jesus. What, then, might she tell us about that fiery, windswept day? Listen . . .

> I couldn't help it. The memory of that day suddenly returned: was it really over thirty years ago now? That urgent, compelling voice, yearning for my yes. That overflowing, overwhelming flow of

43. Acts 1:14 and Luke 8:1–3.

passionate love beyond measure. Could I? Would I? Was it really *God* seeking my desire to birth Love-beyond-Understanding in this broken, bruised world I knew so well? It happened in a split second! Yes: "Here am I, the servant of the Lord; let it be done with me according to your word."[44] And now: so many years later . . . so many healings and teachings later . . . so much excruciating suffering later . . . here I was.

I looked around. There were the men: Peter and John, and the rest of the eleven, alongside the women who had followed Jesus from Galilee—Joanna, Susanna, and so many others. Including Mary of Magdala, of course! Oh, how she loved my Jesus! And how he loved her, too! The gifts he called out of her! Could she ever preach! It brought a smile to my lips and a skip to my heart!

Well, as I said, we were waiting. Jesus had said something about sending his Spirit. But, I wondered. What would that look like? How would we know when it happened? Most of all, what difference would it make? Then my eyes landed on Peter. How could he have denied knowing my Jesus . . . *three* times? I was *still* struggling to forgive him.

Then . . . it happened! The rush of a strong, driving wind, rattling the rafters of the house . . . and our very lives. Sifting our hearts. Firing our gifts. Transforming whimpering fear into backbones of courage. Loosening silent tongues, for the sake of the gospel. I saw it all. I felt it all. Forgiveness, and the desire to forgive. (Oh, that was a big one!) Also, Wisdom. Vision. Understanding. And Joy, unbounded Joy. All of it, knitting us together as one!

Now, I could *see* in a whole new way. This was nothing less than a second birth! Each, the result of a very long, hard labor. But *this* one was so different from that first, in Bethlehem: in the dark of night, alone with Joseph. That is, until strangers startled us with their presence. Shepherds, the poorest of the poor, the ones nobody else seemed to want. But on *that* night, their faces were *shining*. And their words *stunned* our hearts! A *Savior* was born! For *them*! For *all*! Had it only been a few short months before that I had prophesied that very truth? God lifts up the

---

44. Luke 1:38; Mary pronounces this same promise again, at the very end of her story, as told here.

lowly, brings down the arrogant. *Everyone* matters! Ah, it's taken me a lifetime to really understand those words.

But *now* . . . the possibilities were endless! For *now* a much larger body was being born. The body of Christ: male and female, rich and poor, saint and sinner. A body *full* of gifts . . . as the *Spirit* doles them out . . . for one and for all . . . for the entire world, as far as the heart can see. Would it be easy to birth this body? Oh, no! My life had taught me otherwise. There would *always* be fear. Resistance. Raw and open wounds just ready to pounce and create havoc. But *now* there would be so much more! The Spirit of Jesus at work. *Already*, in hearts that see. *Already*, in souls fueled by compassion. In feet that follow his way. In hands that settle for nothing less than human dignity for everyone. We surely aren't there yet, but the Spirit is still moving and shaking. *Still* rattling the rafters of many a house. *Still* giving birth to the body of Christ. Again and again and again. This much I know. Giving birth is always painful. *And*, it's *always* worth the struggle. So, then. Who among us, right here . . . and right now . . . is ready, willing and able to help give birth, yet one more time, to this magnificent body of Christ? To proclaim: "Here am I, a servant of the Lord: let it be done with me according to your word."

The People of God, at Pentecost Today: What Do You Say?

Well, folks? Here we are: today's one hundred and twenty. Saint and sinner alike, the people of God. Can you feel the tremors of God's Holy Spirit, still moving and shaking in us? Still groaning with all creation? Still rattling the windows and blowing open the doors of God's dreams for us all, yet one more time? Can you touch them? Taste them? Believe in them? Perhaps even work for them? What do *you* say?

6

Ordinary Time, According to Mark
(Cycle B)

An Introduction to the Season

Here we are, in Ordinary Time, once again. That long stretch, nearly half the year, from the Feast of the Most Holy Body and Blood of Christ (sometime in June) until the end of the church year in November. But, lest you think you're in for some "ordinary, ho-hum" stuff, think again. The "Ordinary" refers to the everyday stuff of Jesus' life and ministry. How could *that* ever be ordinary? At the same time, it refers to *our* everyday stuff. With all the twists and turns, ups and downs, good times and tough ones, days of putting one foot in front of the other, days of anguish, days of celebration, you get the picture. Looking back, is any of that "ordinary"? Truly, I doubt it. And, looking back, how does *our* everyday connect to that of Jesus? Come and see. First, however, let me share the letter I wrote to our very first Gospel writer, the one we name Mark.

> Dear Mark,
>
> You remain a shrouded figure, one left open to our imaginations. We simply don't know what you look like, where you're from, or even your name, beyond a shadow of a doubt. Yet *this* we *can* say with absolute certitude: you are a passionate follower of Jesus Christ! Somehow, in some way, he has touched your life profoundly. Somehow, in some way, he has given utter and total meaning to your life, impossible before his coming. We know that your writing lacks polish, elegance, and flourish. At the same time, the starkness of your writing, the simplicity of words wasting nothing, convey great power.

Your introduction of This-One-without-Equal is absolutely stunning: "The beginning of the Good News of Jesus Christ, the Son of God." Wow! Surely, you realized, and in fact intended, to take on the power of the Roman emperor himself! For *he* continually professed to bring good news, with every great military victory. *He* continually professed to be the son of god. (Yes, I use small letters deliberately.) Yet, from the get-go, you proclaim the ultimate truth of Jesus Christ. With such courage, with such seeming fearlessness and conviction. At a time when your community, wherever it was and however small, could have been squashed by yet one more military exploit of that same Roman emperor. Where does your courage originate, except in and through Jesus Christ, in whom you so profoundly believe?

Furthermore, it is *abundantly* clear that you and your community were wrestling with something almost beyond imagining. How could such a totally good, healing, loving person—who only brought the power of a merciful God to bear on every imaginable human difficulty—end up on a cross? Attacked, broken, beaten, bloodied, sneered at, totally rejected by so many who thought *they* had power! How could this *be*? All the expectations of the Promised One never, ever, included such a miserable death! *And yet*, this beaten up, left-to-die Jesus would have the last word. The ultimate Word of God. For he would not, *could* not, stay dead! No, God had the last word by raising him up to new life. Not just him, but all of us! It is absolutely breathtaking, isn't it? Beyond human imagining, isn't it? The power for so much goodness in the face of so much sin and death and rejection.

Is that why you simply *had* to write? Tell the story as best you could, as simply and truthfully as possible? So that others might see . . . might come to understand . . . might come to believe? Yes, that's it, so that others might come to believe in a goodness beyond our ability to create, yet alone even begin to imagine. For all that, I thank you, endlessly.

Sincerely yours,

Gloria Ulterino, in the Year of Our Lord 2020

An Introduction to Mark's Jesus

So it is that we begin . . . with Mark. Why? Because scholars generally agree: Mark's Gospel was first! First to develop the form we name Gospel, or Good News. First, according to commentator Ched Myers, to take dead

aim at the Roman emperor and all the trappings of empire.[1] No genealogy
here. No infancy narrative. Nothing but the daring claim that Jesus Christ
alone is the true, only Son of God! In Mark's urgent, breathless style, we are
driven into an encounter with Jesus, not unlike the Spirit *driving* Jesus into
the wilderness to be tested for mission.

We know many of the stories. But, who is Mark? We can't be sure.
Where is his community? Again, we don't know. The most respected scholars
tell us is that it was a mixed community of gentile and Jew, probably beyond
Palestine, maybe somewhere in today's Syria, or even Rome. When was the
Gospel written? Again, the best guess is the late 60s, when tiny communities, followers of "the Way," were popping up around the Mediterranean
world. Wrestling with making sense of a crucified Messiah. Contending
with the reality of Nero's persecutions in 64 CE and the devastating destruction of the Jewish revolt against imperial Rome (67 to 70 CE). Yes, Rome
hammered Jerusalem, leaving the Second Temple in a pile of rubble. (Today,
from a panoramic perspective at the top of the Mount of Olives, one beholds
a majestic golden dome atop a mosque in its place. Known as the Temple
Mount—veiling centuries of bitter feuds—this magnificent plot of ground is
sacred to Jews, Christians, and Muslims.) Into this scene, the Jesus of Mark's
Gospel shows up. Ernest. Urgent. Breathless. "Straightway"—"immediately,"
as the translation goes—driven by mission.[2] To make God's ways straight.
For time is short. *His* time! And *ours*!

Is that why Mark's Gospel—in its original format—is unfinished, at
16:8? (Scripture scholars have repeatedly assured us of this strange phenomenon.) Yes, indeed, the women were there, at the empty tomb. But, they
"went out and fled from the tomb, for terror and amazement had seized
them; and they said nothing to anyone, for they were afraid." Huh? How
can this be? *Someone* must have said *something!* For this we know: by the
late 40s and on into the 50s, Paul had formed communities in places like
Corinth, Ephesus, and Philippi. And his ministry colleagues—women as
well as men—nurtured and sustained them. There were women like Prisca
(Priscilla in Acts of the Apostles) and her husband Aquila, his coworkers,
who "risked their necks for my life" and led the house church in Rome.[3] Also

---

1. Myers et al., "*Say This to the Mountain*," 5–6.

2. Marie Noonan Sabin, in her 2006 commentary on Mark, notes that Mark uses
this word forty-three times, most often translated as "immediately." But, she claims, that
misses an important point: the message of John the Baptist in 1:3 to "prepare the way
of the Lord, make his paths straight." Jesus is all about making God's ways straight. See
Sabin, *Gospel According to Mark*, 11.

3. Rom 16:3–5. See also Acts 18:1–4, 18–21 regarding their house church in Ephesus and 1 Cor 16:19, reaffirming their house church in Corinth.

Lydia, who prevailed upon Paul to baptize her entire household, was known to be a leader of the house church of Philippi.[4] We can't leave out Phoebe, a "deacon" in Cenchreae, near Corinth.[5] Additionally, so many other women were praised by Paul in chapter 16 of his Letter to the Romans. And yet, according to the original ending of Mark, the Gospel is unfinished.

Almost immediately, an image came to my mind, of Michelangelo's magnificent sculpture of the Gospel writer Matthew. Why? Because the head and upper torso are complete, down to the finest detail. But the rest remains unfinished. Just like Mark's original, abrupt "ending." Was the Good News (according to Mark, according to Michelangelo) to be continually unfinished? Left to each generation? Left to us, right here and right now? Maybe, just maybe.

Here's one more "thought" on Mark's Gospel, inspired by Marie Noonan Sabin, author of a commentary on Mark. She probes the Marcan Jesus from the perspective of Proverb's Wisdom Woman of old (emerging out of the sixth-century exile, BCE). For *this* Jesus—just like Wisdom, in chapters 8 and 9 of Proverbs—is bold. Brash. Eager to share food, drink, maturity, and insight. True enough. And yet, is there not an even closer affinity between Mark and the apostle Paul? Did not each wrestle mightily with the wisdom of preaching a crucified Christ? How could this be? Wasn't it utter nonsense? Total foolishness? Listen to Paul's "take" on these questions.

> Where is the one who is wise? . . . Has not God made foolish the wisdom of the world? For since, in the wisdom of God, the world did not know God through wisdom, God decided, through the foolishness of our proclamation, to save those who believe. For Jews demand signs and Greeks desire wisdom, but we proclaim Christ crucified, a stumbling block to Jews and foolishness to Gentiles, but to those who are the called, both Jews and Greeks, Christ the power of God and the wisdom of God. For God's foolishness is wiser than human wisdom, and God's weakness is stronger than human strength. . . . He is the source of your life in Christ Jesus, who became for us wisdom from God, and righteousness and sanctification and redemption, in order that, as it is written, "Let the one who boasts, boast in the Lord."[6]

---

4. See Acts 16:9–15 and 40.

5. Rom 16:1–2; Paul used the same word for some men, all of whom were charismatic, servant leaders. Also, it is generally believed that she delivered Paul's Letter to the Romans.

6. 1 Cor 1:20a, 20c–25, 30–31. This letter, one of Paul's first, was written in the early 50s.

Wasn't it possible that these two—Paul and Mark—knew each other, since Paul wrote in the 50s and Mark in the late 60s? Might they even have worked together at some point? I don't know. But this I do know: Mark's Gospel has often been called a passion narrative with a long introduction. And Paul has unfailingly proclaimed "Christ crucified" as the *Wisdom* of God.

Getting to Know Mark's Jesus in the Everyday

Now as we enter Ordinary Time, what might an "ordinary" day in the life of Jesus look like, according to Mark? On any given day, he taught "with authority." Healed, even on the Sabbath, a serious "no-no" to Jewish religious leaders. Invited some men to "follow" him, even Levi, the tax collector. Became the center of controversy, not only to some religious leaders, but even to his hometown folks and his very own family. Told stories about the reign of God in the most ordinary terms, in images everyone could understand. Trained his disciples in healing and compassion, even revealing how a huge mob of five thousand hungry souls could be fed. Then, pivoting toward Jerusalem, the place of the cross, he named his Gospel's core: "Whoever wishes to become great among you must be your servant, and whoever wishes to be first among you must be slave of all. For the Son of Man came not to be served but to serve, and to give his life a ransom for many."[7] How the male disciples wrestled with *this* teaching! Only Bartimaeus, newly healed of his blindness, *enthusiastically* cast off his cloak to follow Jesus "on the way."[8] A question rears its head. Can we—like Bartimaeus—eagerly cast off *our* old cloaks of confinement, "same old, same old," to follow a *crucified* Messiah? One whose mission is to serve others, no matter what?

Who, then, perceived . . . really grasped . . . the truth of Jesus? The male disciples follow him but keep coming up short in the understanding department, as Mark tells it. Usually it is people without a name, especially women without a name, who seem to "get it." Like Simon's mother-in-law, early in the Gospel (on the Fifth Sunday in Ordinary Time). We are only told this: she's in bed with a fever. Jesus "came and took her by the hand and lifted her up. Then the fever left her, and she began to serve them."[9] Of *course*, we might say! She does her *woman's* work, as so many have done, age after age. True enough. But, is there also a hint, early on, that "diaconia"—service—is at the very core of Jesus' life? And that, as we serve others, we will be "raised up" to new life. Just as *she* was. Just as *Jesus* was. Perhaps!

7. Mark 10:43–45.
· 8. Mark 10:52; the whole story of Bartimaeus is told in vv. 46–52.
9. Mark 1:31.

In fact, on the eve of Jesus' passion, we encounter another unnamed woman in Mark 14:3. This woman barges into an all-male dinner party at the home of Simon the leper, in Bethany, just outside Jerusalem. *Somehow,* she knows Jesus. *Somehow,* she knows what is coming. *Somehow,* from the depths of her heart, she simply *must* tenderly pour out her profound love on this man who has made all the difference in her life. Who is she? We have no idea. *But her actions are just like those of Jesus, who pours out his life for all.* Her actions are those of a prophet, even a priest, as she lavishly anoints him, head to toe, with "very costly ointment of nard."[10] The disciples' anger at her "waste" is immediately corrected by Jesus' profound gratitude: "Wherever the good news is proclaimed in the whole world, what she has done will be told in remembrance of her."[11] But. We have forgotten her, haven't we? Have we also forgotten the *Jesus* she knows so well?

Now, back to another ordinary day in the life of Jesus. Another healing—two, in fact—each filling out the other's story. (This doubling of stories is one of Mark's consistent characteristics.) There's the woman with the hemorrhage, whose healing story is encased in the life-giving story of Jairus's daughter.[12] Both Matthew and Luke also tell this story in their Gospels, though Mark uncharacteristically paints many more details, compelling us to enter into this moment. Jairus, a leader of the synagogue (one of the few religious leaders who really *knows* Jesus), is desperate, for his twelve-year-old daughter is near death. He *throws* himself at Jesus' feet, *begging* him to *come . . . quickly . . .* and *heal* his daughter.

Jesus comes then, only to be momentarily halted by another distraught person, the woman who has been incessantly bleeding for *twelve . . . very . . . long . . . years.* Hidden in the crowd, she simply reaches out for his garments, absolutely certain of the healing that has eluded her all this time, as she has gone from doctor to doctor to doctor. *This* time she is *healed!* Instantly! Aware that healing power has been drained from him, Jesus stops: Who did this? "*Who touched my clothes?*"[13] His startling question calls her forth, trembling in fear. For she—a bleeding woman, unclean in traditional Jewish eyes—has dared to make him unclean. But, no; Jesus tenderly calls her "daughter."[14] Family! Does the recent stinging rejection of his blood family—determined to "restrain him" from his mission—wash over him?[15] Does

10. Mark 14:3.

11. Mark 14:9.

12. See Mark 5:21–33, told on the Thirteenth Sunday in Ordinary Time.

13. Mark 5:30.

14. Mark 5:34.

15. Mark 3:21; as a result, Jesus keeps them "outside" the circle of his followers.

he recall his response? Who is family to me? "Whoever does the will of God is my brother and sister and mother."[16] Just like this woman in front of him. Whose faith in *him* has made her well, insists Jesus.

After what must have felt like an eternity to Jairus, they are on their way again, to his house. Jesus only brings along Peter, James, and John: the same three who would accompany him to the mountain of transfiguration, as well as his passionate agony in the garden. In shades of the passion, Jesus is jeered by the crowd, who are convinced that the girl is dead. But no, once again, Jesus takes her by the hand and lifts her up (an unclean corpse?) to new life, not unlike his early-on healing of Simon's mother-in-law. Met with others' astonishment, Jesus charges everyone to feed the girl. And then, most of all, to tell *nobody* of this. For who would understand that Jesus is *not* a wonder-worker? Who would *ever* understand that the ragtag followers of Jesus would become the new Israel (the renewed twelve tribes)? Nobody! At least, not until *after* the crucifixion, death, and resurrection (raising up) of Jesus himself.

Thankfully, our lectionary includes this amazing story of faith in the crucified Christ. But it leaves out another healing story on another day in the life of Jesus: the healing of the Syrophoenician woman's daughter.[17] Yes, it is true that Matthew's version of this story *is* included in the lectionary on the Twentieth Sunday of Ordinary Time, Cycle A.[18] But the gentler Luke leaves it out of his Gospel altogether. So it's worth a mention here, perhaps because it raises more questions for us than answers. As Mark tells it, Jesus is exhausted. Worn out from arguing with some of the religious leaders once again, this time over true defilement, or what makes us "unclean."[19] And *this* controversy comes not long after rejection by his hometown folks.[20] Oh, he *has* continued to heal . . . even continued to show his disciples how an enormous crowd of five thousand men (and how many women and children?) can be fed. For they "are like sheep without a shepherd."[21] By now, however, he is *drained*. Out of gas. Running on empty. In need of quiet, in a place outside Israel: Tyre and Sidon. In need of rejuvenation. And yet, no sooner does he arrive than word gets out. A mother, who will do *anything* to have her daughter healed, pleads with him, begs him on bended knee

16. Mark 3:35, where Jesus clarifies that blood relationship does not make family; rather, it is the faithful following of God's will that matters.

17. Mark 7:24–30.

18. Matthew's story of Jesus' encounter with the Canaanite woman is found in Matt 15:21–28.

19. See Mark 7:1–23.

20. See Mark 6:1–6a.

21. Mark 6:34.

(just like Jairus) to "cast the demon out of her daughter."[22] *But* we are left speechless at his *insult* to this woman: "Let the children be fed first, for it is not fair to take the children's food and throw it to the dogs."[23] What?! Where did the *real* Jesus go? This determined woman, however, will have none of it and comes right back at him. Does her immediate, respectful response bring him to himself? Does he glimpse his God in this woman of great faith? Does he even learn from *her* that his family is much bigger than he first imagined? Much bigger than the people of Israel? Is that why he pronounces the truth: that her daughter is healed because of *her* words? All I can say is this. We repeatedly claim our belief that Jesus is fully human. What, then, does exhaustion do to *us*, fully human people? To the parent awakened yet one . . . more . . . time . . . in the middle of the night to feed a hungry baby? To anyone who's given everything to a family . . . to a job . . . and comes up short? Don't we snap? Become short? Let someone "have it"? Is Jesus *really* fully human or *not*? Can *he* grow and expand, as we all must do? What do we really believe about that?

Connecting the Marcan Jesus to Dorothy Day

So it is that the Marcan Jesus, in his "ordinary" days, can be brash and abrasively sandpaper-like, as well as compassionate. Without a doubt, he is prophetic. Intent on proclaiming and acting out of the God he knows, loves, trusts, and passionately believes in. Intent on serving, intent on pouring himself out for this God and for God's people. Who comes to mind today for you? For me, it's none other than Dorothy Day.

Confession time. I was never drawn emotionally to Dorothy Day, though I have greatly admired her life's mission in developing the Catholic Worker movement. For one thing, there were too many grim-looking pictures of this woman staring back at us. But then I read her granddaughter Kate's biography and a new Dorothy emerged for me.[24] Intensely human. Intensely honest. Intensely searching out God's path for her. Intensely caring of the most vulnerable among us. Yes, even joyful, despite those photographs. Here are some snapshots, then, of some moments in Dorothy's life. For she has challenged me beyond measure.

---

22. Mark 7:26.

23. Mark 7:27.

24. Hennessy, *Dorothy Day: The World Will Be Saved by Beauty*. In the footnotes that follow, the title will appear as *Day: Saved by Beauty*.

Perusing Snapshots of Dorothy Day

First, however, allow me to introduce Dorothy. Born in Brooklyn on November 8, 1897, to John and Grace Day, she was their third of five children.
A big-city girl. For John, the journalist, moved his family from Brooklyn
to Oakland, to Chicago (after the San Francisco earthquake), then back to
New York in 1916, always in search of work. Grace, though from a family
of limited means like her husband, always believed in putting on a good
dress for dinner and a good face for the world. It was said that Dorothy inherited her "Pop's" looks. *And* his stubbornness. To the point of "knowing"
what was best for everyone else! At the same time, Dorothy's poured-out
generosity of heart, time, and money for anyone in need became legendary.
Day in, day out, she doggedly pursued this mission through the Catholic
Worker movement, from age thirty-five to her death at age eighty-three.
Now, for a closer look . . .

> **It is 1917, and we discover two very different snapshots:** In one,
> she's often accompanied by her friend Eugene O'Neill (who
> taught her to listen carefully to people's stories), other writers,
> and/or her then-fiancé Irwin (Itzok) Granich. We catch sight of
> her restless, radical nature, often attracted to socialists and com-
> munists in her youth. Days find her writing, nights drinking in
> Greenwich Village bars. By then, she has claimed the path of her
> journalist father, her "Pop." In the other snapshot, she is alone. It's
> early morning, after all the bars have closed. Having just entered
> Saint Joseph's Church on Sixth Avenue, she finds herself kneel-
> ing there in the dark. Is she discovering some unacknowledged
> need? No stranger to New York's slums, she already sees more
> than misery; she also perceives "the dignity and courage of ordi-
> nary people in extraordinary circumstances."[25]
>
> **The year is 1924, sometime during the summer:** There's Doro-
> thy—attractive, slender, at peace, full of youthful energy, yet on
> the cusp of maturity—walking along a beach in Staten Island.
> Now several months shy of her twenty-seventh birthday, she's
> feeling rich! For she has just received twenty-five hundred dollars
> from a movie studio for a possible film of her book *The Eleventh
> Virgin.* She splurges then on the purchase of a small beach house
> for twelve hundred dollars in one of her favorite spots. (While
> there is no movie, Dorothy is already becoming recognized as

25. Hennessy, *Day: Saved by Beauty*, 10.

a proficient writer.) Here at the beach she embraces her craving for the sea, the peaceful lapping of the waves on the shoreline she loves to walk, and the opportunity to reflect on all that has been and all that is yet to be. Her deepest desires, often in conflict with one another. Her wrestling with it all. Her calling.

It is March 4, 1926: Nestled in Dorothy's arms is her newborn daughter, Tamar Teresa (after Teresa of Avila). Oh, how passionately she loves this child! *And* Tamar's father, Forster Batterham! This birth finally convinces her of God's forgiveness for an earlier abortion, from another time, of darkness and desperation. However, the forever joy of a blissful marriage is not to be. Forster, the man she deeply loves—the atheist, anarchist, and naturalist—is true to himself; he is *adamantly* opposed to religion! Dorothy, on the other hand, having stepped a toe into Catholicism, is on her way to full immersion. The time comes, late in 1927, to make a choice: God or the man she loves. What agony! But she can find no other way.

December 8, 1932, the Feast of the Immaculate Conception: Dorothy is in rapt prayer in the crypt of the National Shrine, on the Catholic University campus. The church building was still under construction, as was Dorothy's primary calling in life. She had been sent by *America* magazine to cover the Hunger March in Washington, DC, organized by the communist Unemployed Council. Impressed and deeply moved by the convictions of the marchers, she prayed, with tears and anguish, that God would open up some way to sate her ravenous hunger "for me to use what talents I possessed for my fellow workers, for the poor."[26]

December 9, 1932: A middle-aged man (fifty-five years old), with rumpled clothes, weather-beaten face, and calloused hands awaits Dorothy's return. Peter Maurin (Pierre Joseph Orestide Maurin, born in the Languedoc region of southeastern France) was given her address from *Commonweal* magazine. She finds him "intensely alive, on the alert, even when silent, engaged in reading or in thought. When he talked, the tilt of his head, his animated expression, the warm glow in his eyes, the gestures of his hands, his shoulders, his whole body, compelled your attention."[27] Could *he* be the answer to her impassioned prayer?

26. Wright, *Dorothy Day: An Introduction*, 41.
27. Ellsberg, *Dorothy Day: Selected Writings*, 42.

Would *she* respond by joining him in serving the poor, according to the Gospel and Catholic social justice teachings?

How could she *refuse* this "troubadour of Christ," as he loved to call himself?[28] Singing his love song of compassion and justice for *all* people. Even though she knew virtually nothing—yet—about Catholic social justice teachings. *"Yes, oh yes!"* Had her whole life up till now been yearning for this vision? Dorothy, the practical one, the gifted journalist searching for purpose in life, joined forces with Peter, the dreamer and teacher. Thus began the Catholic Worker movement, and a seventeen-year partnership, lasting until Peter's death. In time, *here* is what Dorothy would learn about Peter. Born into a peasant family, he was educated by the Christian Brothers and worked many jobs as a day laborer in western Canada and across the northern United States. Totally unassuming, yet continually learning, reading, and teaching, he rooted his entire being in this dream: changing people's hearts, so as to build a society "where it was easier for people to be good."[29] Anywhere, to anyone, at any time, he bubbled over with the need for roundtable discussions on making life better for everyone. Building houses of hospitality in cities for the homeless and unemployed. Creating farms in the country—"agronomic universities" he called them—to support a caring environment.[30] Getting these ideas "out there" through a newspaper. *Always* for the good of all.

May 1, 1933: Dorothy holds up the very first copy of the newspaper *The Catholic Worker*. Not so much about patching up old systems as creating a more just world, it sold then—and continued to sell—for a penny. Dorothy's stirring invitation rang out: "For those who are sitting on spring benches in the warm spring sunlight. For those who are huddling in shelters trying to escape the rain. For those who think there is no hope for the future, no recognition of their plight—this little paper is addressed."[31] For the Catholic Church now has a way, a program, to reconstruct the social order. By 1936, the circulation had increased to one

28. Day, *Long Loneliness*, 124.

29. Wright, *Dorothy Day: An Introduction*, 45; also Ellsberg, *Dorothy Day: Selected Writings*, 126; also Hennessy, *Day: Saved by Beauty*, 73.

30. Hennessy, *Day: Saved by Beauty*, 71.

31. Wright, *Dorothy Day: An Introduction*, 63.

hundred fifty thousand from its initial twenty-five hundred, and early-on twenty-five thousand.

Thanksgiving week, 1936, at the first farm in Easton, Pennsylvania: "The trees are getting bare, but still it stays warm. Coming down at night from the city, the warm, sweet smell of the good earth enwraps one like a garment. There is the smell of rotting apples; or alfalfa in the barn; burning leaves; of wood fires in the house; of pickled green tomatoes and baked beans. Now there is a warm feeling of contentment about the farm these days—the first summer is over, many people have been cared for here, already. From day to day we did not know where the next money to pay bills was coming from, but trusting to our cooperators, our readers throughout the country, we went on with the work. Now all our bills are paid and there is a renewed feeling of courage on the part of all those who are doing the work, a sense of confidence that the work is progressing."[32] In this month of Thanksgiving, we are even learning to be "thankful for the trials of the past."[33]

February 1937, a day in the life of the House of Hospitality, at Mott and Hester Streets: A tiny Italian village within the great city of New York. In Dorothy's words: "Every morning about four hundred men come to Mott Street to be fed. The radio is cheerful, the smell of coffee is a good smell, the air of the morning is fresh and not too cold, but my heart bleeds as I pass the lines of men in front of the store which is our headquarters. The place is packed—not another man can get in—so they have to form a line. Always we have hated lines, and now the breakfast which we serve of cottage cheese and rye bread and coffee has brought about a line. It is an eyesore to the community."[34] But it sustains these men, who are *not* derelicts, as they spend the day searching for work.

February 1940: Dorothy, at her desk in the Mott Street House, pondering their work. By then there were thirty Houses of Hospitality and several farms. How could she live with the noise, confusion, and chaos? Day in and day out? Where was her strength? Her hope? Listen. Yes, there are the daily reminders that leaders are hard to come by. That my own leadership

32. Ellsberg, *Dorothy Day: Selected Writings*, 76, written by Dorothy.
33. Ellsberg, *Dorothy Day: Selected Writings*, 76.
34. Ellsberg, *Dorothy Day: Selected Writings*, 80.

is faulty. That discouragement often raises its ugly head. That "even the best of human love is filled with self-seeking."[35] There was the time when two coworkers constantly quarreled, giving all of us a headache. For "the work becomes difficult only when there is quarreling and dissension and when one's own heart is filled with a spirit of criticism."[36] Yet, "the one thing that makes our work easier most certainly is the love we bear for each other and for the people for whom we work."[37] "Love and ever more love is the only solution to every problem that comes up. If we love each other enough, we will bear with each other's faults and burdens."[38] The question is: how can we keep before us the call to build a new heaven and a new earth, a Christian social order? Only through daily Mass, daily prayer. "And as we pray that our faith be increased, we will see Christ in each other, and we will not lose faith in those around us, no matter how stumbling their progress is. It is easier to have faith that God will support each House of Hospitality and farming commune and supply our needs in the way of food and money to pay bills, than it is to keep a strong, hearty, living faith in each individual around us—to see Christ in him. If we lose faith, if we stop the work of indoctrinating, we are in a way denying Christ again."[39]

January 1942: Inside a church on Mott Street, Dorothy writes a letter to Catholic workers, imploring God for wisdom. It is wartime, her country has been attacked, and yet she proclaims:

> We are still pacifists. Our manifesto is the Sermon on the Mount, which means that we will try to be peacemakers. Speaking for many of our conscientious objectors, we will not participate in armed warfare or in making munitions, or by buying government bonds to prosecute the war, or in urging others to these efforts.
>
> But neither will we be carping in our criticism. We love our country and we love our President. We have been the only country in the world where men and women of all nations have taken refuge from oppression. We recognize that while in the order of intention

35. Ellsberg, *Dorothy Day: Selected Writings*, 87.
36. Ellsberg, *Dorothy Day: Selected Writings*, 85.
37. Ellsberg, *Dorothy Day: Selected Writings*, 85.
38. Ellsberg, *Dorothy Day: Selected Writings*, 87.
39. Ellsberg, *Dorothy Day: Selected Writings*, 91–92.

we have tried to stand for peace, for love of our brothers
and sisters, in the order of execution we have failed as
Americans in living up to our principles.

We will try daily, hourly, to pray for an end to the
war.[40]

While we totally understand that there are profound differences
among us, regarding this so-important issue of conscientious objection, we continue to "beg that there will be mutual charity and
forbearance among us all."[41]

> *A brief reflection: Dorothy's passionately held pacifism
> cost her and the Catholic Worker movement dearly. She
> was standing up for what she profoundly believed; she
> could do no other. Nevertheless, many in the movement
> did not agree. Indeed, she felt attacked on all sides! Ac-
> cording to her granddaughter Kate, the years 1942 to
> 1944 were especially painful. "Many of the houses and
> farms around the country were closing down, and people
> blamed it on Dorothy. Even the town of Easton (Penn-
> sylvania) turned against them, and the police were on
> the lookout for any reason to arrest those on the farm."[42]*

**The 1940s, Dorothy's "severe-and-pious decade," so named by
Tamar:**[43] For both women, it was a grieving-the-loss-of-a-dream
time, a coming-to-terms-with-reality time. This will require four
snapshots.

First Tamar, her wedding on April 19, 1944, to David Hennessy:
It was never right. In truth, it would take Tamar thirty years to
finally admit to her youngest of nine, daughter Kate: "Within
weeks of the wedding, I knew I had made a terrible mistake."[44]
He was controlling; he was difficult. But she endured: birthing
and loving nine children and cultivating life on a farm: digging
her toes and her fingers into the good earth she loved, growing
food, spinning, and weaving.

Then Dorothy, so much promise before, so much stress now: Perhaps it was the intense struggle within the movement. Perhaps

40. Ellsberg, *Dorothy Day: Selected Writings*, 262.
41. Ellsberg, *Dorothy Day: Selected Writings*, 262.
42. Hennessy, *Day: Saved by Beauty*, 134.
43. Hennessy, *Day: Saved by Beauty*, 122.
44. Hennessy, *Day: Saved by Beauty*, 162.

it was Dorothy's continual wrestling with her own leadership
. . . *and* her mothering. How could Tamar or any child share a
mother with the whole world? Yes, Dorothy made careful ar-
rangements for Tamar's care whenever she responded to worldwide invitations. How could she *not* speak on the mission? How
could she *not* ignite the flame of her passion? Even though
Tamar *missed* her mother. Even when Dorothy *insisted* that she
knew what was best for her daughter. Then there was the inser-
tion of Father John Hugo, into the mission's ongoing retreats.
For Dorothy, his leadership offered perfection and joy! In the
form of his preaching staples: austerity and penance, hardship
and severity. Tamar found them cruel! Unbearable! Yet Dorothy
persisted in her choice of Father John . . . until, *finally,* her generous, loving, abundant nature won out over severity. But not
before driving a wedge between mother and daughter, already a
complicated, although loving, relationship.

**For both, the slow, painful death of Easton, the first communal
farm:** It started out with such promise. The first property owned
by the Catholic Worker, it had been purchased back in 1936 as a
working farm to support the bread lines on Mott Street, as well
as the forty or fifty retreatants who come for a week at a time.
In Dorothy's words: "It is a place to develop spiritual resources,
a place to think. It is a place of *action*, because we believe that
spiritual action is the hardest of all—to praise and worship
God, to thank Him, to petition Him for our brothers, to repent
our sins and those of others. This is action. . . . And just to lie in
the sun and let God work on you is to be sitting in the light of
the Sun of Justice."[45] For we are all called to be saints—"that is,
witnesses to the eternal."[46]

Tamar loved the place. She even had her very own tiny
cottage, built just for her by the skilled carpenter, Mr. McCon-
nell. Dorothy loved it, too. *For Peter it was his dream come true*:
the place "where it was easier for a people to be good." A place
of hard work, tilling the good earth, reading, conversation, and
feeding the hungry. With a "glorious" view besides, "overlook-
ing New Jersey and Pennsylvania, the Pocono Mountains, and
the Delaware Water Gap."[47]

45. Ellsberg, *Dorothy Day: Selected Writings*, 104.
46. Ellsberg, *Dorothy Day: Selected Writings*, 102.
47. Hennessy, *Day: Saved by Beauty*, 103.

Despite the hope from which it was birthed, the decade of the '40s witnessed its intense suffering, before its death knell. Easton suffered from lack of focus: working farm or retreat house? It suffered from the wartime loss of strong, young men to work the land. It suffered from lack of leadership. It suffered, finally, from the darkly tyrannical influence of a lawyer named Guy Tobler. In 1945, he moved in, little by little enslaving the couple in charge of the upper farm. They were Dorothy's friends, and she could find no way out of the mess. Except to retreat, heartbroken and defeated.

May 15, 1949, a final great loss of this decade, the death of Peter Maurin: He had been dying by inches, physically and then mentally over the previous five years. Indeed, it was as though he had suffered a stroke in his sleep, after which he "became silent," when "his great brain failed."[48] The words to his great love song . . . that profound passion for the good of each and every person created by God . . . simply would no longer come. Dorothy's only consolation was that "he had finished his work before his mind failed."[49] How she had *loved* him, despite their differences. In fact, Peter had left the *Worker* in 1939 for a year, truly believing that he was unwanted. Thankfully, for both, they reconciled. Truth be told, the strong-willed Dorothy realized—yet one more time— that she continually depended on his wisdom. For Tamar he was a kindred spirit, unfailingly kind, totally incapable of "small talk." His funeral Mass in New York City's Church of the Transfiguration was packed with people who celebrated his life's purpose. "Blessed are the pure in heart, for they will see God."[50]

December 27, 1957, from an article for *Commonweal* on being jailed: We are pacifists, so "we refused to take part in the war maneuvers, if you can call them that, the compulsory civil defense drills of the past three years . . .

"And so on three occasions we have been imprisoned. Each time we have gone through the grueling experience of torturous rides in the police van, sitting for long hours in prison cells awaiting booking or trial. In the first year, we had only an overnight

48. Ellsberg, *Dorothy Day: Selected Writings*, 124.

49. Ellsberg, *Dorothy Day: Selected Writings*, 125.

50. Matt 5:8, one of Matthew's beloved Beatitudes; this was an apt description of Peter Maurin.

experience of jail (which necessitated, however, the examinations for drugs, the humiliations of being stripped and showered and deprived of clothing and belongings). The second year the sentence was five days, and this last summer it was thirty days (with five days off for good behavior)."[51]

In the last imprisonment, we "passed through an experience which was as ugly and horrifying as any I may ever experience. We had been processed, and as we got off the elevators on the seventh floor to be assigned to our cells, clutching our wrappers around us, we were surrounded by a group of young women, black and white, who first surveyed us boldly and then started making ribald comments."[52] Judith, one of the three of us, was young and beautiful. "Put her in my cell," shouted one of the roughest. . . . No, another called out, "Let me have her."[53] Dorothy continued, "It was a real hubbub, ugly and distracting, coming as it did on top of contact with prison officials, officers, nurses, and so on."[54] I demanded that Judith be put with me, in my cell, and she was. Incredibly, these same prisoners gathered some clothes together for us so that we could go to Mass. "Prostitutes, drug addicts, forgers, and thieves had more loving-kindness toward us than our jailers, who had no sense of the practice of religion being a necessity to us, but acted as though it were a privilege which they could withhold."[55] Yes, Dorothy confessed, I had been judgmental. "Yes, we fail in love, we make judgments and we fail to see that we are all brothers, we all are seeking love, seeking God, seeking the beatific vision."[56]

November 29, 1980: A physically frail Dorothy gently exhales her last sigh, her final breath. She is attended during those tender hours only by daughter Tamar, just as Dorothy had wished. From this tiny circle of love overflowed circle around circle around circle of so many who held Dorothy in their hearts. There was Forster: Tamar's father and Dorothy's passionate love, who had long before reconciled with her. And hundreds, if not thousands, of Catholic Worker family members from around the globe. And

51. Ellsberg, *Dorothy Day: Selected Writings*, 278–79.

52. Ellsberg, *Dorothy Day: Selected Writings*, 290.

53. Ellsberg, *Dorothy Day: Selected Writings*, 290.

54. Ellsberg, *Dorothy Day: Selected Writings*, 290.

55. Ellsberg, *Dorothy Day: Selected Writings*, 292.

56. Ellsberg, *Dorothy Day: Selected Writings*, 293.

so many more, inspired by Dorothy "to do justice, and to love kindness, and to walk humbly with your God," despite the cost.[57] After her funeral liturgy at New York's Church of the Nativity, and burial on Staten Island at the Cemetery of the Resurrection, her tombstone was fitted with the most appropriate words of all, "Deo Gratias" (Thanks be to God).

In the end, what can we say? On September 24, 2015, Pope Francis said this. As he spoke before the United States Congress, he claimed her as one of four influential Americans, alongside Abraham Lincoln, Thomas Merton, and the Rev. Dr. Martin Luther King Jr. Earlier, *America* magazine had devoted its entire November 11, 1972, issue to her, on the occasion of her seventy-fifth birthday. In the words of the editors: "By now, if one had to choose a single individual to symbolize the best in the aspiration and action of the American Catholic community during the last forty years, that one person would be Dorothy Day." That passionately human disciple of Jesus. That prophet of peace, justice and nonviolence, intent on serving the most vulnerable among us and insistently advocating for them. That loving servant of God, on the first step of being considered for sainthood, as of March 16, 2000. That strong-willed, courageous, mistake-making woman of fierce, poured-out love. For one and for all.

In Conclusion

One word immediately comes to mind: *brave*, beyond all telling. Mark's Gospel was the very first! Written during a time of intense persecution. Written at a time when the emperor was *intent* on squashing the life out of these newly formed, pesky, but profoundly faithful communities of believers in Jesus, the Christ. Would Mark, whoever he was, be destroyed, as well? No matter. He was determined to proclaim his truth: Jesus, the Christ (*not* the emperor) was the *true* Son of God. *Only* Jesus, the Christ (*not* the emperor) was the ultimate Good News! How would he tell this story? Plainly, in spare fashion, without flourish, leading up to and including the passion of Jesus himself. Is it possible to even begin to imagine his courage?

In contemplating Mark's style and mission, one contemporary woman immediately came to my mind: Dorothy Day. She was a perfect fit! At exactly the right time, when she was searching for the best way to respond to her life's purpose, Peter Maurin sought her out. Together, with the courage of conviction, they set about creating something totally new: the Catholic

57. Mic 6:8.

Worker movement. Would this cost her? Yes. For it would mean giving up the human love of her life: Forster Batterham. It would also mean leaving her much-loved daughter Tamar in good hands, while she responded to calls to speak. Yes, the Catholic Worker movement was her passion, her best way of responding to God's call upon her life, often despite criticism, especially in the face of her conscientious objection to the Second World War. Like Mark, her style was direct, without flourish, intense, and always faithful to the center of her life: Jesus, the Christ.

7

Ordinary Time, According to Matthew (Cycle A)

A Beatitude for Teachers

Blessed are the teachers,
    whose heart-eyes penetrate the depths and dreams
    of their students.
Blessed are the teachers,
    whose blazing love can nurture and nudge
    their students' potential into being.
Blessed are the teachers,
    whose eager desire to inspire their charges
    and impart their hard-won knowledge
    can breathe new life into an exhausted, war-weary world.
Blessed are teachers forever etched in my heart:
    Mrs. Kimmel, teacher of history and kindness personified,
    Fr. Sebastian Falcone, whose passion for Scripture
        was matched only by his profound care for his students,
    David Turner, who took a chance on hiring a brand-new,
        green teacher.
Blessed, too, are the ones who have
    nourished *your* hearts with gladness.
Blessed are inspiring and generous theologians,
    like Elizabeth Johnson, who mentor their students
    into becoming their very best selves.
Blessed are our Evangelists: Matthew, Mark, Luke, and John,
    Profoundly in love with Jesus the Christ and

Profusely overflowing with God's Holy Spirit.

In collaboration with their own community,

They summoned stories, like pieces of a puzzle,

Fashioning them into unique, enlivening portraits,

Brilliant Creations of Love, Gospels bearing their names.

So that we might never forget . . .

So that we might be inspired to live . . .

More like this Jesus, the Christ,

Both now and forevermore. Amen!

Introducing Matthew, Theologian and Teacher: Enlivening Us with His Gospel of Jesus, the Christ.

Matthew. Who, exactly, was he? Maybe the scribe "who has been trained for the kingdom of heaven," or "the master of a household who brings out of his treasure what is new and what is old."[1] Or, perhaps the tax collector called by Jesus, as some have suggested.[2] We simply don't know, except to say this. He's Jewish, just like Jesus. Yet open, at the same time, to gentiles knocking on the door of his community. A brilliant and sometimes disturbing storyteller, he paints pictures of human desolation, depravity, and despair—the worst in people—alongside the best. Rooted in the Jewish law and the prophets, he's first and foremost a teacher. Inspired by Jesus to challenge all of us to live the law as God intends. Explaining it in so many different ways, that we might understand. Taking a full twenty-eight chapters to do so!

Curiously, while we know that Mark's Gospel was written first, Matthew's is given pride of place. Why? Perhaps because Matthew repeatedly quotes from the Hebrew Scripture, assuring us that Jesus fulfills the law and the prophets.[3] Or, maybe it is to call attention to his Jewish roots, and *ours*, as well.

Of this we can be fairly certain: the place and the time from which Matthew wrote. It was Antioch, in the 80s and 90s CE. Yes, we know about the fierce, ill-advised Jewish revolt of the late 60s. We know about the Roman army's revenge—the horrendous decimation of the Second Jerusalem Temple—that crushed the mortar and stone citadel of Jewish identity. We know about the Romans' final punctuation mark left on the Second Temple,

---

1. Matt 13:52.

2. Matt 9:9.

3. See Matt 1:22; 2:15, 17, 23; 4:12–16; 5:17; 8:17; and 12:17, for example.

well into Matthew's day: a pile of rubble, as the only visible reminder of its former glory.

Who, then, are the people for whom Matthew is writing? What, exactly, is going on in his community? Nothing less than this: a messy, brutal, nasty family feud. For the future of Judaism is at stake: the Jewish Pharisees pitted against the Jewish followers of Jesus. You see, the Essene communities, like the one at Qumran, had disappeared. So it was that a Pharisee named Johanan ben Zakkai gathered sages around himself to rebuild Judaism at the town of Jamnia. Locked in a contentious struggle with them for the hearts and souls of their neighbors were the Jewish disciples of Jesus, the Christ. Each of them vigorous. Each of them intense. Each determined to reign victorious.[4] The struggle back then was intense, often brutal, with unmistakable consequences for the future. We know, all too well, the anti-Semitism that has plagued human existence ever since. And yet, according to Scripture scholar Donald Senior, Matthew's Gospel also reveals the richness of our Jewish heritage, serving as a link to the Hebrew writings we once named the "Old Testament."[5]

What Is Unique about Matthew's Gospel?

The time has come for all of us to imagine ourselves in this Gospel. Imagine a dialogue between Matthew and each of us. Like you, I am a learner, one who longs to breathe life into Jesus of Nazareth, with and for us today. Like you, I long to better understand Jesus, in his world and the world of Matthew. Like you, I long to better understand the unique contributions that this evangelist makes to our experience of the One-beyond-All-Understanding. Like you, I long to worship Jesus in ways that penetrate the depths of my heart. So it is that I offer this dialogue with Matthew the Evangelist, as one way to approach Jesus. In this dialogue, Matthew and I will offer comments and raise questions, always for the purposes of revealing *his* unique understandings of Jesus and deepening our own. Please join me in this dialogue, with my sincere hope that we will *all* come to know Jesus, the Christ, more faithfully and more lovingly.

4. Jensen, *Preaching Matthew's Gospel*, 20; in this, he credits R. Smith, *Matthew*, 19–20.

5. From my memory of a talk given by Donald Senior at a June Institute, Georgetown University, 2016.

Matthew's Infancy Narrative, Chapters 1 and 2

Gloria: What truths about Jesus mattered most to you? In your day, nobody was still alive from the very beginning of Jesus' life. Yet you had stories, so many stories passed on from person to person and generation to generation. Like Luke, another evangelist, you took this raw material and fashioned a magnificent Gospel, complete with a two-chapter introduction of Jesus' beginnings. We call it an infancy narrative. How different they are from each other! And yet, each of you speaks truth about Jesus. What inspired *your* portrait?

Matthew: In my Jewish tradition, genealogies matter. Where do I come from? Where do I belong? What does that say about who I am? All the great people of our past were given a genealogy. So, of course, I began with Jesus "the Messiah, the son of David, the son of Abraham."[6] And I divided the generations from Abraham to King David, then David to the exile in Babylon, and finally the exile to the Messiah into fourteen generations each (or double the number seven, which signals perfection). I also tossed in a few surprises: five in fact, all women! Unheard of, in my day!

Gloria: Yes, I know them well! Please tell everyone else about them!

Matthew: There is Tamar, a widow, assured in the tradition of another marriage within the family for her protection. Yet when Judah, her father-in-law, refuses to honor her predicament, she takes matters into her own hands. Veiling herself, she plots to have sex with him—we call it incest—to secure her progeny and livelihood. In the end, however, Judah proclaims her "more in the right than I, since I did not give her to my son Shelah."[7] Then there is Rahab, the prostitute. *She's* the one who saves the people of Israel by assisting Joshua's two spies in the conquest of the promised land. She's *also* the very same one who becomes the great-great-grandmother of King David! There's the sainted Ruth, the Moabite, an outsider. Descended from a people *detested* by my ancestors, *she*—more than any other—embodies all that it means to live the covenant. There's my unnamed "wife of Uriah" the Hittite, whom you know as Bathsheba; she became one of

6. Matt 1:1.

7. Gen 38:26; her entire story is told in ch. 38, interrupting the story of Joseph.

David's wives and the mother of Solomon. But, how did this happen? Was it the result of *her* plotting to attract his attention? Or, was it David's predictable lusting desire, against her wishes? Or even both, in some measure? We simply don't know. And of course, ultimately, there is "Mary, of whom Jesus was born, who is called the Messiah."[8]

However, as I see it, Joseph—not Mary—takes center stage. This Joseph, the Just, is surely not unlike Joseph of old, the youngest of Jacob's twelve sons, the "dreamer," born of Rachel. Both are dreamers. Both heed the messages of their dreams. I couldn't help but wonder: What was he feeling? Was he totally confused? Even stunned? Unwilling to take Mary as his wife?

Gloria: According to one scholar I've discovered, Joseph is "fuming"! "Justly" angry at the news of Mary's pregnancy.[9] How could she! Even so, as you say in your Gospel, Joseph's compassion prevails; he will simply divorce her quietly. Until an angel of God speaks to him in a dream: "Do not be afraid to take Mary as your wife, for the child conceived in her is from the Holy Spirit."[10] Could it possibly be that he remembers words he knows well, words he has internalized, from Isaiah 42:1–6? According to scholar Kenneth Bailey, Joseph is now willing to become a "suffering servant" for Mary, whose situation he simply does *not* comprehend.[11]

Matthew: So it is that Jesus is born! Not just for Jews. But for *all* seekers, no matter *who* they are, no matter *where* they are from. What stories, what images could I create to proclaim *that* truth? Then I *knew*! Tell the story of the magi, those following light in the midst of any and every human darkness and division, struggle and strife. Where are they from? Somewhere east of us, definitely outsiders.[12] Where do they go for information about the newborn "king of the Jews," whose star they are following? To Herod the king, of course, in Jerusalem! And he's *terrified*: "Frightened, and all Jerusalem with him."[13] Herod's response?

---

8. Matt 1:16.

9. See Bailey, *Jesus through Middle Eastern Eyes*, 44–45.

10. Matt 1:20.

11. See Bailey, *Jesus through Middle Eastern Eyes*, 43–46.

12. Bailey, *Jesus through Middle Eastern Eyes*, 51–52; he believes the magi are from Arabia.

13. Matt 2:3.

Kill the child! Not only that: savagely slaughter *all* the innocents, just to make sure. We can *still* hear the agonizing wailing
of Rachel (the mothers of Israel) for their little ones . . . *who
are no more.* I *had* to tell the truth about the depths of human
depravity! For even in the joy of Jesus' birth, some *child* . . . some
children . . . some *families* suffer horrific pain.

Gloria: Oh, yes, how true! To this very day! For "Herod" is still
breathing murder on oh, so many children: physically, emotionally, and every which way. We *still* pause today with heavy hearts
on December 28, the Feast of the Holy Innocents. At the same
time, there are *still* dreamers today intent on listening to God.
Showing up on behalf of many stranded immigrants. *Refusing
to* collude with such butchery, the kind *still* capable of nailing
Jesus to the cross.

Matthew: While nothing can ease the profound grief of "Rachel,"
God *does* intervene on behalf of Jesus, directing Joseph through
yet another dream: "Flee to Egypt and remain there until I tell
you."[14] That is, *until* it is safe to return with the family, to Nazareth,
where Jesus grew up. As a faithful Jew, I *had* to proclaim that Jesus
follows in the liberating footsteps of Moses, servant of God, "for
he will save his people from their sins."[15] As for the magi, having
been warned about Herod's intentions in yet one more dream,
they "left for their own country by another road."[16] We can only
imagine the stories *they* might tell upon their return home.

Gloria: Indeed! What stories might *we* tell of following "another
road" in our *own* lives, a road totally unplanned, beyond our
wildest imaginations?

A Special Name for Jesus

Gloria: I know that you have a special name for Jesus: *Emmanuel,*
meaning "God is with us." Can you tell us why this name means
so much to you?

---

14. Matt 2:13.
15. Matt 1:21.
16. Matt 2:12.

Matthew: Yes, of course! It goes back to my Jewish roots, back to the eighth century before Jesus. As early as chapter 1, I assure everyone that Jesus fulfills God's promise of old to King Ahaz, as told by Isaiah, "Look, the virgin shall conceive and bear a son, and they shall name him *Emmanuel*, which means, 'God is with us.'"[17] Now, Ahaz was weak, under pressure both from the cruel Assyrians *and* a coalition of neighboring kingdoms arrayed against the Assyrians. A weakling in faith, as well, he refused the offer. But God honored it anyway! It seemed possible, then, to fairly *shout*: God's promise is true! In Jesus! *He* is *Emmanuel*, God with us! Not only that, I ended my Gospel with the risen Jesus commissioning his first disciples, and all of us: "And remember, I am with you always, to the end of the age."[18] In between, Jesus assures us all: "Again, truly I tell you, if two of you agree on earth about anything you ask, it will be done for you by my Father in heaven. For where two or three are gathered in my name, I am there among them."[19] What comfort it was for our community, simply struggling to survive! How about for you?

Gloria: Yes, I have surely needed to know that God *is* with me, through thick and thin. Sometimes I imagine Jesus as an older brother, the very *best* older brother, one I've craved as an only child. In fact, I have experienced your invitation of Jesus to each of us as a brotherly summons: "Come to me, all you that are weary and carrying heavy burdens, and I will give you rest. Take my yoke upon you, and learn from me; for I am gentle and humble in heart, and you will find rest for your souls. For my yoke is easy, and my burden is light."[20] This much is certainly true: *anything* is possible with Jesus at my side.

The Beatitudes: Beginning of the Sermon on the Mount
(First of Five Sermons)

Matthew: This teaching sets the tone and content of the entire Gospel. For I must tell you: I deliberately patterned my five

---

17. Matt 1:23 and Isa 7:10–14; some translations say "young woman" rather than "virgin."

18. Matt 28:20.

19. Matt 18:19–20.

20. Matt 11:28–30.

discourses after what was thought to be the first five books of the
so-called Old Testament, traditionally assigned to Moses.[21] Jesus
is Jewish, the fulfillment of our tradition, even greater than Moses himself. So, of course, he continually quotes from the Jewish
law and prophets. And he *must* deliver five great sermons (or discourses). At the same time, gentiles keep knocking on our door.
Could they come in? Would it be proper? What would Jesus say
about that? Is my community meant to be Jewish? Gentile? Both?
At first, it seemed to me that we *are* meant to be Jewish. For Jesus
sends his disciples only to "the lost sheep of the house of Israel."[22]
However, not long afterward, Jesus encounters a Canaanite woman, from a race "hated" by Israelites. It's quite the conversation!
He's insulting! She's intent on her purpose: to wrest from Jesus
the healing of her daughter.[23] She kneels before him. Pleads with
him. Pursues her need, undaunted by his insult. Until *finally*, she
elicits these words from Jesus: "Woman, great is your faith! Let
it be done for you as you wish."[24] It is *not* by accident that I place
this encounter near the very center of my Gospel. For it reflects
my *community's* wrestling with its *own* change of heart, to reach
out beyond itself. To strangers, gentiles, to *any* who are insulted.
Wounded and in need. Do *you* know what I mean?

Gloria: Do we ever! Think of all our refugees! Our immigrants!
But first, back to the Mount of the Beatitudes. I was actually there!
It was May 2008, and I was on pilgrimage in the Holy Land with
some thirty or so other women. It was our first stop, of course.
Sunny and in the eighties, it seemed that the whole world was in
bloom! Not far in the distance, we caught a glimpse of the Sea
of Galilee. Imagine with me, then, the crowds of people. Some
curious, others on the verge of following Jesus. But his disciples,
like us, are up close. Hanging upon every word.

Matthew: Blessing upon blessing upon blessing: on the poor in
spirit, the mourning, the meek, those hungering and thirsting
for righteousness, the merciful, the pure in heart, peacemakers,
even the reviled.[25] The very ones so often left out . . . ignored . . .

---

21. We now realize, of course, that there were other hands and hearts at work creating those five books.

22. Matt 10:6.

23. Matt 15:21–28.

24. Matt 15:28. We are told that "her daughter was healed instantly."

25. This is the only place in Scripture where the word "peacemaker" is used.

shunted aside . . . even despised! Did he really mean *them*? Are the blessings "for real"?

Gloria: I am reminded of a contemporary author of Celtic spirituality, John O'Donohue, now deceased. Here's what he says about blessings. "A blessing is a circle of light drawn around a person to protect, heal, and strengthen. Life is a constant flow of emergence. The beauty of blessing is its belief that it can affect what unfolds."[26] Blessings can even serve as "sheltering walls" during life's tough times, holding out hope for transformation.[27]

Matthew: Yes! What profound truth! For Jesus immediately . . . and boldly . . . proclaims: these very folks sitting before him are "salt of the earth" and "light of the world."[28] I could not help but wonder. Does Jesus pause . . . for a moment . . . to let that truth soak in? Before issuing challenge upon challenge upon challenge that he sets before them (and us)? Like, living as *God* intends. Making tough choices, lined up with God. Setting things right in our broken, heartbroken world. Even going beyond the righteousness "of the scribes and Pharisees."[29] *Here* is what I proclaim, at the conclusion of this first of Jesus' sermons: "the crowds were astounded at his teaching, for he taught them as having authority, and not as their scribes."[30]

Gloria: What about us? Whose preaching has moved us, in our day, with the authority, integrity, and purpose of Jesus? With what results?

---

26. O'Donohue, *To Bless the Space between Us*, 198. This author was born in 1956 and raised in Ireland; an extraordinarily gifted writer of spirituality, he died while still in his fifties, leaving behind much wisdom for the world.

27. O'Donohue, *To Bless the Space between Us*, 203.

28. Matt 5:13–14.

29. Matt 5:20.

30. Matt 7:28–29; can you not hear these words emerge from the conflict going on in his community?

To What Extent Have We Lived the Beatitudes?
The Last Judgment Scene (25:31–24);
Gospel for the Last Sunday of the Year,
(Feast of Christ the King, Cycle A)

Matthew: Remember, now: the Beatitudes set the stage for this entire Gospel.

Gloria: Likewise, they set the stage for our liturgical year according to your Gospel, normally showing up on the Fourth Sunday in Ordinary Time of Year A (early in February). By year's end, *you* are asking *us*: Who is *our* king? Whom do we worship? Does *our* king match up with *your* portrait of Christ the King?

Matthew: What do we make of this vulnerable king? He's hungry, thirsty, sorrowing, suffering in so many ways, even to the point of being reviled. For I deliberately follow this scene of judgment with the passion, whereby Jesus is the most reviled of all: condemned, bloodied, beaten, writhing in pain, left to die nearly alone, except for the women. Where do *we* enter in? Is this "last judgment" scene meant to be put off until the end of our lives? Or, in fact, might it be the measure of our lives each and every day for the entire year? Have we, in fact, sought out the hungry, the sorrowing, and those suffering in so many ways? Have we tried to console and heal, comfort and advocate for their needs? And, in the process, have *we* come to terms with our *own* vulnerability, our *own* poverty, our *own* need for this God who is within us and among us? In other words, have we become capable of witnessing Christ in *all* the most vulnerable, including ourselves? Yesterday, today, tomorrow, *each and every* day?

The Passion

Matthew: My passion account follows Mark, but is longer, more thorough. I *must* include some significant pieces that he left out. In a Gospel where human sin, even degradation, is boldly named, repentance and forgiveness are absolutely essential. In a Gospel where dreams urge human response, I paint yet one more dream as a warning to Pilate. In a Gospel where human machinations abound, I unabashedly proclaim the beyond-all-imagining power of God, over which humans have absolutely no control.

In a Gospel where God shatters human conniving, earthquakes signal that nothing will ever again be the same! The end times are here! So it is that:

1. Jesus calls Judas "friend," as the latter is about to betray him, highlighting the magnitude of the betrayal;

2. Judas profoundly repents, attempting in vain to return the thirty pieces of silver, before hanging himself;

3. the wife of Pilate—in one final dream of this Gospel—warns her husband, "have nothing to do with that innocent man, for today I have suffered a great deal because of a dream about him";[31]

4. Pilate attempts to wash away his guilt by washing his hands of the crucifixion;

5. the earth quakes at the death of Jesus, instantly bursting open the tombs of ancient saints;

6. and a human guard is set at the tomb of Jesus, utterly useless in the face of God's unsurpassed power in raising Jesus from the dead.

Gloria: As contemporary writer Jim Dunning has pointed out, in your Gospel there's a lot of "quaking" going on, beginning to end: massive disturbances, shattering human expectations, the "birth pangs of a new world."[32] Announcing the One and Only Jesus, the long-awaited Messiah, rooted in the Jewish people (the son of David, the son of Abraham). Announcing the One and Only Jesus, the Christ, who would *not* stay dead!

(*Gloria: Here are two related questions that Matthew cannot answer, for I have not discovered any scholarly comment on them. Why is Matthew alone in saying that Judas repented of his betrayal? Surely, God would forgive him, but the Pharisees would have none of it. Was this because of the bitter family feud with the Pharisees? I wonder.*)

---

31. Matt 27:19.

32. Dunning, *Echoing God's Word*, 227. He points to the "quaking" fear of Herod "and all Jerusalem with him" (Matt 2:3) at the wise men's question: "Where is the child who has been born king of the Jews?" (Matt 2:2).

Living in-between Times as Church (Ecclesia)

Gloria: You may not realize, Matthew, that you are the only Gospel writer who devotes an entire chapter to "ecclesia," to an ordered Church life.[33] Why was this so important to you?

Matthew: In my day, some fifty years after Jesus, small communities of his followers were sprouting up here, there, and everywhere, needing strength and courage. For persecution was always around the corner. We *had* to be faithful to the hopes and dreams of Jesus.

Gloria: How did you set out this ordering?

Matthew: "Who is the greatest in the kingdom of heaven?"[34] That question, so often pressed upon Jesus by the disciples, set the stage for my ordering. Disciples ever since have wrestled with Jesus' response. "Truly I tell you, *unless you change* and become like children, you will never enter the kingdom of heaven."[35] In other words, forget privilege. Become humble. Become one of the "little ones." For in *them* you will find *me. Welcome* them. And *never,* ever, put a stumbling block in their way. Even amputate a foot or an eye, if those get in your way. Do whatever it takes to restore a lost little one. For that is what God would do. Finally: *forgive.* Go out of your way to forgive; take the initiative. Go to the one who has caused offense. If that doesn't work, return, with a couple of witnesses. If *that* doesn't work, take it to the Church. And, if *that* doesn't work, "let such a one be to you as a Gentile and a tax collector."[36] (We might squirm at this, for we all know how Jesus treated gentiles and tax collectors, don't we?)

But always, always know this: the community *must* be involved in the process of forgiveness. "Truly I tell you, whatever you bind on earth will be bound in heaven, and whatever you loose on earth will be loosed in heaven."[37] *The community itself,* gathered in prayer, has the power to retain or forgive, bind or loose! *Peter* gets it. Or *thinks* he does. After all, Jesus has just recently pronounced Peter as "the rock," upon whom I will build

---

33. See ch. 18 of Matthew's Gospel.
34. Matt 18:1b.
35. Matt 18:3; my emphasis.
36. Matt 18:17.
37. Matt 18:18.

my Church.[38] Believing himself to be extravagant when Jewish custom only demands forgiveness four times, Peter asks: Do I even have to forgive *seven* times? Uh, no, Peter, says Jesus. Instead, how about seventy-seven times . . . or seventy times seven times . . . or endlessly? Oh . . . then, for final emphasis, I drew upon a Jesus story to conclude my chapter on Church life.[39]

Gloria: Yes, it is sometimes called the Parable of the King's Accounting, or, The Unforgiving Servant. I've wrestled with it myself. Would you tell the story?

Matthew: It seems that a king wanted to settle accounts with his slaves. One of them owed him ten thousand talents: the largest number in Greek vocabulary, and the heftiest of monetary units. In effect, more money than could ever possibly be imagined! Let alone repaid! So much, in fact, that the king ordered him—along with his family—to be sold! But, the slave *pleaded*, on his knees, for patience to repay (an impossibility, given the size of the debt.) The king, then, mercifully forgave his debt!

Yet, that very *same* slave *immediately* refused to forgive another slave's much smaller debt (a hundred denarii, the wage for one hundred days' work). Witnesses to this cruelty were "distressed"! So much so, that they reported it directly to the king.

Gloria: Not unlike today's "whistleblowers"!

Matthew: So, then, his wrath stirred up, the king handed him over to be tortured with these words: "Should you not have had mercy on your fellow slave, as I had mercy on you?"[40] Jesus concludes: "So my heavenly Father will also do to every one of you, if you do not forgive your brother or sister from your heart."[41]

Gloria: Ouch! Is this "harshness" too much for us?

Matthew: Remember now, what *is* going on in this chapter. Recall Jesus' praise of the "little ones" as "greatest" in the kingdom of heaven. Recall God's compassion, like a shepherd retrieving the one lost sheep.[42] Recall Jesus' urgent, constant, continual call

38. Matt 16:18.
39. Matt 18:23–34.
40. Matt 18:33.
41. Matt 18:35.
42. Matt 18:10–14.

to forgive. Recall Jesus' assurance as Emmanuel: "For where two or three are gathered in my name, I am there among them."[43] Finally, recall Jesus' handing over of binding and loosing to the *community*.[44]

Gloria: Oh! God will honor human decisions! Maybe that's it! *Does Jesus intend to give us responsibility for treating others with God's generosity?* If so, isn't it possible that the "king's" inability to forgive is more reflective of *human* inability to forgive rather than *God's* unwillingness to forgive? And, if *we're* unwilling to forgive as God does, who gets hurt the most? In the end, aren't *we* the ones who suffer from remaining bound up? I wonder.

His Parables as Guides to Our Common Life

Matthew: How could I get people to take a second . . . third . . . or fourth look at themselves? To consider other possibilities? Do what Jesus did, of course! Tell parables! My parable of the net is pretty straightforward.[45] Yes, there *is* a sorting out that happens in the end. But in other parables, not so much. Take the story of the merchant in search of fine pearls (13:45–46). Most see this as encouragement to pursue what's most valuable. True. But, it's the only one that deals with a member of the upper class, for pearls point to great wealth. Might it also warn against being greedy? And, encourage the holding of gifts lightly, that they might be shared? What if the merchant loses everything in the end, since he's already spent *all that he has* on this pearl?

Gloria: Or, consider the parable of the weeds and the wheat (13:24–30) . . . *and* its interpretation (13:36–43). Certainly, this parable seems to suggest the patience of God, who simply longs for our repentance, our turning . . . again and again and again. And yet, there's a fire-and-brimstone ending. So, what's this about? Is it an urgent plea to remember that evil will be punished, in the end? And, that God alone is judge of good and evil?

Matthew: Indeed, *here* is the ultimate question: how does God decide? Righteousness—what's right in God's eyes—is a thread

43. Matt 18:20.
44. Matt 18:18, where Jesus is speaking to the entire community.
45. Matt 13:47–50.

running throughout my Gospel. I couldn't help but reflect on Judas. He *must* have profoundly repented of his betrayal.[46] For he throws down the "thirty pieces of silver," trying to make it right. But the chief priests and elders will have none of it! Only then does Judas—utterly hopeless and despondent—commit suicide. *How does God greet Judas, in the end?* I do not know. All I can do is trust in God's goodness.

Gloria: Another of your parables leaves me scratching my head, saying, "What do you suppose Jesus meant by that?" Let's take a closer look at the parable of the Landowner Who Went Out Early,[47] otherwise entitled "Am I Not Doing You Right?" by Scripture scholar Bernard Brandon Scott.[48] I imagine that the story might go like this, if told by one of the first-hired men.

"It's not fair! I go out, every morning, with my buddies, to get work for the day. To keep house and home together. To feed our families. Oh, we'll never get rich, not even close, but we manage to get by. We're strong. Healthy. Always chosen first by the steward who comes out to hire for the day. And off we go, to put in a hard day's work. In the blazing sun. Until our necks, our hands, our backs, and our muscles everywhere, simply ache. That's just how it is. Except for one time, a time I'll never forget. All I could do, along with my buddies, was simply howl in protest: It's not fair!

"This one day was different, that's for sure. As it turns out, the landowner *himself* came out, looking to hire. Not just once, first thing in the morning . . . but also at the third hour (nine o'clock) . . . then again at the sixth hour (noon) . . . at the ninth hour (three o'clock) . . . and *finally*, one more time, at the eleventh hour (five o'clock). Why?! He has a manager who does that kind of work. But there's even more! He showed up to dole out the payment for the day. He *never* does that! Then, as if adding insult to injury, he had us all stand around, waiting for our pay, starting with the last ones hired. Already, we're restless. Exhausted. Aching, from a full day's labor. Shouldn't we just receive our pay so we can get home and rest? But, no! To our utter amazement, everyone—starting with the last one hired, and ending with us, who labored long and hard in the heat of the day—we *each*

46. See Matt 27:3–5.
47. See Matt 20:1–15.
48. See Scott, *Hear Then the Parable*, 281.

received the *same* full day's wage! I ask you, is that fair?! I didn't stick around to enjoy the glee of the ones who came in last. No way!"

    In reply, someone might say: "But it was a just wage. You agreed to it. Did you ever stop to think what it might have been like for the last ones hired? Here they were, worn out and sickly . . . with no marketable skills . . . with only the tiniest shred of hope that *someone, anyone*, would come along and have pity on them, so that they wouldn't have to slink home yet one more time with nothing to offer a waiting wife and children. No? Then consider this: now they can burst in the door with a triumphant, 'Look! We can eat! At least for a little bit!' Can you put yourselves in their shoes, even for a moment?"

Matthew: We can all whine, complain, and protest, can't we? Whenever *our* sense of justice (the question raised three times in this parable but never answered) doesn't seem to fit. Where *do* we fit in this story? Remember, now, we *are* talking about the kingdom of heaven.[49] About a landowner who doesn't act like one. Who keeps on returning to hire the ones left behind. Who even doles out paychecks to everyone, in plain sight. How do *we*, who so often place such an emphasis on *earning* what's right and good and just, deal with the grace of God? This *inexplicable, overflowing grace* of God. Even for the ones who squeak into the kingdom of heaven at the very last moment. Aren't we all here in the first place by the grace of God? True enough: we hone and develop our God-given gifts with hard work; but they *do* come from God. Don't they? And, we know *joy* in the use of them? Don't we? Oh, and one more question: can we possibly *rejoice* in being part of that kind of kingdom, even for the ones who don't "deserve" it? Isn't Jesus trying to correct our eyesight? Or, more accurately, our *heart-sight*? Especially for the "little ones," the vulnerable ones, the ones who are "greatest" in the kingdom of God? The ones who aren't trapped in ego and power. The ones for whom he gives thanks to his Father (in Matt 11:25). I wonder. Maybe you do, as well.

---

49. I, Gloria, always prefer the word "kin-dom," which expresses community, while also being inclusive. But I continue with the word "kingdom," since it references Matthew's use of the word.

Gloria: It has been noted, Matthew, that you continually refer to the *kingdom of heaven*, rather than the kingdom of God, in these parables and throughout the Gospel. Why is that?

Matthew: As a faithful Jew, I was taught to refrain from using God's name out of reverence. Yet in Jesus, the kingdom of heaven was being established.

Gloria: Yes, just like Jesus, you told us stories—parables—about this kingdom. Powerful enough to draw us in. To engage us. To imagine where we belong in the story. To *name* our place in the story. In doing so, to answer for ourselves the all-important question: what is the reign of God like? Or, as one contemporary commentator says, "The parable suggests, but it leaves to its hearer the responsibility for meaning."[50]

Commissioning of Disciples of Every Age,
as Guides for Others

Matthew:

> Now the eleven disciples went to Galilee, to the mountain to which Jesus had directed them. When they saw him, they worshiped him; but some doubted. And Jesus came and said to them, "All authority in heaven and on earth has been given to me. Go therefore and make disciples of all nations, baptizing them in the name of the Father and of the Son and of the Holy Spirit, and teaching them to obey everything that I have commanded you. And remember, I am with you always, to the end of the age." (28:16–20)

The first disciples are sent to *all* people, to outsiders and gentiles, to anyone and everyone who is "different." A generation later, the apostle Paul—himself a Pharisee—had come to this realization. Recall that in the 50s he had written to the feisty Galatians: in baptism, "there is no longer Jew or Greek, there is no longer slave or free, there is no longer male and female; for all of you are one in Christ Jesus."[51]

---

50. Scott, *Hear Then the Parable*, 280.
51. Gal 3:28.

Gloria: And *your* generation, Matthew, in the 80s, wrestled with this truth, as has every generation ever since. Today we gustily sing "All Are Welcome," but do we really mean it? Do we really believe it? Do we really live it?

Matthew: Please be sure to note, as well, that the first disciples *worship* Jesus on this *mountain*. Was this the scene of his transfiguration? Or, can they now see in the risen Jesus what was only hinted at earlier? In any case, they simply *had* to worship him! Not unlike the magi, first to visit the child Jesus, who "knelt down and paid him homage"[52] before offering him "gifts of gold, frankincense, and myrrh."[53]

Gloria: Only in your Gospel, Matthew, is Jesus continually worshiped, beginning to end.

Matthew: Finally, Jesus—Emmanuel—leaves us with these words: "Remember, I am with you always, to the end of the age."[54] They are *not* words to perfect people. They *are* words to his first disciples—sinners all—for they worshiped, "but some doubted."[55]

Gloria: They are also words to *us*: sinners all, with our warts and flaws and doubts. Along with our abiding desire to worship Jesus. For he proclaimed to *us*, as well, "I am with you always." To which we respond, loud and clear: Amen!

Elizabeth Johnson: Extraordinary in her Teaching, Theologizing, and Humanity

I struggled to imagine what it must have been like for our first evangelists. Here they were, human just like us, left with so many stories of Jesus. Did they say to themselves, "We *must* remember Jesus! And his stories! We simply cannot forget!" How did they possibly take upon themselves, in conversation with their community, the enormous task of probing the Mystery of God in the person of Jesus Christ? They only knew this: he meant the whole world to them. They had to get it right! And they did, different as they were from one another.

---

52. Matt 2:11.
53. Matt 2:11.
54. Matt 28:20, the very last words of his Gospel.
55. Matt 28:17.

As I considered their vast contributions to us, as I specifically considered Matthew and *his* Gospel, I questioned: Who models for us today that
same dedication? Who has that same ability to teach, profoundly, having
probed for herself the Mystery of God as found in Jesus, the Christ? Who
today stands out as an extraordinary theologian, continually nourishing us
at Jesus' Feast of Life? One woman immediately came to mind: Elizabeth
Johnson. I had heard her speak. I have devoured most of her books. And I
have been impressed with her ability to "bring out of" her "treasure what is
new and what is old."[56] In this, she is like "every scribe who has been trained
for the kingdom of heaven."[57] I just love and deeply appreciate the way she
probes our tradition, only to faithfully raise new questions. New thoughts.
New possibilities, always within the scope of what we already believe. To all
this, I add her generosity of spirit. Elizabeth and I really don't know each
other, though she once told me that my two earlier books on women in
Scripture and tradition helped create a bridge of understanding for her
students. When I tentatively asked if she would consider answering a few
questions for this book, she agreed.

Introducing Elizabeth Johnson, for Those Unfamiliar with Her Work

A relatively new book, *Elizabeth Johnson: Questing for God*, by Heidi
Schlumpf, brought to life the humanity and magnificence of this woman I
would love to know better.[58] Indeed, I had experienced Elizabeth's engaging
speaking ability, along with her brilliant, yet clear, scholarship. But this book
helped root me in the person behind her books.

From the first, she is a Sister of St. Joseph of Brentwood, having entered her beloved order in 1959, just prior to the Second Vatican Council.
While the rigid rules of community living, early on, raised doubts about her
choice, the liberating wind of Vatican II convinced her of its rightness. Like
some other sisters, she pursued college studies at Brentwood College, before becoming a teacher, first to elementary kids, then to middle and high
school students. How impressive, I thought, that she could excite and teach
youngsters of all ages! But it was the study of theology that would become her
passion, while earning a master's degree in religious studies from Manhattan
College in the Bronx. During most of the 1970s, then, she ignited the flame
of theological questioning in her high school students before doing the same
at St. Joseph's College. By 1977, it became obvious that she would study for

56. Matt 13:52.
57. Matt 13:52, again.
58. See the bibliography; this book was published in 2016.

a doctorate in theology. Her choice? Catholic University of America, with its first-rate professors in systematic theology. Listen to her words: "I have a desire to make a contribution myself in the field of systematic theology, dialoguing with our ancient tradition from the standpoint of the American experience, of the American woman's experience. There is a dearth of good women theologians in our Church, in all the churches, and I would expect that in some way I could make an enriching contribution."[59]

What a colossal contribution she has made! Brilliance of mind, humility yet confidence of purpose, hard work, kindness and nonviolence of spirit along with the courage to speak her truth would merge and continually grow in her. *But* not without a struggle! One major obstacle was earning tenure at Catholic University of America (CUA), where she had begun teaching in 1981. Because CUA was a pontifical university, its board of trustees included six American cardinals. All were positively disposed toward Elizabeth, except for Cardinal Bernard Law. Hostile is not too strong a word about his attitude toward her, but he did not prevail. She was tenured; but, in the end, Elizabeth sought a place where she could freely and faithfully ask the questions she simply *had* to pursue. That place was Fordham, back in her beloved New York City, where she has served with distinction since 1991. Despite the heft of her teaching and writing, she is no academic prima donna, according to Christine Firer Hinze, director of the Curran Center for American Catholic Studies at Fordham. On the contrary, she rolls up her sleeves and contributes to her share of departmental work. Above all, she loves mentoring her students!

One more controversy is worth mentioning. The year is 2011. The date, March 29. The book is her *Quest for the Living God*, written primarily—like *Consider Jesus*—for people studying to pursue ministry, a broader audience than a strictly academic one. The United States Bishops' Committee on Doctrine began investigating this book, though it had been out in people's hands for four years at that point. Why the investigation? Nobody knew. But on that date Cardinal Timothy Dolan delivered that information to Elizabeth and Fordham's president, Fr. Joseph M. McShane. Had the committee followed its own guidelines for pursuing such an investigation? No. There was no advance dialogue. Did it come "out of the blue"? Yes. Was there room for discussion? Apparently not. The committee simply warned: this book "completely undermines the Gospel and the faith of those who believe in the Gospel."[60] Elizabeth chose not to respond at first. Then, believing that

59. Elizabeth A. Johnson, "Statement of Purpose," Application to the Catholic University of America, Spring 1977, Elizabeth A. Johnson Papers, box 1, file 10, University of Notre Dame Archives, Notre Dame, IN, in Johnson, 42.

60. Committee on Doctrine, statement on *Quest for the Living God*, in Schlumpf,

there might be a dialogue and an opportunity for teaching, she submitted a carefully worded thirty-eight-page paper, addressing each concern. But, there was no response; the committee only repeated its charges in October. The author of these charges, Doctrine Committee Chairman Thomas Weinandy, OFM Cap., had publicly rebuked five prominent theologians in his eight years as committee chair, angering many competent theologians. Some even questioned: Had his misreading of Elizabeth's book been willful? There never was an answer to that question.

As for Elizabeth? It only brought award after award and accolade upon accolade; loving support by Elizabeth's colleagues at Fordham, the Catholic Theological Society of America, and elsewhere; the eternal gratitude of her Sisters of St. Joseph; the 2015 LCWR (Leadership Conference of Women Religious) leadership award in profound appreciation for her entire ministry; the devotion of many students; and even lots of flowers and chocolate. Elizabeth Johnson: what a gift to our Church and to our world!

My Questions and Elizabeth's Response

Question 1: *It occurs to me that your theological ministry of probing the Mystery of God is not unlike that of the Gospel authors, who plumbed the depths of God's incarnation in Jesus. Their work and yours is faith-filled, faithful, and passionate, intending to inspire others into ever deepening levels of believing. Would you be willing to comment on this?*

Elizabeth's Response: The way Edward Schillebeeckx put it, Christians of every generation need to be writing the fifth gospel. All should do it with their lives; some in each generation have the skill and desire to express the good news in a new idiom. Writing the fifth gospel is essential because culture changes, and so do people's anxieties and grief, joys, and hopes. What made sense in one time and place can lose it relevance in another. The ancient wisdom needs to be heard anew so it can be lived out with a new justice.

The context for this gospel writing, both in the first century, through the ages, and again now, is the community of faith. With an ear to the questions of four different early Christian communities, the original evangelists (the fab four!) crafted four different tellings of the story of Jesus. Theologians in every

---

Elizabeth Johnson, 104.

age since have taken to scroll and quill, paper and pen, or computer keyboard to interpret the good news afresh. The joy and challenge of my life has been to participate in this centuries-long sweep of a vocation to bring faith into meaningful relationship with contemporary culture.

Question 2: *By the time the Gospels were written, there were already several layers of understanding swirling around Jesus, the Christ. And you, some twenty centuries later, face the awesome task of unveiling many more such layers, always to reach more truth about Jesus. How do you approach your work in this regard?*

Elizabeth's Response: What is essential for my own work is listening, listening, listening to the questions and insights of people today about Jesus; then thinking in a discerning way about what is going on in their minds and hearts; then searching for a good word that will bring forth truth.

For example, women's distress over how Jesus is used to shore up patriarchal structures which exclude them from ministry, and their need to "redeem" him; the discovery of Jesus' liberating intent by the poor church of Latin America; African American's critique of the cross as payment for sin, and their insistence that it shows Jesus accompanying the victims of racism, suffering with them in order to bring about victory; the connection of Jesus with all flesh, including animals and plants, which leads to ecological care—all these and many more angles of vision become starting points for interpreting Jesus today. Without listening, though, I would just go on repeating the ancient pieties which would grow more and more irrelevant.

Question 3: *As a woman who longs for the full participation of women in my beloved Roman Catholic Church, I am deeply grateful for your work on images of God in* She Who Is *and for your consideration of saints as Wisdom-filled people in* Friends of God and Prophets. *What feeds your hope for women's full and equal participation in our Church?*

Elizabeth's Response: What feeds my hope that the movement of women for full participation in the church will succeed is that in the most profound sense this is the work of the Holy Spirit. And she will not be quenched.

Question 4: *You have all the qualities of a gifted teacher who cares deeply for her students. What would you most want to pass along to other teachers regarding this ministry?*

Elizabeth's Response: In a conference I gave to the current crop of theological students at my university, I said it comes down to this: you teach with your whole self. If you are just going through the motions, bored with the routine work, you will not light a spark. But if you attend to the wonder at the heart of it all, you will be energized afresh for every encounter with students. You teach with your whole self. If you love your students as well as the subject, they will catch the spirit of it. You teach through loving, even if now and then you have to give some student an F.

Question 5: *What other words of Wisdom do you have for us at a time such as ours, when clericalism, sex abuse, and the ongoing struggle for women's equality can challenge our hope for the future?*

Elizabeth's Response: We cannot choose the times we live in. For every human being who wants to live a meaningful life, the call is to be aware of what is going on, and respond with one's gifts in ways that make a contribution. As you say, our time has more than enough scandals that could lead one to despair. But note the good things that are happening; search out community; lend your voice to the compassion of God in the world. In our day the global character is becoming more apparent, with long silent voices beginning to be heard; this can have unforeseen good effects. How things will develop is not at all clear. But reform of the church is the work of infinite Love who has already raised the crucified Jesus from the dead. Reason enough to hope, despite the current mess.

Thank you, Elizabeth Johnson!

In Conclusion

One word immediately comes to mind: *thorough.* Matthew, the teacher, simply *had* to get his story right. Would this mean adding to Mark's account? Yes, absolutely! Would it mean creating the longest of the four canonical Gospels? Yes, once again, though that was not necessarily his intent. For *his* purpose was to create the most *complete* version. The most exhaustive. The version that would include new parables, new stories, new ways of describing Jesus. His painstakingly exact style could on occasion even become inspiring: as in his Sermon on the Mount and his account of the last judgment. At the same time, Matthew—rooted in Judaism—*had* to begin with a genealogy of Jesus. In his tradition, all men (yes, it was always men) of importance had a genealogy. From the beginning, then (1:1), Matthew was absolutely clear: this was "the genealogy of Jesus the Messiah, the son of David, the son of Abraham."

What contemporary woman reflected that same exactitude, that same desire to share her knowledge abundantly with her students? One woman stood out for me: none other than Sr. Elizabeth Johnson, brilliant and thorough professor of the good news of Jesus, the Christ. A prolific author of theology, she has challenged so many—myself included—to probe the person of Jesus ever more deeply, ever more truthfully, ever more lovingly. Elizabeth has the ability to closely examine our tradition, all the while faithfully raising new questions and new approaches to what we already understand to be true. She persistently approaches every subject this way, always in love with Jesus, the Christ, and always with a deep regard for her students' benefit. Clearly, she is one of the extraordinary teachers of our day.

8

Ordinary Time, According to Luke
(Cycle C)

A Blessing as We Set Out with Luke on
Jesus' Journey to Jerusalem and Beyond

Jesus Proclaimed:
Blessed are those who hear the word of God and obey it:[1]

May we who have heard and seek to obey, set out expectantly
    on pilgrimage to Jerusalem, with Luke as our day-in, day-out guide.
May we tread openheartedly with this Gospel's first prophets:
    Elizabeth, mother of John the Baptist; Mary, mother of Jesus;
    Anna, aged widow who spread the good news of the infant Jesus;
    Zechariah, father of John the Baptist; and Simeon, upon *finally*
    seeing the Saving Instrument of God in Jesus.
May we, like them, attend to unexpected stirrings in our own souls,
    and give voice to their murmurings.
May we, like the woman anointer, dare to shatter the customs
    that would stifle our profuse love, birthed out of forgiveness.
May we, like the woman rejoicing at finding her lost coin,
    and the prodigal father, who never gave up on his wayward son,
    grow into the image of the prodigally merciful God of Jesus.
May we, like the widow, doggedly demanding justice
    from the unjust judge, reveal yet one more face of
    our Never-Giving-Up-on-Us God.
May we, like the women at the empty tomb,

---

1. Taken from Luke 11:28.

remember everything about Jesus,
and proclaim it with our every breath.
May we, like the two disciples on the road to Emmaus,
be startled and transformed by a glimpse of Christ,
in strangers along our way.
May we, like Dorcas, the only woman Luke names as disciple,
follow in the footsteps of Jesus.[2]
May we, like female and male disciples of every age,
recognize, affirm, and wholeheartedly pursue
God's unique call upon each of us.
May we—mystics and artists, plumbers and "techies,"
scholars and diplomats, parents and caregivers,
servant-hearted people who heed the cries
of the earth
and all baptized into the dignity of Christ—
trust in the fuel of God's Holy Spirit to heal
our tiny world into connection.
May we all persist on our God-given paths, no matter the cost.

For Jesus proclaimed:
Blessed are those who hear the word of God and obey it.

Part 1: The Gospel According to Luke

Introducing Luke the Evangelist and His Gospel

Luke the Evangelist: my first favorite Gospel author. Dissatisfied with the
many accounts of Jesus' good news which had already been served up, he
simply *had* to recount *his* version to Theophilus, lover of God. (That's *us*,
folks.) He *had* to tell the story with elegance, authority, challenges clothed
in tenderness and forgiveness, and unique stories of Love seeking out the
lost. He *had* to mention women, unheard of elsewhere, even though he
often muted their words and actions. (To fit in with the culture of his day?
So as not to call undue attention to himself?) He *had* to travel that once-
in-a-lifetime journey with Jesus to Jerusalem, the ultimate place of salvation. Ah, "Jerusalem, Jerusalem, the city that kills the prophets and stones
those who are sent to it! How often have I desired to gather your children
together as a hen gathers her brood under her wings, and you were not

2. Acts 9:36–43. Dorcas is her Greek name; Tabitha is her Jewish name.

willing!"[3] For Jerusalem *was* the very place where Jesus was crucified, died, and then raised up to new life. It was also the very place from which faith in Jesus, the Christ, was propelled to the ends of the known earth. Only Luke, of all the evangelists, continued the story in his Gospel sequel, the Acts of the Apostles. *This* part of the journey begins on one violently fiery, windy day, as the Holy Spirit births a fledgling Church. We call it Pentecost, that explosive day of empowering female and male disciples for mission. Luke alone recounts the spread—from there—of tiny, yet mighty, communities, to the ends of the known Mediterranean world.

Who is Luke? When was he writing? And to what community? We simply do not know, with certainty. Often thought of as "the beloved physician" of Col 4:14, perhaps because of his healing stance on Jesus, we only know that he was well educated and familiar with Greek culture. While it is thought he might have been a gentile, writing to a mixed community of gentile and Jew, his community's location remains a guess. As for the timing of his writing, the best guess is some time in the 80s CE. By this time, it was clear that Jesus was not "coming again" any time soon; for Luke, this meant enduring in and through the tough times.

Jesus, According to Luke

Jesus loved to eat! Indeed, Luke situated him at more tables, around more food, with more people than any other Gospel writer. Not only for the food but for the companionship, of friend and challenger alike. I couldn't help but delight in this possibility: Jesus would have loved being around my grandma's table. What a great cook Grandma was! When I would stay with her and my grandpa occasionally as a youngster, I was often awakened by the smell of dough rising on her old black wrought iron stove. In all my days, I've never found any oatmeal bread that could even *begin* to rival hers! Then, too, I remember the dinners she put on for family and friends. Chicken, German potato salad, and pies, always followed by card games on into the night. I can imagine Jesus being there, loving it all, whether he knew how to play "High Low Jack" or not. Perhaps there's a table in *your* family that Jesus would have loved to join?

3. Luke 13:34.

Yes, Jesus' meals are essential to this Gospel, along with his mission and purpose, *always* fueled by prayer. Before any of his "red-letter days," as my Scripture professor used to say, Jesus was always to be found in prayer. Yet the story line unfolds as a journey. The journey of a prophet and more than a prophet: the "Son of the Most High."[4] The One whose kingdom will have no end.[5] Geographically a mere seventy miles, from Nazareth—up north in Galilee—to Jerusalem of Judea, the city on the heights and core of Jewish faith. Propelled by the Spirit, Jesus began in Nazareth, only to immediately encounter rage and rejection. For his very own neighbors tried to "hurl him off the cliff."[6] Early on, he pivoted with determination from Galilee to Jerusalem,[7] once again moved by prayer. Along the way, he called and molded disciples. Continually sought out the least and the lost. Forgave and healed, taught, feasted with the least and the greatest, and persisted. Despite continual carping by his critics . . . and even deceit, betrayal and denial by some friends. *His* is the story of human rejection, inordinate cruelty and suffering—the cross—only to encounter the God who can make all things new!

Metaphorically, it's *our* journey, too. From striving, straining, and dying . . . to joy, fulfillment, and new life beyond imagining. It *seemed* like the end. But *no*! He's *alive*! Appearing to two disciples on the road to Emmaus! Appearing to *all* his disciples, commanding them to proclaim "repentance and forgiveness of sins . . . in his name to all nations."[8] Pivoting from Jerusalem to the ends of the earth. Luke alone tells "the rest of the story," in his Acts of the Apostles, now become *our* story. *Our* empowerment by the Holy Spirit. *Our* commissioning to set out on the journey of a lifetime. And, oh, the people we meet along the way, just like Jesus.

How best to unpack this unique Gospel? (1) I begin by writing a letter to Luke, extolling his infancy narrative of unmatched beauty. (2) Then we journey together with Jesus, faithful to Luke's unique stops along the way. Mary of Magdala and Joanna, who provided for Jesus and the twelve "out of their resources,"[9] serve as our guides. (3) Because many questions have been raised about Luke's treatment of Martha and Mary, I "pen" a second letter to Luke about this story. (4) Finally, I reflect on our own walk with Jesus today. With that, we begin.

4. Luke 1:32; these are the angel Gabriel's words to Mary.
5. Luke 1:33; again, Gabriel's words to Mary.
6. Luke 4:29.
7. Luke 9:51.
8. Luke 24:47.
9. Luke 8:1–3.

Luke's Infancy Narrative,
Told through a Letter from Gloria to Luke

Dear Luke,

Your infancy narrative is a masterpiece! Elegant. Charming. Tender, yet full of difficulty and challenge, all at the same time. Calling forth the best that people can give: faith, courage, stamina for an unknown future, and committed love. Thanks in some measure to St. Francis of Assisi, we know, love, and tell many of your stories. Our favorites include Jesus' birth during the world's first census and his being laid in a manger (a feeding trough for animals) because there was "no room for them in the inn."[10] If only you could see our Christmas pageants on Christmas Eve, complete with a young Mary, Joseph and baby Jesus, a host of angels, and a couple of shepherds, as well!

Did you write these two chapters *last*, only *after* having researched and created your magnificent Gospel? For you needed real people, with real hopes, dreams and struggles, not unlike all of us, to whet our appetite for the story that would unfold. In any case, you surely planted the seeds for your entire message right from the start. For example:

1. The Spirit of God hovers, activating people at every turn, until it explodes at Pentecost.

2. Prophesy has once again staked its claim on the land, beginning with three women, though you never name the first two as such. Elizabeth, mother of John the Baptist, is *first* to proclaim Jesus (in Mary's womb) as Lord: "And why has this happened to me, that the mother of *my Lord* comes to me?"[11] In response, *Mary* is first to proclaim the upside-down nature of Jesus' entire Gospel, which we call the Magnificat.[12] Shortly thereafter, the elderly Anna, living in the temple during the infancy of Jesus, "began to praise God and to speak about the child to all who were looking for the redemption of Jerusalem."[13] You join *their* prophesies to those of Zechariah, father of John the Baptist, and

10. Luke 2:7.

11. Luke 1:43; my emphasis. Elizabeth, the first prophet of this Gospel, is the first to name Jesus as Lord.

12. See Luke 1:46–55. Actually, Mary's Magnificat was already in the Jewish tradition, as Hannah's prayer. See 1 Sam 2:1–10. Hannah was the mother of Samuel, the last of Israel's judges, and a fine one.

13. Luke 2:38.

the aging Simeon. Through the power of the Holy Spirit, Simeon is able to recognize Jesus as the promised Messiah: "for my eyes have seen your salvation" (i.e., your saving instrument), "a light for revelation to the Gentiles and for glory to your people Israel."[14]

3. Prayer is constant; prayer is essential. Anna, for example, a witness to Jesus at his circumcision, along with Simeon, "never left the temple, but worshiped there with fasting and prayer night and day."[15]

4. Jesus is "Bread for the World" from the first, when he is laid in a manger, a feeding trough for animals. As an adult, he will relish many a meal, serving up many lessons in the process. Like this: the "nobodies" of this world matter. Yes, shepherds—unwanted in "polite company" because they cared for animals out in the fields and couldn't follow ordinary Jewish cleansing rituals—were first to see Jesus. And this: Jesus "welcomes sinners and eats with them,"[16] much to the whining complaints of religious leaders.

5. Forgiveness wends its way through your entire Gospel. Early on, Zechariah announces that his son, John the Baptist, will prepare the way for the Lord, "to give knowledge of salvation to his people by the forgiveness of their sins."[17] You alone give voice to Simon Peter's ardent protests of sinfulness, before heeding Jesus' call to follow him.[18] Once again, you are the only evangelist to place a final forgiving prayer on the lips of Jesus, as he hangs in agony on the cross. "Father, forgive them; for they do not know what they are doing."[19] And, at the very end, the risen Jesus (now the Christ) proclaims to his puzzled, yet thrilled disciples: "Thus it is written, that the Messiah is to suffer and to rise from the dead on the third day, and that repentance and forgiveness of sins is to be proclaimed in his name to all nations, beginning from Jerusalem."[20]

14. Luke 2:30, 32.

15. Luke 2:37.

16. Luke 15:2.

17. Luke 1:77.

18. See Luke 5:1–11, esp. 5:8–10; he acknowledged his disbelief in the power of Jesus to create a huge haul of fish.

19. Luke 23:34; this is *only* found in Luke's Gospel.

20. Luke 24:46–47.

I still quietly marvel at how profoundly you know the hearts and souls of Mary, Elizabeth and Zechariah, Anna and Simeon, and the nameless but openhearted shepherds, almost as though you know our own hearts, as well. You have no idea of the magnificent art, music, teaching and theology you have inspired from then 'til now! Thank you, Luke, for such a noble beginning.

Sincerely,

Gloria Ulterino

The Journey, Beginning in Galilee: An Introduction

Who or what is urgently calling to us? Tugging at our hearts? How do *we* prepare to go on such a journey? We pack. Determine what we *must* take. *Decide* what we can leave behind. As we reflect on these questions, I return to Jesus' ultimate journey to Jerusalem. In doing so, I speak in the present tense, hoping to create the immediacy of connecting with his sacred story.

How does Jesus prepare? Surely, he has heard God's Holy Spirit stirring insistently at his core. Has he also been captivated by the whispers of Isaiah? That tenderhearted prophet alive among exiles in Babylon some five hundred years before Jesus, the one we name Second Isaiah? How these exiles had *yearned* to come home, for seventy long years! But no: all seemed futile. To everyone but Isaiah. He alone could see it coming! Yes, they *were* released, through King Cyrus of Persia. They arrived *home*! Only to be heartbroken, once again. For seventy years is a very long time. Their land had been snatched away by others. Even worse, their temple had been *destroyed*. Where, oh *where*, was the hope for which they had longed?

Finally, some years later, Third Isaiah would rub balm into their wounded souls by proclaiming *these* stirring words: "The Spirit of the Lord is upon me," anointing me "to bring good news to the poor . . . to proclaim release to the captives and recovery of sight to the blind, to let the oppressed go free, to proclaim the year of the Lord's favor."[21] It was to be the Jubilee Year! When all would be forgiven and made whole!

In *his* day, Jesus *himself* is weighed down by his people's heavy burdens. Oppressive taxation. Bare-bones survival. So, when handed the scroll of Isaiah in his synagogue at Nazareth, Jesus proclaims those same stirring words, importantly adding: "Today this scripture has been fulfilled in your

21. Luke 4:18–19; compare to Isa 61:1–2, leaving out "the day of vengeance of our God." We attribute these words to Third Isaiah, the prophet living at the time of the return home from Babylon.

hearing."[22] Today! Yes, only Luke—that eloquent lover of language—places such soaring, hope-filled words in the mouth of Jesus. For folks back then, and folks of every "today."

So it is that Jesus prepares to set out. He has been "led" by the Spirit into the wilderness. At the devil's hands, he has known ravishing hunger. Temptations to earthly power. Temptations to be like God. Yet Jesus prevails, despite Luke's uneasy warning that the devil will return at "an opportune time."[23] Then, fortified with the strength of his mission—to fulfill Isaiah's words in *his* day—Jesus calls his first disciples. The men, whom he calls apostles: Simon Peter, Andrew, James, John, and the rest of the Twelve. The women followers, too, including some "who had been cured of evil spirits and infirmities: Mary, called Magdalene, from whom seven demons had gone out, and Joanna, the wife of Herod's steward Chuza, and Susanna, and many others, who provided for them out of their resources."[24] (Were their resources only monetary? Or, did they include strength, love, and encouragement? We know Mary Magdalene, but who is Joanna? Was she from a wealthy family? Did she leave Chuza because she simply *could not* stomach Herod, for whom he worked? We simply do not know. Nevertheless, there she is, along with Mary, along with the twelve men.)

Stops along the Galilean Journey, According to Luke

Thus companioned, Jesus begins his teaching and healing, early on, in Galilee. What follows is an imagined conversation between Mary of Magdala and Joanna, looking back on their experiences of the stops along the way, as told by Luke alone. In this imagining, their voices are faithful to the Gospel and scholarly research. Places along the way are included.

In the village of Nain, in Galilee (7:11–17).

Joanna: Oh, Mary, how could we *not* follow this man Jesus? Surely you were as astounded as I, when we first encountered Jesus. Here was this helpless widow: without a husband, without any means of support, and now without a son, stretched out on a funeral bier. That is, until Jesus—so strong, yet so viscerally moved to compassion—*commanded* that her son's breath be restored! We had *never* experienced anything like it!

---

22. Luke 4:21.
23. Luke 4:13.
24. Luke 8:2–3.

Mary: Oh, yes! Jesus was different from *anyone* we'd ever known! So alive, so at home in his own skin, so sure of himself, so in love with God, people, and a good meal! Only days later, it seemed, we heard about his meal at the home of Simon the Pharisee. Remember?

Jesus' meal at the home of Simon the Pharisee (7:36–50).

Joanna: Of course I do! Much to the chagrin of his host, Jesus welcomed a "sinful" woman. Somehow, she had been forgiven by Jesus. All she could do in return was to gratefully, tearfully, profusely anoint Jesus on his feet.[25] In commending her, it was as if Jesus was saying to all gathered, "Now, *that is* love!"

Mary: You're right! *We* could even say, it's *true* love. *Belonging* love. *Family* love.

Jesus' words, in response to a woman blessing his mother: "My mother and brothers are those who hear the word of God and do it" (8:21).

Joanna: How we longed to be part of Jesus' family! One event after another only deepened our faith in Jesus. Like his feeding of five thousand people. Remember how Peter—who could make his share of mistakes—was inspired to declare Jesus as "the Messiah of God"?[26] Yet Jesus cautioned us against celebrating, knowing that he would be betrayed.[27]

Mary: Even so, he now seemed ready to face whatever would lie ahead. By now, there was something about him: a deeper, more confident determination. A profound love that propelled him. We could see it. We could feel it. Had God anointed him in a special way? Only much later would we hear about his transfiguration before Peter, James, and John. Only much later would we come to know his ultimate sense of purpose: "When the days drew near for him to be taken up, he set his face to go to Jerusalem."[28]

---

25. In Mark and Matthew, this unnamed woman does not show up until Jesus' passion is about to begin; with love-poured-out, she anoints Jesus on the head, for all that lies ahead.

26. Luke 9:20.

27. Luke 9:44.

28. Luke 9:51. According to Luke, Jesus understood his fate of being "taken up" on the cross for the sake of us all.

The Singular Journey to Jerusalem, According to Luke

Jesus' unique story of the good Samaritan (10:25–37), a response to the lawyer's question: "Who is my neighbor?"

Joanna: For now, however, we were entering Samaria. "Enemy" territory to most Jews. Despite having descended from common parents way back when, Jews and Samaritans had developed a deep religious divide. The lawyer meant to test Jesus. But Jesus turned the tables on him! With yet one more powerful story. Remember? The Samaritan, the "enemy," became the model for neighborly living!

Jesus' visit to Martha and Mary (10:38–42).

Mary: Yes, Joanna, I remember it well! I also remember our next stop, to the home of Martha, sister of Mary. What a puzzlement for us! He *seemed* to divide these two sisters, his dear friends. Why? Only later on could we begin to understand.

(From Gloria: I will explore this question further, at the conclusion of Jesus' stops along the way to Jerusalem. Words of some Scripture scholars today will help "make sense" of this story.)

Another story, often called "the friends at midnight," raised questions about God's response to prayer (11:5–8).

Joanna: How true! At the same time, we *both* remember how Jesus *always* rooted himself in prayer. How often he prayed, especially before a big decision. Then he taught us all to pray what we came to call the Lord's Prayer.[29] Almost as if to make his point, he followed that up with yet another story. A person in need arrives at midnight, with nothing to offer his host. So he cries out to the one inside, snuggled down with his family, sound asleep. Will the latter get up to provide bread? Yes, he absolutely *must*! Either because of the needy one's *persistence* . . . *or* because the one inside would be *shamed* if he didn't hospitably respond.[30] Probably both are true, don't you agree?

Mary: I do, indeed. Of course, he kept doing God's work. Like healing a bent-over woman.

29. See Luke 11:1–4.
30. Joanna's words reflect two different scholarly opinions.

Jesus healed a bent-over woman on the Sabbath, in a synagogue (13:10–17).[31]

Mary: This particular healing means so much to me! She never says a word, but Jesus *had* to heal her crippled posture, which she had endured for eighteen . . . very . . . long . . . years. It was the Sabbath, but no matter. While the leader of the synagogue was *irate* at the healing of Jesus, the *crowd* "was rejoicing" at all his works! So were we!

Joanna: Yes, indeed! I remember another time, as well, around another table, where some religious leaders *insisted* that their rules came before God's healing love!

"And the Pharisees and the scribes were grumbling and saying, 'This fellow welcomes sinners and eats with them'" (15:2).[32]

Joanna: But Jesus just kept telling his great stories. How far will God go to save us when we get lost? *This* far! Like a good shepherd, he will *leave* his flock to search high and low for the *one* sheep who gets stuck. Like a "housewife," a woman without means, God searches . . . sweeps . . . the house, high and low, until she finds her precious lost coin. And then? What a party! For the entire neighborhood! Or, like a "prodigal" (lavishly loving) father, God takes his post. Day in, day out, he's standing at his gate, waiting . . . and waiting some more . . . until he *finally* spots his sin-weary, "dead" son emerging just over the hill. And then? What a great celebration! *Nothing's* too good for this long-lost son! Sandals for his feet! (His days of enslavement are over!) The best robe! The family's ring for his finger!

Mary: Yet a question hangs heavy in the air. Will the *older* son— the one who's stayed, who's nursed a *titanic* grudge over all these years—will *he* come to the party? What about the grumbling Pharisees and scribes? What about us, on our penny-pinching, worst days? Here is another story that just won't leave me alone. It challenges me. Even disturbs me.

---

31. See Luke 13:10–17.

32. This begins the "lost and found" ch. 15, in which Jesus describes several images of God: the shepherd seeking the lost sheep, the woman searching for her lost coin, and the father never giving up on his lost son(s).

The story of the unjust steward (16:1–9).

Mary: This story asks each of us: what *is* the right use of power? At first, I could identify with the steward, somehow trying to protect his turf at the expense of the powerful "rich man" in charge.[33] But then, suddenly, we see that the steward has clay feet! He's not so great after all! Now what? Who's in the right? Is *anyone* here in the right? What kind of power can be *found* in God's kingdom?[34] Is Jesus suggesting that *no* human scheming is any match, in the end, for the mercy of God? That we are *all* vulnerable? That only trusting in *God's mercy* will save us? I wonder.

The parable of the rich man and Lazarus (16:19–31).

Joanna: Yes, Mary, so do I. This much I know. We see the mercy of God in Jesus! We see *everything* of God in Jesus! Who *knows* where the mercy of God will take us in the end.

For now, here's another story, easier for us to understand. An ultimate reversal of fortunes. Like Jesus' upside-down teachings. Like Mary's Magnificat in action. Think of the richest man in town. Just outside his gate is someone he refuses to notice. Lazarus, by name. So downtrodden is he that "even the dogs would come and lick his sores."[35] Each one dies. Lazarus is nestled in the bosom of Abraham, but the rich man is sent to the everlasting fire of Hades. *Pleading* with Abraham for the chance to warn his five brothers of *their* certain fate, the rich man is given an emphatic *no.* As Abraham puts it, "If they do not listen to Moses and the prophets, neither will they be convinced even if someone rises from the dead."[36] We looked at each other, remember? What did he mean, "even if someone rises from the dead"? Later on, of course, we would understand the truth about Jesus. But for now, we just knew that so many of Jesus' stories ended in surprise.

33. Scott, *Hear Then the Parable*, 255–66.

34. Scott, *Hear Then the Parable*, 266. "The kingdom is for the vulnerable, for masters and stewards who do not get even." I prefer the term "kin-dom" but have used the traditional "kingdom" in my quote and in Mary's question.

35. Luke 16:21.

36. Luke 16:31.

Jesus' healing of the ten lepers (17:11–19).

Mary: Yes, indeed. Here's another surprise. Only one of the ten lepers—healed by Jesus as they make their way to the priests for confirmation of his healing—returns to offer profound thanks to Jesus. *This* one is a "foreigner," a hated Samaritan, an *outsider*. However, as Jesus so often proclaims to *all* who are healed: "Your faith has made you well."[37]

His parable of the unjust judge and the gutsy widow (18:1–8).

Joanna: Yes, Mary, how true. But *here* is the story I just love! It's about one very gutsy woman. In the Jewish tradition, judges were expected to be fair. Just. Out to help the most vulnerable. In effect, they were to be images of God. In truth, of course, judges did not always act like God. *This* one, however, is particularly egregious, making it known that "he neither feared God nor had respect for people."[38] Who, then, acts like God? Why, it's the *widow*! *She* is the one who works for justice! *She* is *not* dependent. Or silent. *Not* the expected image of a widow. On the contrary, *she* is very sure of herself. She *persists*, just like God. I just *love* this woman!

In Jericho, an oasis town on the edge of the wilderness, Jesus is about to encounter Zacchaeus (19:1–10).

Mary: So do I! What a model of *determination*, despite everything. *Now*, after all we've seen and heard, we're *finally* getting closer to Jerusalem. We're in Jericho, and Jesus is about to encounter Zacchaeus. Can't you just picture this man, this chief tax collector? Maybe he's overcharged people in the past. Or defrauded them. Yet, he's heard of Jesus, now passing through his city. He *must* see this man! So, short in stature, Zacchaeus clambers up a tree to get a good view. At which point, Jesus—spotting him at the top of the tree—invites himself to dinner. What follows is yet one more dinner party, complete with one more grumbling audience about Jesus eating with sinners, *and* one more total transformation. As Jesus puts it, "The Son of Man

---

37. Luke 17:19.
38. Luke 18:2.

came to seek out and to save the lost."[39] What good news on this day, Joanna! And yet, not without a warning. Remember?

Jesus wept over Jerusalem (19:41–44).

Joanna: Oh, yes, Mary, I remember it well. "If you, even you, had only recognized on this day the things that make for peace! But now they are hidden from your eyes."[40]

Mary: I could feel the depth of his heavyheartedness.

Joanna: Yes, his burden was truly beginning to weigh him down. Weighing us down, too, along with him. We *never* could have imagined what would lie ahead, for him and for us.

Finally, I return to Jesus' visit with Martha and Mary (10:38–42). Because I find it troubling, along with so many women, I must probe it in detail, through another letter to Luke.

> Dear Luke,
>
> I have tried to understand! But I can't! In fact, this story has troubled me. Disturbed me. And I'm not alone. Ask any woman: with whom do you identify? Most will say "Martha!" Of course! Women lead busy lives! So . . . where does that leave *them* when Jesus seems to pit Martha against Mary? To compare Martha *unfavorably* to Mary. What is *really* going on here?
>
> I begin with the *location* of Martha's home. Tradition tells us (as does John the Evangelist, a few years after your Gospel) that Martha and Mary lived in Bethany, just a stone's throw from Jerusalem. *Not* somewhere up in Galilee. (John tells us that it is a safe and friendly place for Jesus to lay his head on any trip he makes to Jerusalem.) However, *you* insist that it's in "a certain village" somewhere in Galilee, at the *beginning* of Jesus' journey to Jerusalem.[41] Why?

---

39. Luke 19:10.

40. Luke 19:42; Luke alone expresses Jesus' profound sadness just before entering Jerusalem.

41. In John's story, Jesus restores Lazarus (brother of Martha and Mary) to life. Martha, the "take charge" sister, is the one in this Gospel who proclaims Jesus "the Messiah, the Son of God" (11:27), not Peter. Mary is at home weeping, but her tears elicit the same response from Jesus. All three siblings are important; all three are beloved of Jesus. Luke's story, on the other hand, emphasizes the importance of prayer.

Your story begins simply enough. Both Martha and Mary welcome Jesus, each in her own way. Martha welcomes Jesus, along with his word, *into her home*; Mary welcomes his word by sitting at his feet, prayerfully taking in all Jesus has to say. So far, so good. Apparently, you are making the point that daily, persistent prayer is absolutely essential to life! Of course!

At the same time, anxiety fills the air. For Jesus is there, taking *Mary's* side. Why? (As women often say, in defense of Martha: *someone* has to put food on the table! *Someone* has to make the guests comfortable!) What do we make of this tension? Scripture scholar and professor Barbara E. Reid—one of my contemporaries—offers an answer that rings true to me.[42] The real issue, she says, is one of translation. And that change in translation changes *everything* in the story. The phrase usually translated as "distracted by her many tasks," can have another meaning. Reid maintains that the primary meaning is "to be pulled or dragged away."[43] In short, she maintains, Martha is complaining about being pulled away from her *diakonia* (Greek word for service) by those who oppose her ministry. Furthermore, frustrated that her sister does not take her part, she looks to the Lord for approval. Reid adds to this picture by her translation of Martha's "worry," on the lips of Jesus. A more accurate translation of this word, she says, connotes a community disturbance. Or, as Reid puts it, "the whole community is in an uproar" over her ministry.[44] (Surely, this is very different from what we normally hear!)

Here is the point. Both Reid and another contemporary Scripture scholar, Eugene LaVerdiere, agree that this story most likely takes place in *your* day, Luke, rather than the time of Jesus.[45] Why? Because you continually refer to Jesus in this story as Lord, the commonplace reference to Jesus in your day. Also, it's well known that inclusive memories of Jesus' treatment of women were receding by the time of your writing. Might it not be true, then, that you are not

42. See Reid, *Choosing the Better Part?*, 144–62.
43. Reid, *Choosing the Better Part?*, 157.
44. Reid, *Choosing the Better Part?*, 158.
45. LaVerdiere, *Dining in the Kingdom of God*, 73–86.

only changing the *location* of this visit, but the *time*, as well, from Jesus' day to yours?

If so, might not this story represent the tension over women's *diakonia*—ministerial service—in the 80s, when *you* are writing? By your day, some fifty years after Jesus, small faith communities had cropped up in homes (house churches) all over the Mediterranean world. By then, women had already become leaders of their faith communities.[46] In fact, early on, in the 50s, Paul had praised women's leadership. But *later* pastoral letters to Timothy and Titus (written in the 80s and 90s) often took exception to it.[47] Indeed, Paul could *never* have written those letters, since he died in the late 50s.

Was Martha's "home," then, the place of a house church in *your* day? To acknowledge that truth makes no attempt to "rescue" Jesus' rudeness to Martha, as some have tried to do. To acknowledge that truth might well explain *your* seeming unease with *women's servant leadership*. Or with *anything* that might call attention to the fledgling Christian communities at a time of possible persecution. To acknowledge that truth accepts the many twists and turns of women's leadership in the Church over the centuries. For example, from the fourteenth through the sixteenth centuries, there was a resurgent interest in Martha, reclaiming her strong faith in Jesus. In some paintings, she became the female version of St. George and the Dragon, only without bloodshed. A painting of Fra Angelico (1387–1455) places Martha and Mary at Gethsemane. While Mary is reading a book, Martha's pose imitates that of Jesus, "praying with uplifted hands."[48]

So, then, what are we to make of *your* story? Clearly, your *entire* Gospel points to the both/and of prayer and activity, not either/or. Jesus was *always* at prayer before significant events. The same *must* be true

46. Phoebe was deacon of Cenchreae; Prisca and her husband, Aquila, were leaders of house churches in Corinth, Ephesus, and Rome; Junia and her partner, Andronicus, were "prominent among the apostles." See also Acts 16:11–15, 40 on Lydia, who became leader of the church in Philippi.

47. See ch. 16 of Paul's Letter to the Romans (probably written around the year 58) and his Letter to the Philippians (written about the year 55; see esp. 4:2–3), revealing his high regard for his women coworkers. See also 1 Tim 2:8–15 for the later development.

48. Reid, *Choosing the Better Part?*, 161.

for us! Immediately upon leaving Martha and Mary, Jesus enters into prayer, once again. Then he responds to his disciples' request—"Lord, teach us to pray"[49]— by teaching them the Lord's Prayer. However, the tension remains—most likely the tension in your day over the ministerial role of women. Along with the tension down to *our* day, in the twenty-first century. Luke, how I would love to hear your response to this letter!

Sincerely,

Gloria Ulterino

The End of Jesus' Journey to Jerusalem Is *Not* the End: His Death, Resurrection, and Commissioning of Disciples Continues in Us and Beyond

In the end, Jesus experienced utter, total degradation. I admit: only in the last few days of June 2020, has the horror of Jesus' crucifixion hit home in me. I saw it all over the news. Jesus was crucified again, when a few—intent on utter depraved destruction—overran peaceful demonstrators and ripped open new wounds. Violently destroying small businesses. Looting. Crushing people's dreams. It was precisely into this kind of devastation that Jesus breathed his last words of love, self-giving, and total surrender. "Father, into your hands I commend my spirit."[50]

Was this the end? No! For vulnerable, giving, sustaining Love *crushed* the seeming stranglehold of death. Both *then* and forevermore! The women were the first to know. For they remained at the cross. Watching. Coming with spices to anoint the body of Jesus. Only to be terrified by two men in dazzling clothes, standing beside them.[51] "Why do you look for the living among the dead? He is not here, but has risen. Remember how he told you, while he was still in Galilee, that the Son of Man must be handed over to sinners, and be crucified, and on the third day rise again."[52] Mary and Joanna remembered, as we have seen.

49. Luke 11:1.

50. Luke 23:46.

51. Luke 24:4–5; this is the beginning of the resurrection account, according to Luke.

52. Luke 24:5b–7.

Words Essential to Luke:
Remembering, Eucharist, and Holy Spirit

Remembering: From his own cross, having repented of his crimes, the "good criminal" next to Jesus pleaded: "Jesus, remember me, when you come into your kingdom."[53] Having been urged to remember Jesus' words by "two men in dazzling clothes," the women at the empty tomb "*remembered his words, and returning from the tomb, they told all this to the eleven and to all the rest.*"[54]

Here's what Presbyterian spirituality writer Frederick Buechner says about remembering:

> When you remember me, it means that you have carried something of who I am with you, that I have left some mark of who I am on who you are. It means that you can summon me back to your mind even though countless years and miles may stand between us. It means that if we meet again, you will know me. It means that even after I die, you can still see my face and hear my voice and speak to me in your heart.
>
> For as long as you remember me, I am never entirely lost.
>
> . . .
>
> If you forget me, one of the ways I remember who I am will be gone. If you forget me, part of who I am will be gone.[55]

How do his words land on you?

Eucharist: The documents of Vatican II have maintained that there are two essential parts of Eucharist: (1) the word of God/the stories, and (2) the Breaking of the Bread. In his unique story of the two disciples on the road to Emmaus (24:13–35), Luke describes Eucharist. Now it is the risen Lord who encounters two utterly despondent, "we-had-hoped" disciples, heading back home after the crucifixion. Perhaps a married couple, they simply *cannot* see, hear, or understand. Until, in a flash . . . in the Breaking of the Bread at their home with Jesus, they suddenly know! Astounded, their hearts burn within them! They *remember* all he told them on the road. They dash back to Jerusalem! How can they keep the good news to themselves? How can we?

The Holy Spirit: From the first, the Holy Spirit hovers over this Gospel. Now, after the resurrection, the followers of Jesus gathered, as the risen Jesus commanded. All the men "were constantly devoting themselves to prayer,

53. Luke 23:42. This is only found in Luke's Gospel.
54. Luke 24:4, 8–9.
55. Buechner, *Whistling in the Dark*, 100.

together with certain women, including Mary the mother of Jesus, as well as his brothers."[56] Until suddenly, it happened! Pentecost! That fiery, windy, mind-blowing, heart-enlarging commissioning day, fueled by the power of God's Holy Spirit! Only Luke tells this story, in his continuation of the Gospel, the Acts of the Apostles. These men and women were to be Jesus' "witnesses in Jerusalem, in all Judea and Samaria, and to the ends of the earth."[57] That was then! Now, it's our turn!

Part II: Discerning Women's Service in the Church: Should Women's Ordination to the Diaconate Be Restored?

This question has come to the fore, of late, in the Roman Catholic Church. A question that could well further the full and active participation of women's service in our beloved Church. A question that surfaces from the Lucan emphasis on Jesus' service to all people. A question that I will now explore as follows: (1) A question rooted in Luke's Gospel; (2) Contemporary experience, specifically in Mexico in the 1970s and the Amazonian Synod of 2019; (3) What does Scripture say? (4) A brief history of women in the diaconate over the centuries; (5) What, then, do *we* say?

Diakonia. Service: A "What-Matters-Most-Word," Rooted in Luke's Account of the Last Supper

"For who is greater, the one who is at the table or the one who serves? . . . But I am among you as the one who serves."[58] Specifically, as the Son of Man, Jesus had served, over and over again, by seeking out and saving the lost, including Zacchaeus. Claiming this "lost" tax collector as his own. Telling stories of reclaiming the lost sheep, the prodigal son, and the lost coin. And extending his service to each and any of us: "lost" physically, emotionally, spiritually, every which way. Like being stuck in addictions of one kind or other . . . to alcohol, drugs, harsh judgments made on others, self-righteousness, or anything else. Or, feeling utterly hopeless, as in the "good" criminal, pleading with Jesus on his cross next to Jesus, "Jesus, remember me, when you come into your kingdom."[59] Even here, one breath

56. Acts 1:14.
57. Acts 1:8.
58. Luke 22:27.
59. Luke 23:42.

away from dying himself, Jesus could proclaim, "Truly I tell you, today you will be with me in Paradise."[60] His service complete, Jesus could breathe his last: "Father, into your hands I commend my spirit."[61]

What does it mean to serve God and others? Especially in a sacramental order of service? What does such an order of service look like? For women, as well as for men? How and why did it exist? Was it truly sacramental? (In other words: did it come into being through the prayer of the community, led by the local bishop?) Is it needed today? How can women live out their call from God *now*?

We begin with personal experience, with your stories and mine, over the past fifty years or so, still basking in the eruption of the Holy Spirit at the Second Vatican Council.[62] Then we hold them up to the light of Scripture before turning to our history. What does all this mean for us today? Many of us still believe in the yet-to-be-fulfilled promises of Vatican II. We yearn for them . . . hope in them . . . trust in them . . . advocate for them.

One Woman's Story from the New Mexico
Diocese in the 1970s

The year is 1972, the place New Mexico. At that time the state was one diocese served by Archbishop James Peter Davis, a man alive with the promises of Vatican II. Why not restore a permanent diaconate? A young and enthusiastic priest, Spencer Stopa, became the first director of the archdiocesan deacon training program. His second class (of 1978) included five women, with his good friend Catherine Stewart-Roache among them.[63] Yes, they could be prepared, along with the men; it was their only way of preparing women for ministry in the diocese at that time. A year into this process a new bishop was appointed, Robert F. Sanchez. At first seemingly agreeable to including women in the preparation, he later waffled. But Catherine persisted, pressing her case before the deacon board, which advised the bishop on diaconate matters. After an exhausting three-hour meeting, the board unanimously agreed with Catherine's position, thanks in no small part to the statement of a

60. Luke 23:43.

61. Luke 23:46.

62. Beginning with our experience is essential to feminist scholarship; indeed, it is to all liberation scholarship.

63. Ratigan and Swidler, *New Phoebe*, 34–42.

young priest toward the end of the meeting: "I am ashamed that women must beg in our church."[64]

Is Catherine's story not unlike the Martha/Mary story of old, only this time with a both/and? Catherine, like Martha, knew herself called to serve her community. At the same time, like Mary, she had prayed her way through every struggle, of which there were many. Fast-forward to the day of the men's ordination. The five women were to be part of the ceremony, to be commissioned for ministerial service. But it didn't work out that way. The women looked like an afterthought. *After* Communion, *after* the men had been addressed by the bishop, *after* they had been ordained, each woman was to kneel before the bishop and kiss his ring, while he promised to give her a book of the Gospels. Four of them did so. But Catherine could not; she *had* to speak her truth. "Robert," she said, "I have something to say and I need your microphone." "Do you have to?" "Yes," she replied.[65] Her brief statement expressed the truth that "separate but equal" would never create equality. Indeed, she "prayed for the day that the Holy Spirit of God could blow freely among women and men and true equality would be a reality for all."[66] Shaking but at peace, she heard loud applause erupt . . . and continue . . . and continue. Until *finally* the bishop laughed and said, "I guess the people have spoken."[67]

A Story of Our Day: The Amazonian Synod, October 6 to 27, 2019, "New Pathways for the Church and for an Integral Ecology"

Has the day finally come, some forty years later? The short answer is no! Women are being asked to wait . . . yet one . . . more . . . time! At the same time, I offer profound thanks to Deborah Rose-Milavec, codirector with Russ Petrus of FutureChurch, a leading Church reform group in the United States. Deb was in Rome for the duration of this Synod and reported daily on its unfolding. She agreed to share her reporting notes with me, for this purpose.

This Synod sparked promise in many of us *yearning* for the voice of women to be spoken and heard, equally with men. It was the third of three

64. Ratigan and Swidler, *New Phoebe*, 36.
65. Ratigan and Swidler, *New Phoebe*, 39.
66. Ratigan and Swidler, *New Phoebe*, 40.
67. Ratigan and Swidler, *New Phoebe*, 40.

recent Synods initiated by Pope Francis, each one reflecting the pope's desire to call forth, walk with, and listen to the people of God. Yet this Synod on the Amazon—with its focus on a nine-nation region—was different from earlier ones on family and youth. New voices surged, demanding to be heard. For the "lungs" of our planet are seriously ill! Indigenous peoples have been largely ignored! As one observer noted, "The great novelty of this synod is that indigenous peoples will be the teachers; Catholic priests the students."[68] At the same time, some leading official Church voices articulated their openness to new thoughts. Take Cardinal Claudio Hummes, the Brazilian chair of this Synod, for example. He announced that there was a request from communities in Amazonia that the service [of women] "be acknowledged and there be an attempt to consolidate it with a suitable ministry for the women who live in these communities."[69] On day three—October 9, 2019—Bishop Erwin Krautler, CPPS, of Brazil, one of the authors of the working document, spoke eloquently about the destruction of the Amazon, the need for an indigenous Church, and the centrality of Eucharist. He is, by the way, under constant police protection because of his "tell-it-like-it-is" behavior. The people, he assured us, do not understand celibacy; they would gladly accept a married priesthood. As for women? "Two thirds of our communities are animated by women. We have to think about this. We have to proclaim the women and their work. We need concrete solutions. So why not women deacons?"[70] Finally, in answer to a question about women priests, he replied, "Why not?"

Nevertheless, this Synod had its drawbacks, revealing the long distance that must *still* be traveled before the dream of women's equality becomes a reality in this Church. This Synod included 40 women, alongside 230 men, for example. Predictably, none of the women could vote!

But they could speak, openly, in small group conversations: five Spanish and four Portuguese groups representing the Amazon region, two Italian, and one English/French group. As Deb noted on the fourth day of the Synod: "The bishops, women religious, and others who have sat on the panels in press briefings . . . know and love their people and they are fearless, faith-filled innovators who know that God does not live in a rule-bound institution, but in the faces of Her people and in the rivers, trees and skies that hold them."[71] Furthermore, their voices were often supported by some church officials. For example, Deb reported on October 25

68. Rose-Milavec, notes, October 17.

69. Rose-Milavec, notes, October 7, day 1 of the Synod.

70. Rose-Milavec, notes, October 9.

71. Rose-Milavec, notes, October 10.

that Bishop Evaristo Pascoal Spengler, OFM, "offered the most lucid and compelling pitch for ordaining women deacons that I would venture to say has ever been heard at a synod."[72]

1. "We need an official ministry for women in the church. Sixty percent of all ministry in the Amazon is led and coordinated by women."

2. "Evidence from the Hebrew Scriptures show women on par with men as judges, matriarchs, prophets, etc."

3. "There is a huge presence of women throughout the history of the church."

4. "It is not for lack of holiness that we do not ordain women."

5. "In the history of the church there were women deacons and that role should be expanded today."

6. "Vatican II opened up the diaconate for men because it was recognized that they were doing diaconal work. The same is true of women."

7. "There is a path open for women to become deacons. Pope Benedict opened it in 2009 when he changed Canon Law to make it clear that the diaconate is a ministry of the word, liturgy, and charity—a separate ministry from the priesthood."

8. "Galatians says there is no longer Jew or Greek, slave or free, female or male, but all are one in Christ Jesus" (see Gal 3:28).

All true, every last point!

The final document approved all one hundred twenty paragraphs, as reported on October 26 (the last day of the Synod) by Gerard O'Connell, Vatican correspondent for *America* magazine, and Luke Hansen, SJ, a former associate editor of *America*. After exploring a multitude of ecological and pastoral concerns facing this sprawling Church, most of the final segment (ch. 5, paras. 86–119), focused on "New Paths of Synodal Conversion":

Of primary importance was the Church's commitment in the Amazonian region "to seek new ways to preach the Gospel and to promote justice and stand in solidarity with its thirty-four million inhabitants, including some two and a half million indigenous people."[73]

Examples abounded! See for yourselves.[74]

---

72. Rose-Milavec, notes, October 25. The quotes that immediately follow are all taken from that day's notes.

73. This quote and others from O'Connell and Hansen are taken from their report, "Synod Votes to Ordain Married Men."

74. To see the full text of the final document of the Synod on the Amazon, see

- In upside-down fashion, it proclaimed (in para. 93) that the laity, by virtue of their baptism, must become "privileged actors" in creating "a society of justice and solidarity in the care of our common home." In fact (in para. 95), the Amazon Church must "promote and confer ministries for men and women in an equitable manner."

- Indeed, the Amazon Church wants to "create still broader opportunities for a more incisive female presence in the Church." (See para. 99, quoting *Evangelii Gaudium* [2013] of Pope Francis, 103.) For example, in many consultations throughout the Amazon, "the permanent diaconate for women was requested," making it "an important theme of the Synod." (See para. 103, which also named the desire to interface with the results of Pope Francis's 2016 commission on this issue.) Indeed, the need to promote "a permanent diaconate" in the Amazonian Church was named as "urgent" in paragraph 104.

- Recognizing the already significant work of the laity, the document noted (in para. 96): "In the absence of priests, the bishop may entrust the pastoral care of a community to a lay person 'with an official mandate through a ritual act.'"

- Paragraphs 116–19 explored the need for creating "a liturgical rite for the indigenous peoples of the Amazon" so that folks everywhere might fully celebrate their faith.

- In order to coordinate all recommendations, it was deemed necessary to create "an office for Amazonia in the Vatican Dicastery for the Service of Integral Human Development" (see para. 85).

Yes, many folks appreciated the diaconal service of women. Indeed, it can, and must, continue! Ah, but when?

What Does Scripture Say?

It all began with Phoebe, commended by Paul as a "deacon of the church at Cenchreae," just outside Corinth in present-day Greece. So says Paul, in his Letter to the Romans, perhaps early in the year 58.[75] By this he meant that she was a servant leader of her community and a charismatic preacher, just like the eleven men he also named as deacons in his authentic letters.[76]

Synod of Bishops, "Amazon."

75. Rom 16:1.

76. This is Paul's last authentic letter. According to Bernadette J. Brooten, of the twelve times this word *diakonos* is used in the authentic Pauline letters, it refers eleven

Why, she might even have delivered this letter herself to ministry colleagues Prisca and Aquila and their house church in the ancient part of Rome, for such delivery later became part of women's diaconal service.

Yes, in those days, when memories of Jesus "in the flesh" still pulsed in people's hearts, women were still recognized and named as coworkers with men, partners in ministry. They were leaders of house churches, like Prisca (Priscilla in Acts) and her husband Aquila (where her name usually appears first). They were apostles, like Mary of Magdala (apostle to the apostles according to John the Evangelist, 20:1–18), and Junia, along with her partner Andronicus ("prominent among the apostles" in Rom 16:7). All gifted by God's Holy Spirit for spreading the good news and building up the infant Church communities.

But, little by little, much of this would change. By the end of the first century, the male-dominating (or patriarchal) supremacy, with accompanying legal dependence of wives and children, took root. Little by little, it encroached upon the inclusive certainty of the gospel that everyone matters. Rather, "I permit no woman to teach or have authority over a man; she is to keep silent."[77] Nonetheless, "Timothy" goes on to concede that women deacons, like their male counterparts, "must be serious, not slanderers, but temperate, faithful in all things."[78]

The Tradition, Beginning in the East
(Contemporary Syria and Turkey)

So it was that the women persisted. Followed their call. And were ordained by their bishops, through a sacramental laying on of hands and anointing. We know this because of the *Didascalia*, written early in third-century northern Syria, the earliest liturgical document of the Eastern Church.[79] Remember now, we are talking about real people, with real dreams. Can you see them? Many older, most likely over fifty. Serious. Compassionate. Faith-filled, with a wisdom forged from life's struggles. Can you see them in action? They *must* serve God and their people. Assist women in their baptismal immersion, essential for the sake of modesty. Do they reverently,

---

times to a man and once to Phoebe. See Brooten, "Women and the Churches," 52.

77. 1 Tim 2:12, likely written early in the second century.

78. 1 Tim 3:11, following 1 Tim 3:8–10; while some scholars believe that women refers to the wives of deacons, more conclude that the whole section is about deacons, men and women, in parallel form.

79. See Corrado Marucci, "History and Value of the Feminine Diaconate in the Ancient Church," in Zagano, *Women Deacons?*, 33.

perhaps tearfully, describe placing the white garment of new creation on these women? Without a doubt, they pray with and for them and their children, at this very moment of their new life in Christ. Continue to form them in their newfound faith. Visit them, and other women, whenever illness would strike. And always make themselves available to the bishop to deliver correspondence of importance or some other suitable task.

We will never know the names of most of these women deacons, but there are a few—especially treasured by significant male clerics—who stand out. In the East, there's Olympias, for example, born into a wealthy and influential family. Married in 385 CE to Nebridius, prefect of Constantinople and widowed a year later, she vowed never to remarry. So it was that Bishop Nectarius ordained her a deacon while she was still in her thirties; not only that, she became one of his personal advisors. And Amproukla, woman deacon in Constantinople, to whom John Chrysostom (who died in 411 CE) wrote letters of thanks for supporting him during his exile. And Anastasia, recipient of letters from Severus, bishop of Antioch, after he was exiled in 518 CE. Their correspondence often included scriptural reflection.

Of course, as baptism by immersion gave way to infant baptism, the ministry of women deacons receded, little by little. While the canonical collection of the Patriarch Photius of Constantinople reveals that there were still forty women deacons in the ninth century, by two hundred years later, women were no longer being ordained deacons.

In the West

They arrived on the known scene later than in the East and in fewer numbers. For example, the *Apostolic Tradition* of Hippolytus (ca. 215 CE) made no mention of women deacons. Why? For starters, misogyny was continually rearing its ugly head. Tertullian (who died ca. 220 CE) was vociferously opposed to any liturgical teaching ministry by women. Ambrosiaster insisted that men alone are made in the image of God; therefore, it would "be a shame if women dared to talk in church."[80] Even so, the women persisted, at least until the eleventh century. We know, for example, that there were continual condemnations of ordained women by religious authorities in fourth- and fifth-century Gaul. By the sixth century we can honor, by name, several ordained women deacons: Helaria, called diaconia by her father, St. Remigius of Reims; Anna of Rome; Theodora of Gaul; and Ausonia of Dalmatia. But one woman dramatically demands

80. Corrado Marucci, "History and Value of the Feminine Diaconate in the Ancient Church," in Zagano, *Women Deacons?*, 42.

our attention, above all others: St. Radegund, wife of Clothar I (or Lothair I), king of the Franks (511 to 558 CE). Upon leaving the king (ca. 550), she demanded ordination to the diaconate at the hands of Medard, bishop of Noyen. Fearful of the king's wrath, terrified by nobles "attempting to drag him brutally through the basilica from the altar," he waffled.[81] Understandably! Until some holy women intervened, clothing their queen in monastic garb. She then imperiously proclaimed: "If you shrink from consecrating me, and fear man more than God, Pastor, He will require His sheep's soul from your hand."[82] Bishop Medard ordained her!

Over time, as in the East, the ordination of women to the diaconate receded with increasing infant baptism. But not before the powerful advocacy in the twelfth century of the theologian Abelard, on behalf of his wife, Abbess Heloise of Paris. At her urging, Abelard wrote "possibly the most thorough and passionate defense of the ordination of women in the High Middle Ages."[83] Husband and wife considered abbesses to be the successors to the ancient order of women deacons, "an ordained clerical office established by Christ himself."[84]

This Question Remained: Were These Women Authentically, Sacramentally Ordained?

Indeed, of this we are certain: there *were* women deacons in the East and the West. And yet, much ink has been spilled over a very important question. Were they authentically, truly, *ordained* as deacons? By the laying on of hands and anointing of oil by the bishop? Or, were they only blessed, as were the widows, and not really ordained? While there is no absolute consensus among scholars, many clearly contend that genuine ordination took place.[85] Once again, the *Didascalia* is first to be instructive in this regard. Speaking of bishops, deacons/deaconesses, and presbyters in Trinitarian terms, it then equates deacons and deaconesses. "Therefore, bishop, make permanent workers of justice (*diakonous*) who may help your people for life. Elect and make deacons from among your people those whom you like:

81. Macy, *Hidden History of Women's Ordination*, 68–69.

82. See Gary Macy, "Women Deacons: History," in Macy et al., *Women Deacons*, 16.

83. See Macy, "Women Deacons," in Macy et al., *Women Deacons*, 29.

84. See Macy, "Women Deacons," in Macy et al., *Women Deacons*, 30.

85. See Marucci, "History and Value of the Feminine Diaconate," 30–56; also Cipriano Vagaggini, "The Ordination of Deaconesses in the Greek and Byzantine Tradition," in Zagano, *Women Deacons?*, 100–43.

the man so that he might take care of the many things that are necessary, and the woman for ministry among women."[86]

Fast-forward another hundred and fifty years or so to the several documents compiled in the East, known as the *Apostolic Constitutions*. According to Vagaggini, who has probed these documents in exhaustive detail, the position of the deaconess was clarified. She was, indeed, ordained by the bishop's laying on of hands and anointing with oil, as he prayed:

> O Eternal God, Father of our Lord Jesus Christ, creator of man and of woman, you who have filled with your Spirit Miriam and Deborah, Anna and Hulda; you who have not deemed it unworthy that your only begotten Son be born of a woman; you who instituted women as guardians of the holy parts of the tent of the covenant and of the Temple; You, even now, look upon this [female] servant of yours elected to the diaconate; grant her the Holy Spirit and purify her from all sins of the flesh and of the spirit: so that she might fulfill the task entrusted to her for your glory and for the glory of your Christ, with whom and with the Holy Spirit, glory and adoration be to you and forever and ever.[87]

Thus ordained, she was clearly in the upper ranks of bishop, presbyter, and deacon. For her ordination took place in the sanctuary, while those of lower rank (like widows, lectors, and cantors) were blessed outside, in the sacristy. She was to assist women at baptism, continue their formation, and care for them when ill; she was to welcome strangers and serve as a messenger and mediator for the bishop, according to his need.

At the same time, limits were placed on her, because of her womanhood. She was *not* to proceed to priesthood, as reasoned by Epiphanius of Salamis: (1) there was no female priesthood in Scripture; (2) Christ never made Mary a priest; and (3) "women are fragile, weak, and rather unintelligent."[88] Infected with such thinking, the *Apostolic Constitutions* emphasized that "the man is the source of the woman and is therefore her head."[89] Yes, in the Byzantine rite, women *were* ordained to the upper ranks of the clergy, according to Vagaggini. But, their ministry was becoming increasingly constricted, restrained, and controlled. How often in human history had culture *obliterated* the gospel! Here it was again! Jesus had treated women as equals, but *somehow* that message struggled to take root in people's lives.

86. See Vagaggini, "Ordination of Deaconesses," in Zagano, *Women Deacons?*, 104.
87. See Vagaggini, "Ordination of Deaconesses," in Zagano, *Women Deacons?*, 124.
88. See Vagaggini, "Ordination of Deaconesses," in Zagano, *Women Deacons?*, 117.
89. See Vagaggini, "Ordination of Deaconesses," in Zagano, *Women Deacons?*, 119.

Were Women Authentically Ordained in the West?

This we know: the rituals and prayer for ordaining women arrived late, in the eighth century, with the liturgical book of Bishop Egbert of York. In spare Roman fashion, the following words were prayed over deacons, both male and female: "Give heed, Lord, to our prayers and upon this your servant send forth that spirit of your blessing in order that, enriched by heavenly gifts, he [or she] might be able to obtain grace through your majesty and by living well offer an example to others. Through [our Lord Jesus Christ]."[90] At the same time, there were prayers unique to each gender. The women's prayer emphasized their virginity, reflecting back upon the wise virgins of Scripture, awaiting the Bridegroom (based upon Matt 25:1–13); the men's prayer pleaded for God's peace and prosperity, since they were made in God's image.

Despite these differences, the tenth-century *Romano-Germanic Pontifical* (also known as the *Mainz Pontifical*) clearly instructed the women, as well as the men, to receive the stole or *orarium*, indicating their preaching role. The laying on of hands and anointing with oil is once again prescribed. Indeed, about 1148, the scholar Rolandus commented on an enormous collection of church laws amassed in the twelfth century by the monk Gratian: "There is no doubt that it was the custom in the past to ordain women deacons, that is, readers of the Gospel who were not to be ordained before forty years of age, nor were they to be married after ordination."[91]

Male and Female Diaconate Disappeared in East and West by the Thirteenth Century

Why? In the case of women, the need to accompany women into the waters of baptism by immersion had vanished. Also, as the twelfth-century Eastern canonist Theodore Balsamon has maintained: "In times past, orders (*tagmata*) of deaconesses were recognized, and they had access to the sanctuary (*bema*). *But the monthly affliction banished them from the divine and holy sanctuary.* In the holy see of Constantinople, women deacons were appointed to the office, without any participation in the sanctuary, but attending to church functions and directing women's assembly according to church procedure."[92] It was fourteenth-century canonist Matthew

90. See Macy, "Women Deacons," in Macy et al., *Women Deacons*, 20.

91. See Macy, "Women Deacons," in Macy et al., *Women Deacons*, 26.

92. See Macy, "Women Deacons," in Macy et al., *Women Deacons*, 30–31; also in Madigan and Osiek, *Ordained Women*, 137; my emphasis.

Blastares who concurred: "Women deacons then fulfilled a certain service among the clergy (*kleroi*) which is nearly unknown to everyone now. . . . *They were forbidden access and performance of these services by later fathers because of their monthly flow that cannot be controlled.*"[93] (Once again, *ancient* purity laws stubbornly persist.)

Finally, a new theology of ordination emerged in the twelfth century. Up until then, ordination (even with the laying on of hands and anointing) meant an ordering of people's gifts for the good of a particular faith community. However, after continual conversation and reflection, ordination was coming to mean something new: the ordinand received "an indelible character on the soul." He could now serve any community. In short, the "what" of service became the "who" of the ordinand, *as one set apart*; and women were considered unfit matter for such service, with its accompanying authority. This became law circa 1150, when Gratian offered his second reflection on his Decretum. Could a woman, for example, give testimony against a priest? No. Women are in a different ordo. Women, therefore "are not able to advance to the priesthood or even to the diaconate, therefore they are capable of neither accusing priests nor of testifying against them."[94]

How, then, to explain the memory of women deacons? Some said abbesses (like Heloise of Paris) were now the true deacons. Others, that women's ordination had simply been a commissioning for specific ministries but was not sacramental. Indeed, by the end of the twelfth century, Huguccio of Bologna—the most influential canon lawyer of his age—boldly proclaimed that ordination would not "take" on a woman. "The law of the church and sex, that is, the law of the church made on account of sex [impedes it]. If therefore a female is in fact ordained, she does not receive orders, and hence is forbidden to exercise the office of orders."[95]

The Twenty-First-Century Church, Built upon the Second Vatican Council, 1962–1965

Nevertheless, women remembered. Persisted. And never gave up. This we know. Only misogyny stands in the way of our certain knowledge that women were ordained deacons. They met a genuine need in Church history.

93. See Macy, "Women Deacons," in Macy et al., *Women Deacons*, 31, 32; also in Madigan and Osiek, *Ordained Women*, 138; my emphasis.

94. See Macy, "Women Deacons," in Macy et al., *Women Deacons*, 34–35. Macy takes this from Emil Friedberg, ed., *Decretum* C. 15, question 3, princ., in *Corpus iuris canonici* (Graz: Akademisch, 1959), 1:750.

95. See Macy, "Women Deacons," in Macy et al., *Women Deacons*, 36.

The real question, then, is this: *do we need women deacons today*? That's the ultimate question posed by the 1995 report of the Canon Law Society of America. It is also *our* ultimate question, in *our* moment in time.

In a word: yes! Do we not need to see and hear women in the sanctuary? Women called to and prepared for liturgical leadership? Women whose heart's desire it is to preach, to break open that word of God? Women who can witness to the truth: that Jesus came to give life to *everyone*! Women, therefore, capable of serving the gospel of Jesus Christ in God's people.

Don't we know, deep down, that seeing and hearing men alone leaves us bereft, even with so many good, hardworking, and faith-filled men? Especially when Jesus called women as well as men. And women followed . . . year after year . . . century after century. They led house churches in the infant Church. Served, taught, healed, and spoke prophetically. Often despite so many efforts to keep them out. Indeed, year after year, century after century, religious men in power increasingly subdued the voices of women, up to and including the present day. A name for such abuse of power has taken hold. *Clericalism*. Webster defines it as "a policy of maintaining or increasing the power of a religious hierarchy." The symptoms of such illness are everywhere to be found. Sexual abuse of minors. Systemic and systematic cover-ups, protecting the system at all costs, rather than healing the victims. As Pope Francis has so boldly, truthfully proclaimed. Its ugly abuse of power must stop! Now!

Would ordaining women as deacons prevent such abuse? Painful honesty must instruct the task ahead. Clericalism is a *human* temptation, capable of attacking women as well as men. It is a distortion of the use of power. Absolutely essential to our healing is this: awareness of such temptations, along with the desire—through prayer and spiritual companionship—to confront and deal with them. It takes women (as well as men) committed to empowering folks in their communities: noticing their gifts, calling them forth, supporting and challenging them, for the benefit of all. *This* is what ministry is all about.

I ask, then: is it not possible that right now, in this twenty-first century, a new transition is readying for being birthed in our beloved Church? Indeed, is it not a time of lifting up *all* people of whatever color, race, gender, or anyone else we might name "other"? Could it not be true that anyone God so chooses is being called and gifted for service, including liturgical leadership? Indeed, the Second Vatican Council opened up the way by naming the people of God—*not* the hierarchy—as the *primary* image of Church. By restoring a permanent diaconate for men. Since then, the question is increasingly raised: why not for women, as well? Could it not be that the "indelible mark" of twelfth-century ordination has *nothing* to do with an exterior marking of male privilege but *everything* to do with recognizing and affirming the mark that God has *already* placed *within* a person? *Any* person. Then recognizing, calling forth, and *ordaining* that gifted person, as *God* so chooses. Might it not *finally* be time to correct the papal human error of denying ordination to women? Sooner rather than later, when the need for faith-filled servants is so great? Might not this century, our precious moment in time, become a witness to the very reason Jesus came: to serve, often by seeking out and saving the lost? Is it not time—indeed, *past* time—for our beloved Church to witness to the truth, to the extravagant love of Jesus, the Christ, for us *all*? Indeed, is not *this* Jesus the very one we profess to follow?

We have all been here before. In May of 2016 the women's International Union of Superiors General (heads of women's religious orders) questioned Pope Francis about the possibility of restoring a women's diaconate. In response, he appointed an advisory committee of a dozen seasoned scholars, six men and six women. Many of us gazed expectantly upon the shore of hope, since one of the appointees was Phyllis Zagano, a passionate expert on its restoration. January 2019: the report was submitted. May 2019: Pope Francis announced no consensus existed. It would have to wait. October 2019: surely this time, at the Amazonian Synod, with so many women *doing* diaconal work in the Amazon, there would be the restoration of a women's diaconate. But no, not yet, not yet. How long, O Lord? How long?

We are in a new day, for the coronavirus pandemic is leaving its mark on us all. At the same time, thousands—if not millions—of people have walked, sung, and chanted in towns and cities across this country: Black Lives Matter. By now, many have come to the realization that this is not simply a slogan to be chanted. Rather, it is a profound call to help heal and restore the dignity of an entire enslaved people. For example, Jesuit leaders at Georgetown University have just established a project to salve the profound wound of this nation's "original sin." Named as the Descendants Truth and Reconciliation Foundation, this endeavor begins its work with one hundred million dollars to help rebuild the lives of the descendants of 272 slaves who were sold for the establishment of Georgetown University. Such work, wherever it will be found, is the work of justice and restoration.

What, then, will we, the people of God, say and do in this new day about women's leadership in our Church? The following questions might help focus our decisions. What might Jesus say to us today about women's leadership in the Church? What women have *we* known to be called and gifted by God to serve God's people? How has their positive response, in the face of so many odds, inspired us to more truly follow Jesus? If we see the value in women's leadership, what are we called to do about it? How will our response give us courage to more faithfully follow the Jesus in whom we live and love and have our being?

In Conclusion

One word immediately comes to mind for Luke's Gospel: *lyrical*. This evangelist practically sings his way through the story of Jesus. How well we know and love the stories surrounding the birth of Jesus, complete with shepherds and angels. Perhaps, though, the stories that tug at the heartstrings the most are those about finding and reclaiming lost and forlorn people. In fact, Luke's chapter 15 has often been dubbed the "lost and found" chapter. We revel in the stories of the Good Shepherd finding the one lost sheep out of a hundred, the woman turning her house upside down to find the lost coin, and the "prodigal" father, whose love knows no bounds. Who, then, are the lost and found people of *today*? Whose lives are found and restored? As I pondered these questions, it became impossible to focus on just one woman. Rather, a whole host of women occurred to me—women in my beloved Church today who are called to ordination by God and their communities, but whose call is being put on hold by the institutional church. When will these precious calls be heard, and honored?

In response, I chose to zero in on women called to serve as deacons. Why? Because this is ordination to *service*, first and foremost. It is also, to my way of thinking, an ordination whose time has come. Women in earlier centuries have already been sacramentally ordained. Pope Benedict, separating the diaconate out from ordination to the priesthood, has recently opened up a pathway to ordaining women to the diaconate. Is it possible, then, to ordain women to the diaconate *now*? The short answer is yes. What would it take for such ordination to the diaconate to become reality? We *must* answer that question, now, so that the lost might indeed be found.

Jesus proclaimed:
Blessed are those who hear the word of God and obey it!

Addendum

This chapter—indeed, this book—would be incomplete without a brief, yet final, word about women's ordination (both to the diaconate and the priesthood). From my years in pastoral ministry, I genuinely understand that a whole broad spectrum of opinion exists on this subject. Furthermore, I honor every sincerely held view. With an earnest desire, then, to engage all readers in continuing reflection on this subject, I briefly express my own views here.

Since the mid-1970s, women and men have been advocating for women's ordination to the priesthood, as well as to the diaconate. In fact, the Women's Ordination Conference has been a leader among progressive support groups on this very issue. In 2002, seven women were ordained priests on the Danube River by an active bishop in apostolic succession (meaning, connected to ordaining bishops from the time of the early Church). Their numbers, both of women thus ordained, and of the communities they serve, have mushroomed since then. Known as Roman Catholic Womenpriests, information on them can be found at www.romancatholicwomenpriests.org. Suffice it to say that Roman Catholic Womenpriests claim as their mission: "to prepare, ordain in Apostolic Succession, and support primarily women who are called by the Holy Spirit and their communities to a renewed priestly ministry rooted in justice and faithfulness to the Gospel." I deeply admire their courage, strength, and wisdom to follow God's prophetic call upon their lives. Grateful to name a few of them as friends, I am absolutely certain that one day their stories will be cherished by many.

At the same time, I have come face-to-face with folks in parishes who simply cannot accept women's ordination, whether to the diaconate or the priesthood. I recall the man who would sit near the front of the church, arms folded, a look of defiance on his face, whenever I would preach. Then, too, there was the tall woman, in another parish, who would visibly kneel during my reflections on Scripture. But, another person encouraged me with these words: "Every time you preach, I think you shouldn't be doing this; and, every time you preach, you win me over, once again." I am not alone; *many* women know such stories.

Finally, mindful of heartfelt diversity on this subject, alongside God's passionate call on every human life, I ask only for openheartedness in response. As a student of history, I know that changes in the law—including church law—are often preceded by breaking the law. Consider, for example, Susan B. Anthony voting in the 1872 election. Rosa Parks breaking an unjust law by sitting on a bus. And the Rev. Dr. Martin Luther King Jr. training followers in *nonviolent* resistance to unjust discrimination. Unjust laws *must* be challenged, *always* nonviolently. This is one way that we, disciples of Jesus Christ, continually grow into becoming all that God desires for us. This I believe.

9

November, Month of Transition
from Here to There

A "Thin Time," According to
the Celtic Tradition

An Introduction

In November, the days grow short (in the Northern Hemisphere), the sunlight fades, and shadows whisper their secrets. Or, as Cynthia Rylant poetically proclaims, "The world has tucked her children in, with a kiss on their heads, till spring."[1] Those within the Celtic tradition might name it a "thin time," when the veil separating this world from the next stretches to the point of near transparency. Picking up on these cues, our liturgies increasingly point to the end times, beginning the month with celebrations of the saints and all souls. It is also the time when parishes remember the lives of those who have died over the past year. November gives us pause . . . raises questions about meaning and what is to be handed on . . . and calls us to ever deepening levels of reflection about life, death, and transition into becoming "more."

Who, then, might model the spirit of this month? One woman immediately came to mind for me, and her name is Kathie Quinlan. Though she may not be well known outside the Rochester, New York, area, this pearl of wisdom has contributed mightily to the questions raised by this month of transition. What follows, then, is her story.

---

1. Rylant, *In November*, last page. She is a noted author of many fine books for young people.

Hospice and the Ministry of Kathie Quinlan

What, then, is a natural life experience for this time of the liturgical year? Hospice. Webster says this: it is "a lodging for travelers, young persons, or the underprivileged; a facility or program designed to provide a caring environment for supplying the physical and emotional needs of the terminally ill." For many of us the secondary definition is primary. And other words come to mind and heart. Human dignity. Compassion. Comfort care. Reconciliation. Familial and spiritual healing.

Who abundantly models this spirit of hospice in the Rochester, New York, area? None other than Kathie Quinlan. Though she may not be well known elsewhere, Kathie stands out here as an advocate for hospice care. Her smile is wide, her manner gentle, her words articulate, and her spine a rod of steel. For she doggedly pursued a dream, which became Isaiah House, named after that powerfully poetic, compassionate prophet of the Hebrew exile, during the sixth century before the Common Era. (His chapters 40–55 are known to us as the book of consolation.) Here was a man who could envision homecoming when all seemed lost. Here was a man who could offer exalted hope to a people cut off from their land. Here was a man who could inspire so many with the impossibilities of God. Truth be told, he still does!

How did Kathie's dream of hospice emerge? Over a long cup of coffee, Kathie told me her story. And she signed a copy of her book, *Blessing Our Goodbyes*,[2] which fills in so many of the details. It all began in the early and mid-'60s, with the devastating death of two of Kathie and Bill's precious children. Virginia, their third little girl, died eighteen days after her first birthday. And Michael, their only boy, died just before that same marker. Both suffered from a rare and little-known degenerative central nervous system disease. Despite the unimaginable suffering of a parent's heart, or maybe because of it, Kathie began to recognize a "tugging at her heart" to become a nurse, specifically for the dying. But mothering young daughters Linda, Beth, and Dorothy put this heart-tug on hold, until the late '70s. As she cared for her father, dying at home . . . as she read Elisabeth Kubler-Ross's book on the stages of dying for the first time . . . this dream would *not* let her be. Her father's dying taught her so much about saying good-bye. She drank

---

2. See the bibliography for details on the publisher.

deeply from the grieving, reminiscing, and letting go. Would not so many others benefit from all that she was learning? So it was that she entered nursing school at midlife.

But then, as she cared for the dying in an acute care hospital setting, she became frustrated. There *must* be a better way of walking with people from this world into the next! Indeed, there was. In July 1984, a faith-filled couple, Rose and Raoul Grossi, formed Mount Carmel House, the very first two-bed home for the dying in Rochester. Now *this* place of compassion was all that she had envisioned! It so happened that she and her husband, Bill, had recently become parishioners at Corpus Christi, pastored by Father Jim Callan. Father Callan had been the force behind four outreach ministries. Would he support a fifth, a home for the dying? The day was November 29, 1984; the event, her "sharing of the dream day" with Father Callan. His answer? Yes! And on August 6, 1987, Isaiah House was born. In Kathie's words, it is an "ordinary extraordinary" house, a house that welcomes each person with an unmistakable rush of peace and serenity. Quite simply, it is home, complete with a meditation garden. One youngster, in fact, longingly named it her "secret garden." Only two residents can live there at any one time, with preference given to those persons with the greatest needs or fewest options.

From the beginning, Kathie and her coworkers envisioned homes for the dying as "appetizers before heaven," often said with a smile. And, from the beginning, there were so many who made those appetizers possible. There were initial consultants Sharon Bailey and Donna Del Santo, Sisters of St. Joseph who directed Corpus Christi Health Center. There were the volunteers beyond number who met every three to four weeks to bring the vision into reality. There was Irene Dymcar, an attorney, who guided them through all the legal issues. There was Dr. Ferdinand Ona, who pronounced their ministry as "simply building the kingdom of God." There were the folks who contributed furniture, wheelchairs, and money, in small and large amounts. There was Jack Rogers, a fireman, who bought the house for them in memory of his wife, Bea. There was dear friend Arlene Helget, who worked shoulder to shoulder with Kathie for twenty years, as administrator of the house. There was the gifted hospice nurse, Cathy Fanslow, who taught Kathie so much over twenty-five years. And so many more, beyond measure.

And yet, perhaps it was the dying themselves who were Kathie's greatest teachers in "the work of her heart." She learned that the end of life is "anguish . . . sad and even tragic . . . yet joyful and even a blessing . . . awesome . . . beautiful . . . transforming . . . healing . . . life-giving . . . intimate . . . privileged . . . a witness to the courage on how to live . . . a time of palpable grace." Many who minister in hospice, says Kathie, claim they are no longer afraid of death. They learn to live in the moment, knowing with each breath the preciousness of life. Indeed, with trust, hospice can become a time of healing the heart and relationships.

For such healing to take place, though, we first need to come to terms with death as an inevitable conclusion to life in this world, says Kathie. As she puts it: "Death is the end to which we are all born, the ultimate and most universal human experience beyond our birth." But our culture's denial of aging and death can make it so hard on us to reach this destination. Rather, Kathie delights in pointing to the wisdom of John O'Donohue, poetic writer of Celtic spirituality. In his *Anam Cara: A Book of Celtic Wisdom*, O'Donohue suggests this: "If you can come to see aging not as the demise of your body but as the harvest of your soul, you will learn that aging can be a time of great strength, poise, and confidence."[3] Kathie wholeheartedly agrees. For her, the path of our lives can become a rehearsal for the final letting go. Along the way, we can savor each day. Take in all the surprises that can greet us in every moment. Allow the difficult, painful times that are certain to come our way to become a source of wisdom, courage, openness, and generosity of spirit . . . in their own good time. Prepare ahead of time with family and friends the kind of path we would choose at the end.

Lessons Learned

What lessons has this empathetic, openhearted, profoundly compassionate woman gleaned from over twenty years of attentive listening—with ears, eyes, hands, and heart—at so many bedsides, day in and day out? Oh, so many! She learned to ask her residents, "What are you hoping for?" She learned to follow their lead: to offer the quiet essential to the dying process, to listen to their reminiscing that makes meaning of their lives, to watch for the physical signs of a body shutting down in preparation for entering

3. O'Donohue, *Anam Cara*, 167–68.

another realm, to discover the one person who can offer peace with these words, "You can leave now; it's all right." Perhaps, above all, she learned that hospice ministers are none other than midwives, in the birthing of the human spirit. Judith, a young mother of two children, cried out just hours before she died, "I feel as if I'm in labor!"[4] Yes, dying is a time to enter "the heart of the soul," the inner work that becomes the focus at this sacred time. It is indeed, Kathie claims, a most holy time, a "thin place," as the Irish would say, with a veil so transparent that the next world can almost be seen. At Isaiah House, they call it "the nearing time."

But, what about the families, the ones left behind? For hospice is every bit about them, as well. These words, which begin chapter 3 of Kathie's book, serve as a guide above all else, I believe: "We are closest to God in our compassionate moments." At this point Kathie draws from the wisdom of Henri Nouwen in his book *Compassion*: "Compassion asks us to go where it hurts, to enter into places of pain, to share in the brokenness, fear, confusion, and anguish. Compassion challenges us to cry out with those in misery, to mourn with those who are lonely, to weep with those in tears. Compassion requires us to be weak with the weak and powerless with the powerless. Compassion means full immersion in the condition of being human."[5] For those of us who are Christian, these words describe Jesus. And they are also meant to describe us, his followers. Listening, a powerful tool of healing, can get us there. Listening to the stories of the one who is dying . . . listening for their life review . . . listening in quiet to their quiet . . . listening for any "thank you" . . . listening for any "I'm sorry" . . . listening for anything else the dying person offers. And, in this listening, realizing that those left behind may also need to be heard by a compassionate presence.

All this leads us to grieving, a process that must take the time it takes. Grieving is essential, for it speaks of the depth of human love. Kathie offers us the image of a stormy sea to help us out here. At first the crashing waves may seem overwhelming, like we might drown. But, little by little, in time, the waves subside, the sea gradually calms, and the day eventually arrives when the sun breaks through. Perhaps with a smile . . . or a skip . . . or a memory graciously stored in the very fabric of our lives. In all this, Kathie advises, "Be gentle with yourself." And don't be afraid to get any help you may need. Gentle woman that she is, Kathie leaves us with these wisdom words from Macrina Weiderkehr: "To mourn is to be given a second heart."[6]

---

4. Quinlan, *Blessing Our Goodbyes*, 26.

5. Nouwen et al., *Compassion*, 4.

6. Weiderkehr, *Seasons of Your Heart*, 98.

A Prayer for Our November Days

Still in the grip of the fateful COVID-19 pandemic, we grieve. We mourn.
We learn, again and again and again . . . to let go. Don't we also crane
our necks, peering 'round the bend, simply searching for a shred of hope
beyond pandemic? What will our approaching new year look like? Feel
like? Will it be a return to *normal?* Is that what we really desire? A return
to the *same old, same old?*

    Or, perhaps, do our hearts and souls ache for something deeper . . .
something more authentic . . . something more honorable for the human
condition? For what might we pray at this crucial juncture? This time of
possible birthing, yet one more time?

> Let us pray . . .
>
> O Most Holy One,
>
> In whom we live and move and have our being,
>
> You never diminish us by leaving us to our own devices.
>
> Rather, you prod, poke, nuzzle, caress us
>
>   into the More of your dreaming.
>
> May we listen for you at every turn,
>
> In sisters and brothers beyond our recognition,
>
> In unlikely hints and whispers beyond our tiny imaginations.
>
> Where everyone has a place at the Table,
>
> Where everyone tastes your justice, as at a banquet,
>
> Where everyone glimpses your joy, beyond measure,
>
> Where everyone knows what it is to *finally* come home
>
> To You, to Love, to Life, to Being, to Trust, to All.
>
> This we earnestly pray,
>
> Today, tomorrow, and every day given to us, in your unending
> mercy.
>
> Amen!

Epilogue

This book has been a long time in the making. It was some forty years
ago now when the power of my Church's liturgy not only struck a chord
in me, but suddenly burst into song. Where had this power been all my life?
I had no idea. Yet, as leader of the parish liturgy committee, I gobbled up
all I was learning, simply longing to share it with those around me. Where
would it lead? Once again, I had no idea. Yet, bit by bit, after four years of
studying theology, the unmistakable call to parish ministry beckoned.

What joy to serve as a pastoral associate, despite any of the usual human struggles. Furthermore, in my diocese at that time, preaching was a
possibility for women in pastoral ministry. What a gift! For my Scripture
professor had already imparted his passion for God's word, along with his
vast knowledge of it. It became my practice to meet regularly with a "homily
team," a group of a half dozen folks, from whom I would receive a sense of
how the readings connect with and impact their lives.

In time, of course, I realized that this beloved Church of my youth
and my life was simply not doing justice to women. How could I participate
in remedying this negative situation? For me, it meant continued study
. . . advocacy for women's liturgical leadership at every turn . . . working
alongside dedicated people in several Church reform groups . . . creation
of the storytelling team "Women of the Well" . . . and authoring books
and articles. In the process, I researched so many exemplary women. Until
finally, over the past couple of years, my work on this book became labor
intensive. It is now in your hands.

Throughout it all, I have experienced the powerful presence of God.
God-of-Love-beyond-Understanding. God of Relationship, seeping into the
crevice of every human cell, in every human being, so as to connect one to

another to another to another. God of ecstatic intimacy, alongside the God who knows the farthest stardust of the universe. And so much more!

It is my profound hope that each reader will discover some *aha* moments in these pages. Perhaps the realization that God is profoundly and continually creating something new . . . an insight into an ongoing struggle . . . a tender balm for a wound that cries out for healing . . . even cause for great rejoicing. Such newness happens in season and out, with every new day, over and over again. May this book become a blessing and a source of ever-deepening life in our Merciful and Just God, whose love is beyond borders, barriers, and human comprehension.

A Blessing for Our Journey into Another Liturgical Year

Blessed are you, preparing to set out, once again,
    into unknown territory.
Blessed are you, Bundle of Gifts, perhaps still unnamed,
    even by you.
Blessed are you, who has known uncontrollable weeping . . .
    sobbing out loud . . .
    everyday wrestling . . . alongside ecstasy-beyond-imagining.
Blessed are you, person of God, image of the Holy One.
    Really? Yes, even on our worst days,
        though intuited on our best ones.
Blessed are you, willing to "go the extra mile" for a friend, and
    Willing to try—yet one . . . more . . . time
        —to see goodness in an "enemy."
Blessed are you, for God is alive in you!
    Caressing, nudging, challenging,
        moving you to ever more become
        the hopes and dreams of the Divine,
        right here and right now,
Abundantly continue to bless us all, O Saving One,
    not only for our good,
        but for the good of Your ongoing creation,
    in the name of Jesus, the Christ, in whom we trust and believe.
Amen!

Bibliography

Aquinas, Thomas. "Question 92: The Production of the Woman." From *The Summa Theologiae of St. Thomas Aquinas*, translated by Fathers of the English Dominican Province, 2nd and rev. ed., 1920. Online ed. edited by Kevin Knight, 2017. www.newadvent.org/summa/1092.htm.

Baer, Richard A. *Philo's Use of the Categories of Male and Female.* Leiden, Neth.: Brill, 1970.

Bailey, Kenneth. *Jesus through Middle Eastern Eyes.* Downers Grove, IL: IVP Academic, 2008.

Bechtle, Regina, ed. *Collected Writings of Elizabeth Ann Bailey Seton.* 2 vols. N.p.: New City Press, 2003.

Bowman, Thea. "To Be Black and Catholic." *Origins* (former weekly publication of *Catholic News Service*) (July 6, 1989) 114–18.

Brett, Donna Whitson, and Edward T. Brett. *Murdered in Central America: The Stories of Eleven U.S. Missionaries.* Maryknoll, NY: Orbis, 1988.

Brooten, Bernadette J. "Women and the Churches in Early Christianity." *Ecumenical Trends* 14 (1985) 51–54.

Brown, Raymond E. *The Gospel According to John, I–XII.* Garden City, NY: Doubleday, 1966.

Buechner, Frederic. *Whistling in the Dark: An ABC Theologized.* San Francisco: Harper & Row, 1988.

———. *Wishful Thinking: A Theological ABC.* New York: Harper & Row, 1973.

Camp, Claudia V. *Wisdom and the Feminine in the Book of Proverbs.* Decatur, GA: Almond, 1985.

Day, Dorothy. *The Long Loneliness: The Autobiography of the Legendary Catholic Social Activist.* New York: HarperCollins, 2017. E-book.

Delio, Ilia. *Making All Things New.* Maryknoll, NY: Orbis, 2015.

Dunning, James. *Echoing God's Word.* Arlington, VA: North American Forum on the Catechumenate, 1993.

Ellsberg, Robert, ed. *Dorothy Day: Selected Writings.* Maryknoll, NY: Orbis, 2005.

Hennessy, Kate. *Dorothy Day: The World Will Be Saved by Beauty.* New York: Scribner, 2017.

Hillesum, Etty. *An Interrupted Life and Letters from Westerbork.* New York: Holt, 1996.

International Commission on English in the Liturgy, trans. *Roman Missal: The Sacramentary.* New York: Catholic Book Publishing, 1985.

Jensen, Richard A. *Preaching Matthew's Gospel.* Lima, OH: CSS, 1998.

John XXIII, Pope. *"Pacem in Terris"* (April 11, 1963). In *Proclaiming Justice and Peace: Papal Documents from Rerum Novarum through Centesimus Annus,* edited by Michael Walsh and Brian Davies, 125–56. New London, CT: Twenty-Third, 1991.

Johnson, Elizabeth A. *Ask the Beasts: Darwin and the God of Love.* London: Bloomsbury, 2014.

———. *Friends of God and Prophets: A Feminist Theological Reading of the Communion of Saints.* New York: Continuum, 1998.

Kuehn, Regina. *A Place for Baptism.* Chicago: Liturgy Training, 1992.

LaVerdiere, Eugene. *Dining in the Kingdom of God.* Chicago: Liturgy Training, 1994.

Macy, Gary. *The Hidden History of Women's Ordination: Female Clergy in the Medieval West.* New York: Oxford University Press, 2008.

———, et al. *Women Deacons: Past, Present, Future.* New York: Paulist, 2011.

Madigan, Kevin, and Carolyn Osiek. *Ordained Women in the Early Church: A Documentary History.* Baltimore: Johns Hopkins University Press, 2005.

Meehan, Bridget Mary, and Regina Madonna Oliver. *Heart Talks with Mother God.* Collegeville, MN: Liturgical, 1995.

Myers, Ched, et al. *"Say to This Mountain": Mark's Story of Discipleship.* Maryknoll, NY: Orbis Books, 1996.

Nouwen, Henri, et al. *Compassion: A Reflection on the Christian Life.* Garden City, NY: Doubleday, 1982.

Nutt, Maurice J. *Thea Bowman: Faithful and Free.* Collegeville, MN: Liturgical, 2019.

———, ed. *Thea Bowman: In My Own Words.* Ligouri, MO: Ligouri, 2009.

O'Connell, Gerard, and Luke Hansen. "Synod Votes to Ordain Married Men, and to Protect Amazon's Indigenous Peoples and Rainforests." *America: The Jesuit Review,* October 26, 2019. https://www.americamagazine.org/faith/2019/10/26/synod-votes-ordain-married-men-and-protect-amazons-indigenous-peoples-and.

O'Donohue, John. *Anam Cara: A Book of Celtic Wisdom.* New York: HarperCollins, 1998.

———. *To Bless the Space between Us.* New York: Doubleday, 2008.

Quinlan, Kathie. *Blessing Our Goodbyes.* Eugene, OR: Resource, 2011.

Ratigan, Virginia Kalb, and Arlene Anderson Swidler, eds. *A New Phoebe.* Kansas City: Sheed and Ward, 1990.

Reid, Barbara E. *Choosing the Better Part? Women in the Gospel of Luke.* Collegeville, MN: Liturgical, 1996.

Robinson, James M., ed. *The Future of Our Religious Past.* New York: Harper & Row, 1971.

Rose-Milavec, Deborah. "New Pathways for the Church and for an Integral Ecology." Notes taken at October 2019 Synod on the Pan-Amazon Region.

Rylant, Cynthia. *In November.* New York: Harcourt Brace, 2000.

Sabin, Marie Noonan. *The Gospel According to Mark.* New Collegeville Bible Commentary. Collegeville, MN: Liturgical, 2006.

Schillebeeckx, Edward. *Christ: The Experience of Jesus as Lord.* Translated by John Bowden. New York: Crossroad, 1983.

Schlumpf, Heidi. *Elizabeth Johnson: Questing for God.* Collegeville, MN: Liturgical, 2016.

Schneiders, Sandra M. Series of five articles on the meaning of religious life today. *National Catholic Reporter*, January 4–8, 2010. https://www.ncronline.org/news/global-sisters-report/call-response-and-task-prophetic-action.

———. *Written That You May Believe: Encountering Jesus in the Fourth Gospel.* New York: Herder & Herder, 1999.

Schussler Fiorenza, Elizabeth. *Jesus: Miriam's Child, Sophia's Prophet.* New York: Continuum, 1994.

Scott, Bernard Brandon. *Hear Then the Parable.* Minneapolis: Fortress, 1989.

Shapiro, Rami. *The Divine Feminine in Biblical Wisdom Literature.* Woodstock, VT: Skylight Paths, 2005.

Smith, Charlene, and John Feister. *Thea's Song: The Life of Thea Bowman.* Maryknoll, NY: Orbis, 2009.

Smith, Robert H. *Matthew.* Augsburg Commentary on the New Testament. Minneapolis: Fortress, 1988.

Synod of Bishops for the Pan-Amazon Region. "The Amazon: New Paths for the Church and for an Integral Ecology." Final document of the Synod on the Pan-Amazon Region, full text. October 26, 2019. https://www.vaticannews.va/en/vatican-city/news/2020-02/final-document-synod-amazon.html.

Tertullian. "Time Changes Nature's Dresses—and Fortunes." Translated by S. Thelwall. In *Ante-Nicene Fathers*, edited by Alexander Roberts et al., 4. Buffalo, NY: Christian Literature, 1885. Revised and edited for New Advent by Kevin Knight. www.newadvent.org/fathers/0401.htm.

Ulterino, Gloria. *Walking with Wisdom's Daughters.* Notre Dame, IN: Ave Maria, 2006.

Weiderkehr, Macrina. *Seasons of Your Heart.* New York: HarperCollins, 1991.

Wright, Terrence C. *Dorothy Day: An Introduction to Her Life and Thought.* San Francisco: Ignatius, 2018.

Zagano, Phyllis, ed. *Women Deacons? Essays with Answers.* Collegeville, MN: Liturgical, 2016.

Zion, Noam, and David Dishon. *A Different Night: The Leader's Guide to The Family Participation Haggadah.* Jerusalem: Shalom Hartman Institute, 1997.